THE ORGANIZATIONAL WOMAN: POWER AND PARADOX

THE COMMUNICATION AND INFORMATION SCIENCE SERIES
Series Editor: BRENDA DERVIN, The Ohio State University

Subseries:
Progress in Communication Sciences: Brant R. Burleson
Interpersonal Communication: Donald J. Cegala
Organizational Communication: George Barnett
Mass Communication/Telecommunication Systems: Lee B. Becker
User-Based Communication/Information System Design: Michael S.
    Nilan
Cross-Cultural/Coss-National Communication and Social Change:
    Josep Rota
International Communication, Peace and Development: Majid
    Tehranian
Critical Cultural Studies in Communication: Leslie T. Good
Feminist Scholarship in Communication: Lana Rakow
Rhetorial Theory and Criticism: Stephen H. Browne
Communication Pedagogy and Practice: Gerald M. Phillips
Communication: The Human Context: Lee Thayer

THE ORGANIZATIONAL WOMAN: POWER AND PARADOX

Beth J. Haslett
Florence L. Geis
Mae R. Carter

The University of Delaware

ABLEX PUBLISHING CORPORATION
NORWOOD, NEW JERSEY

All illustrations and examples are hypothetical and do not refer to any specific person or events.

Printed in the United States of America

Library of Congress Cataloging-in-Publication Data

Haslett, Beth.
    The organizational woman : power and paradox / Beth J. Haslett,
  Florence L. Geis, Mae R. Carter.
        p.   cm.
    Includes bibliographical references and index.
    ISBN 0-89391-837-7
    1. Women executives.   2. Success in business.   I. Geis, Floren
  L.   II. Carter, Mae R.   III. Title.
  HD6054.H37   1991
  658.4'09'082--dc20   91-35
                                                                       C

Ablex Publishing Corporation
355 Chestnut Street
Norwood, New Jersey 07648

To Pioneer Women—Past, Present, and Future

Contents

Acknowledgments   *x*

Introduction   *xi*

Section I · The Real World of Working Women   *1*

1 What You Don't Know Can Hurt You   *3*

Understanding the Nature of Bias in Work   *5*
Discriminatory Practices   *6*
The Story of Maria and Kristin   *8*
Analysis   *14*
The Win–Win Solution   *20*
Summary   *21*

**Section II · In the Mind's Eye: How Women Are Seen
     and Evaluated   *23***

2 Invisible Barriers: Gender Stereotypes
    and Discrimination   *27*

Perceptual Bias: Stereotypes in Action and Evaluation   *33*
Stereotypes, Sex, Status, and Role Models: A Self-Fulfilling
     Prophecy   *45*

3 Tricks of Mind: The Gender Schema and Other Foibles   *57*

The Social Gender Schema   *57*
The Power of Social Expectations   *64*
The Power of Social Consensus   *67*
Other Mental Loopholes   *71*
What Can We Do? Process Versus Outcome   *76*
Summary   *77*

Section III · Communication and Power: Who, What, Why, Where and When   79

4   Communication, Power, and Paradoxes for Women   *81*

Communication in Organizations   *82*
Critical Organizational Issues   *87*

5   Working in Small Groups: Process, Power, and Peril   *103*

Small Group Dynamics   *104*
Sex Differences in Small Group Communication   *107*
Conflict   *111*
Decision Making   *117*
Feedback   *118*
Summary   *121*

6   Leadership: Myth and Reality   *123*

Leadership in Organizations   *123*
Leadership Gender Mythology   *124*
Leadership Gender Reality   *138*
Summary   *148*

7   The Many Facets of Managerial Style   *151*

Characteristics of Managerial Work   *151*
Tasks   *154*
Communicating with New Information Technologies   *155*
Sex Differences in Managerial Communication   *164*
Toward a New Managerial Style   *172*

Section IV · The Bottom Line: Combining Research and Experience in the Real World   175

8   A Matter of Choice: Some Frequent Problems and Possible Strategies   *177*

Case Study 1—Starting in an Organization: The First Steps   *178*
Case Study 2—The Art of Presenting a Proposal Successfully   *183*
Case Study 3—Subtle Harassment: Discrediting the More Competent Woman   *189*
Case Study 4—A Collision Course: Power Space vs. Job Elaboration   *191*

Case Study 5—The Perils of Rapid Advancement   *194*
Case Study 6—Sexual Harassment, the Unwanted
    Attention   *200*
Conclusion   *204*

9 Overcoming the Barriers to Career Success: Summary
        and Conclusion   *205*

Sexism: What Does It Mean to You?   *205*
Questions that Need to be Asked   *207*
Counteracting Sex Discrimination: Steps Toward
    Solutions   *212*
Conclusion   *231*

REFERENCES   *233*

AUTHOR INDEX   *259*

SUBJECT INDEX   *267*

Acknowledgments

The authors would like to thank the following individuals for their helpful comments and suggestions on earlier drafts of the manuscript: Christin Carter-Su, Sue DeWine, Sam Gaertner, Barbara Kelly, Lila Murphy, Linda Putnam, LaVon Palmer, and Cynthia Secor. Our thanks also to the anonymous reviewers and to Brenda Dervin, our editor, for their comments and assistance. The Departments of Communication and Psychology at the University of Delaware gave us strong support throughout the preparation of the manuscript. To our typists extraordinaire, Judy Fingerle and Myrna Hofmann, our deepest thanks for unfailing good humor and accuracy throughout innumerable drafts! Finally, our thanks to our families, who generously gave time, support, and encouragement on this project.

Introduction

Our lives have all been touched by the changing role of women, both in the United States and worldwide. In the United States and other Western cultures, opportunities for many women have never been greater. However, the reality in today's world is that most women are still not allowed the same opportunities as men to develop to their full potential economically, socially, or politically.

Work includes many kinds of productive activity. Work can mean taking care of a family and a home as well as volunteer or paid employment outside the home. However, in this book, we are focusing on women in paid organizational positions. More women than ever before are working outside the home. More women than ever before have professional and managerial training. Despite this training, women are still not advancing in representative numbers to upper-level positions. Nor are women receiving comparable pay for comparable work. Why is there still inequity in salaries and wages? Why have so few women been promoted to high-level positions? Are women doing something wrong? Or are there other reasons? If you have asked these questions, this book is for you.

Why is there still inequity in salaries and wages between men and women?

Research in psychology and communication on these questions has identified many of the factors that directly affect the status and success of all women in organizations. Women must cope with these issues simply because they were born female and assigned into a "second-status" gender position in society. This book discusses the issues in the context of the working world as it currently exists, because that is the reality that working women must face every day.

The purpose of this book is to interpret relevant scientific research findings in light of practical experience as they apply to the contemporary work world. These findings are presented in nontechnical language understandable to the educated reader who is not a specialist in one of the scientific disciplines involved. The book is written for educated women and men in organizations and for college students in relevant courses.

The terms *sex* and *gender* are used throughout this book. *Sex* refers to the biological distinction defined by anatomy. One is biologically either a male or a female. *Gender* is used to describe those personality characteristics, abilities, or interests that are arbitrarily assigned differently to the two sexes. These stereotypes affect all aspects of women's and men's lives, including social rank, education, and economic status. It can be difficult to distinguish between sex and gender issues, because gender characteristics are not independent but directly assigned on the basis of whether one is born male or female. In fact, a major part of the problem is that, until relatively recently, most people, including scientists, believed that what we now recognize as gender characteristics (learned) were in fact *sex* characteristics (biologically innate and inherent).

> Gender stereotypes affect all aspects of women's and men's lives including social rank, education and economic status.

Through this book, we hope to contribute to greater equity, opportunity, and upward mobility for women. Although many of the problems and principles apply to all women in organizations, the discussion focuses on women who hold positions requiring some responsibility, judgment, and decision making. Organizations can be large corporations or small businesses, profit or nonprofit, public or private, offices or laboratories, social service or education.

For women in blue-collar or pink-collar jobs, sexual discrimination is often more overt and deliberate. We do not attempt to discuss the many additional problems that they encounter. Similarly, we do not attempt to discuss the additional problems of minority African, Latino, Asian, and Indian women who encounter racism as well as a host of other biases that increase discrimination both quantitatively and qualitatively. More research needs to be done in these areas, and a thorough discussion of these issues is beyond the scope of this book. However, the basic concepts we discuss are relevant to *all* women, blue- and pink-collar women and minority women, as well as others, and the strategies we develop can be applied generally.

Men, as well as women, can benefit from reading this book. Men can gain an increased understanding of how unconscious bias operates in society generally, in their women colleagues as well as in themselves and their male colleagues, and, more specifically, how it operates in organizations. As economic pressures increase and the labor pool becomes more limited, organizations need to utilize the talents of all their members, both male and female, in order to remain competitive and successful. Organizational practices, both covert and overt, and organizational structures, formal as well as informal, need to facilitate the productivity of every employee. Existing barriers to the full organizational participation of women must be identified and eliminated. Both male and female managers can manage more effectively if they are sensitive to the issues raised in this book.

The book is divided into four sections. The first section, *The World of Working Women,* deals with the working world as it currently exists. Readers are introduced to some problems women face at work and some research findings about women. The themes established in the first section are elaborated throughout the book.

The second section, *In the Mind's Eye,* deals with social stereotypes about women and how they affect women in organizations. Success in an organization is strongly influenced by how your colleagues "see" you. The mental processes that shape how women are seen and evaluated, and how women are subsequently treated, are examined from a psychological perspective. This section assists women in understanding why apparently "unfair" things happen to them and

> *Knowledge empowers both women and men and permits a choice of action.*

offers some suggestions to counter such behavior. Knowledge and understanding of this behavior is the first step to intelligently examining the available options.

Section III, *Communicating Effectively in Organizations,* presents an overview of communication and power in organizations. Power strategies and barriers to power for women are explicitly discussed. Subsequent chapters deal with three important communication contexts: managerial communication, communication in small groups, and leadership. All four chapters in this section focus on communication behavior and judgments of women's communication, and on suggestions for increased effectiveness.

Finally, Section IV, *The Bottom Line,* presents a series of case studies on critical organizational issues confronting women. Each case study presents an analysis of the situation and offers some alternatives for dealing with the situation. We emphasize that these alternatives are all *matters of choice.* An individual must choose a strategy based on an analysis of the benefits and costs for each alternative and what she is willing to risk. We conclude the book with a summary of specific suggestions for women to empower themselves. It includes a series of questions designed to monitor the environment of an organization.

Knowledge empowers both men and women. It permits a choice of action. Power and choice, however, are mixed blessings. The greater the number and variety of choices one has, the more complicated and anxiety-producing making a decision becomes. However, the alternative is ignorance. Ignorance may provide temporary bliss, but if a woman cannot understand what she sees, and what is happening, then external events and people control her life. If she can identify and understand the power and political dynamics, she can formulate alternative strategies, and make a better choice among her options. The problem of sexism is built into the fabric of our society. One woman, alone, cannot stop the sexism, but knowledge of what it is and how it operates can enable her to develop ways to counter it. Women can stop blaming themselves for the results of individual and organizational sexism. That alone is a liberating and empowering understanding. Also, women can avoid exercerbating the problems, protect themselves, and avoid reinforcing stereotypical actions in other women and men.

Some women may be ambivalent and uncomfortable when they think of holding or using power. Power, per se, is neither good nor evil. It can be used for either. Women also resist the idea of power, because it has traditionally been considered "unfeminine." However, the need for power and use of power is neither "masculine" nor "feminine," but human. Most women want some control over their lives, which is another was of saying that they want some power. There are many kinds and uses of power. Mahatma Ghandi and Martin Luther King are two men who used the power of collaboration to make significant changes in society. Some of the women who have used power on a large scale include Eleanor Roosevelt in the area of human rights, Betty Ford in the area of cancer detection and substance abuse, Mother Teresa working with the poor in India, and Margaret Thatcher as Prime Minister of Great Britain. All women need and use power, often without explicitly labeling it as such, in both their personal and work lives.

The reader should also be alert to a related issue. Previous work on the problems women face in paid employment has taken either of two opposing approaches. In their extreme forms, one attributes women's problems to women's "deficiencies" and advocates "remedial training." This approach blames the victim for her own misfortunes. The other approach attributes women's problems to the prevailing sexism of

> The need for power and the use of power is neither "masculine" nor "feminine," but human.

society. This approach implies that women are just fine as they are. Thus there is nothing an individual woman can do to improve her situation, because no one can change "society."

This book goes beyond either of these simplistic approaches. The research discussed in the following chapters clearly identifies the prevailing sexism of society as a major source of problems for women in the workplace. However, there *are* things individual women can do to improve the situation. Some of these strategies involve individual actions. Many of the behaviors and attitudes required for career success are popularly (and mistakenly) called "masculine" because, until recently, only men were seen displaying them. As noted above, we believe that these behaviors and attitudes are neither "masculine" nor "feminine," but "human." A person of either sex can learn and practice them. We also offer strategies for countering societal sexism as it operates in the workplace.

> *Many of the behaviors and attitudes required for career success are mistakenly called "masculine."*

Although no one can change "society" as a whole, everyone has some influence in her or his particular work situation. "Society" is a fabric woven of all the particular situations that comprise it. If *everyone* changed his or her own bailiwick, then "society" as a whole would be changed. It is, in fact, the proliferation of such incremental changes that has produced opportunities for women today. Obviously, both internal and external improvements can proceed at the same time.

This book offers you an analysis of the world of working women as it currently exists, and some effective strategies to protect yourself and for enhancing your own personal and professional effectiveness. We base this analysis upon years of research in communication and psychology; upon counseling thousands of women about organizational, personal, and professional problems; and upon our own long, personal experience and observation as organizational members. The book thus offers information based upon a strong research and experiential background. In addition to the strategies to enhance one's personal and professional effectiveness, we stress that everyone needs to be aware of alternative actions and to *personally* weigh the benefits and risks associated with various options. There are no quick-fix solutions, such as "Be Assertive," offered here, but rather information to empower you and enable you to reach the most effective solution for yourself.

We hope that the experience and knowledge shared in this book will enhance the real equality of opportunity and advancement that we all, men and women alike, sincerely endorse.

Section I
The Real World of Working Women

More and more women are working in organizations than ever before. The composition of the work force with its great increase of women workers has changed dramatically since the 1950s. Women are entering jobs and professions that were formerly denied them. This large influx of women occurred with little preparation and few changes in the workplace itself. Often women continued to be assigned "women's work" or stereotypical and routine work, even in nontraditional professions.

Although women were employed, it was difficult for both men and women to separate their professional roles from their traditional social roles with the other sex. Men still viewed women as mother, wife, daughter, or sister and continued to treat women that way on the job. Women, also, had trouble recognizing that those social roles were inappropriate in a professional environment and limited their paychecks and advancement. When women recognized that they were receiving, not only the routine assignments, but less money and recognition for similar work, sex discrimination was identified and protested.

Most men and many women believe sincerely that sex discrimination is a thing of the past. It is true that many of the worst abuses have been eliminated. However, sex discrimination is still quite common. It is often so subtle that neither the perpetrator nor the victim recognizes what is happening. The victim usually blames herself for the problems and negative outcomes that seem to "just happen." This section seeks to assist the reader in recognizing some of the many forms that sex discrimination can take. Knowledge of what is *really* going on is the first step in any solution.

1

1
What You Don't Know Can Hurt You

The environment for working women is not the same as that of working men in the same organization. Because of this reality, it is important to begin by examining the influence of societal norms on the working climate of women, men, and organizations.

Although there are 51.7 million working women comprising 45% of the work force (U.S. Department of Labor, 1989), employers' attitudes and most organizations' policies and procedures are still written and interpreted from a male perspective. It is estimated that, by 1995, 81% of all women aged 25–34 years will be in the labor force, compared to 70% in 1986 (Sitterly & Duke, 1988). Stereotypical perspectives held by both men and women directly affect every person in an organization. These stereotypes favor some, usually white males, who receive the better work assignments and the accompanying rewards. They place others, usually females and minorities, at a disadvantage, and cause them to receive the routine, less interesting work with fewer rewards. This discrepancy in job assignments and the resulting rewards occurs even among men and women at the same job level with the same title.

There can be no question that attitudes about appropriate roles for men and women are slowly changing. The traditional roles for women have been expanded beyond daughter, girlfriend, wife, and mother. Now, appropriate roles for women also include paid employment outside the home. In 1988 women comprised 45% of the full-time and part-time civilian work force in the United States (U.S. Bureau of Labor Statistics, 1989). It is estimated that, by the year 2000, women and minorities will comprise 85% of new workers entering the work force. However, the basic test of whether an organization's attitudes have changed requires an answer to the following question: Has behavior on the job toward women who work changed, or has society continued the stereotypical behaviors that result in sex discrimination?

3

The answer is "yes, both." Some behavior has changed, but stereotypical and discriminatory behavior also continues. One basic problem is perceptual bias, the systematic misperception and devaluation of work performed by women. In a number of different situations, evaluators rate a given product or performance more positively when they believe it to be the work of a man rather than a woman. Perceptual bias against women is both the cause and result of discrimination against women. Such bias resulting in sex discrimination is not practiced only by men against women. Women also discriminate against other women and against themselves.

> Women, as well as men, discriminate against other women and against themselves.

Perceptual bias prevents women's intellectual capacities from being used to their fullest because women are kept in more menial, low-paying routine jobs. This underutilization is amply documented by government statistics and scientific research. It is reflected in the phenomena of sex-typed occupations such as elementary teaching, the underrepresentation of women in higher management, and blatant sex discrimination. Even with affirmative action legislation and enforcement, women's actual gains have been more modest than striking. Although much lip service is given to examples of a token woman moving up into senior management, the U.S. Department of Labor (1989) reveals that, in 1988, women held only 39.3% of the higher paying executive, administrative, and managerial positions, and they were heavily concentrated in the lower levels of those categories. This is still short of their labor force representation of 45%, making reality very different from the publicized image (U.S. Department of Labor, 1989). In addition, there is a weekly pay gap between male and female managers: $654 for men vs. $454 for women (U.S. Department of Labor, 1989).

A second bias is in communication, which provides the basis for all collaborative social activity. Organizations require effective multiple networks of communication for their maintenance and growth. However, in communication, females are again negatively evaluated. Women's communicative styles, such as elaborating on the statements of others, tend to be devalued. And even if women communicate like men, their style is still viewed negatively. For example, what is aggressive communication for a man becomes "bitchy" when from a woman.

Biases in perception and communication, usually implicit and unconscious, systemically devalue women's work and undermine their personal and organizational effectiveness. These two key issues, perception and communication, are tightly interconnected because people communicate with others in terms of their perceptions of themselves and others. And in organizations, how individuals perceive and communicate with others is critical for their personal and organizational effectiveness. Thus perception and communication have important consequences for an organization's growth and development.

UNDERSTANDING THE NATURE OF BIAS IN WORK

Research conducted over the past decade has outlined the nature of organizational work for women. The world of work for women is quite different from that of men. It has been suggested that a gender role spillover model accounts for the effects of sex and gender in the workplace (Nieva & Gutek, 1981).

Gender role spillover is the carry over into the workplace of stereotypical gender-based roles that are usually irrelevant or inappropriate for work, but familiar ones, traditionally, in everyday life. Gender role spillover occurs, for example, when women are expected to be more nurturant or loyal than men in the same position, or when men are expected automatically to assume the leader's role in a mixed-sex group.

It is important to understand that sex and gender are basic parts of social identity. In the workplace, they affect how people interact, how they work with one another on the job, and the outcomes they experience. Three significant influences of gender in the workplace have been identified (Gutek, 1985). First, there is sex segregation of work: Three-fourths of employed women work in two job areas, clerical work or the less prestigious—and lower paying—professions. Thus, women's work is less diverse than men's work. Second, there are important power, status, and prestige differences between men and women at work, with men typically holding jobs with more power, status, and prestige. Finally, working conditions and personal characteristics of job holders emphasize the effect of gender in the workplace. Women's jobs usually have more pleasant working conditions and emphasize appearance more than men's jobs. Sex segregation of work leads to the expectation that *only* men or *only* women will perform certain jobs.

Sex segregation of work leads to the expectation that only men or only women will perform certain jobs.

The current numerical imbalances of women and men, both in sex segregation of occupations and in specific work settings, do not allow either sex a wide range of experiences in working together. People usually rely upon stereotypes when they have no such previous experience, and treat minority sex members as "token representatives" of their sex. Dividing labor according to sex leads to specific role expectations for both men and women, and leads to stereotyped skills and beliefs as well. These, in turn, lead to sex differences in social behavior (Eagly, 1987). Thus, sex segregation of work results in women acquiring "feminine" skills and beliefs, and men acquiring "masculine" skills and beliefs.

Any analysis of sex, gender, and power in organizations must acknowledge that organizations are generally dominated by what we have learned to regard as male values, experiences and expectations. Gender expectations and the expression of power are cast within this predominant culture and evaluated by those cultural values. The valued model is thus the model of male rather than female experience. Even though actual behaviors may not be influenced by sex or gender, the *evaluation* of those behaviors will be influenced by gender beliefs. Given the use of sex as an important cultural clue, its influence on judgments appears inescapable.

DISCRIMINATORY PRACTICES

As women entered the workforce in increasing numbers, discriminatory practices limited their employment and promotional opportunities. Perceptual bias and discriminatory workplace practices negatively influence women's work and the perception and evaluation of that work. Benokraitis and Feagin (1985) define *overt discrimination* as that which is readily apparent, visible, observable, and easily documented. In contrast, *subtle discrimination,* both attitudinal and behavioral, is often invisible and difficult to detect. These investigators suggest that sex discrimination can be judged across five dimensions:

1. structural or situational (is it built into the organization and continuous as part of the policy, or does it vary with the circumstances?)
2. cumulative or episodic (is it increasing and continuous, or does it happen periodically?)
3. deliberate or accidental (was it planned or unintentional?)
4. public or private (was it done in front of others or in a one-to-one situation?)

5. formal or informal (was it done in writing, through the channels of the organization, or over a cup of coffee?)

Each of these distinctions has implications for understanding the nature of discrimination and for providing strategies to deal with it.

Sex discrimination is particularly insidious when it becomes internalized by women as, for example, when women blame themselves for failure and credit external factors, such as luck, instead of themselves for their success. Because men's work is perceived as "better" even if it is the same or of even poorer quality, sex discrimination results in less pay, less responsibility, less power, and lower self-esteem for women.

> Women often blame themselves for failure and credit external factors, such as luck, instead of themselves for success.

Some structural sources of discrimination can be found in recruitment practices, screening of candidates, promotional opportunities, and in the benevolent disregard of sexual harassment. Another important source of structural discrimination is that men receive more on-the-job training than women do, which affects subsequent promotions and career opportunities (Gutek, 1985).

Covert discrimination is unequal, harmful treatment of women, including tokenism, containment (qualitative exclusion of women from power and opportunity), manipulation, sabotage (work overload, unrealistic expectations), revenge, and co-optation. Minority women experience more discrimination than white women because they suffer the dual discrimination of race as well as sex.

Many forms of subtle sex discrimination occur via communication. Statements that use hostile humor, psychological intimidation, or condescend and support in a discouraging way are just a few of the mechanisms used to reinforce negative evaluations of women in the workplace. Although superficially friendly or supportive, many of these strategies serve to exclude women or devalue their work.

You may be asking yourself, what does this mean to me? Let us take a look at how this environment and these societal norms affect individual women in the work place. Specific problems will become more evident in the following dialogue between two professional women. The problems presented here that result from stereotypical perspectives are real, prevalent, and illustrate the experience of many women. Perhaps you are not aware of having any of the problems described. However, you may encounter similar situations next month, next year, or you may have encountered them already without recognizing them.

THE STORY OF MARIA AND KRISTIN

At a fashionable restaurant in the heart of the business district, Maria and Kristin are having their monthly luncheon at their regular table. Both young women are very well dressed and project an aura of success.

JANUARY

Maria,   an attractive single woman with long black hair, wearing a bright red dress with chunky gold jewelry: I've got good news! Remember my telling you about Katherine, that fireball in Human Resources. Well, she was promoted to Vice-President 2 weeks ago. She really deserved it. Even the men don't seem to mind working for her. I don't know about you, Kristin, but I think sex discrimination is a thing of the past.

Kristin,   a happily married, striking blonde wearing a tailored black suit: Well, I'm not so sure. I've never experienced any discrimination myself, of course, but I know it happens to others. Alice, that terrific woman in our accounting department, may *not* get the next promotion, even though she's the only accountant anyone trusts up there. She's clearly earned the next promotion, but the grapevine says she won't get it. Rumor has it that a younger man will be promoted.

Maria: Oh, I'm sure Alice will get the promotion—from what you've told me, her work is better than anyone else's in the department. Although . . . would a woman be good at giving orders or firing people, especially men?

Kristin: Alice can do anything that needs to be done. I think she'd be a great boss.

Maria: Guess what? I'm in line for a promotion too, since Clare is retiring. My boss, Bill, has invited me to have a drink with him after work on Thursday to discuss it. He even said that, if I don't meet him, I might not get the promotion. Of course, he didn't mean that part of it. He was only kidding.

Kristin: A promotion! Congratulations! *You* deserve it. I know how hard you've worked. And it shows. You've done a great job. But I'd be careful with Bill if I were you. Maybe he did mean it.

Maria: Oh, no, he was just joking. He wouldn't do that to me.

Kristin: Well, there are some things they *will* do to you. Can you believe it? I've just received the most boring assignment in the department for the third time in a row. At my last conference with Roberto, my boss, he told me that I wasn't showing enough initiative. How can I have time to develop my own initiatives when he keeps loading me down with his stupid projects? Things had better improve! I'm really tired of having to do so much more clerical work than anyone else, too. Especially when all the guys have time to go out to lunch every day.

FEBRUARY

Kristin, with a puzzled look on her face: I need a new perspective! Something really crazy happened to me last week and I'm still trying to figure it out. Maybe you can explain it. We were having a team meeting to plan for the transition to the new computer system. I had been thinking about it in advance and came up with a really good idea, so I suggested it at the meeting. But before I had even finished, the guy from Design interrupted me and began talking about the advantages of the new system—and the group went on from what *he* said, and we didn't get anything done. It was like they didn't even hear me, like I have never spoken.

Maria: Weird. It makes you feel like you don't even exist. The same thing has happened to me. But I saw an even weirder one on Monday. We were having a meeting to discuss bidding on a contract from a new company. Marcia, a woman from Production, analyzed the contract specifications, showing that they were incompatible with our production capacities. It was pretty high level and technical, but Marcia did a great job. But as soon as she finished, one of the guys said, in a really condescending way, "Oh, Marcia, don't be so emotional!" At that point, Marcia, who had been anything but emotional during her presentation, got mad and snapped back at him, saying she was *not* emotional. Well, that finished her. Everyone began talking about what the contract would do for their own units, and Marcia's analysis was completely ignored.

MARCH

Maria, with a smart new haircut but in a dejected tone: I'm glad its our day for lunch. I'm really down. It doesn't look as if I'll be getting the promotion or salary increase that goes with it—if our Vice-President has anything to do with it. Somehow, he doesn't seem to take me very seriously. In my interview, he only talked about all the additional work and responsibility involved in the job. He thought it would be too difficult for me, especially since it includes longer hours . . . Well, maybe it's for the best, but I'm still disappointed. I'm sure I could do it.

Kristin,   wearing her red blazer but equally dejected: I thought Bill was going to put in a good word for you. You're obviously qualified. I think you would do very well.

Maria: Yes, Bill's my only hope now. When I met him for dinner last week, he said he would put in a good word for me. He seems so lonely since his divorce. It's really romantic and exciting to be with him. I'm seeing him again tonight.

Kristin: It sounds like you are really getting involved with Bill. Are you sure that's wise? By the way, I heard that Alice was very disappointed when she didn't get her promotion. I think she's much better than the guy who got it, the one she trained. She'll probably leave the company. Why should she stay?

Maria: If I don't get my promotion, I don't know what I'll do. The thing is, I'm not sure anymore that I even deserve the promotion. Maybe Russ, my competition, really is better than I am.

Kristin: Well, I'm down, too. Unfortunately, I'm still getting the routine jobs. And if that isn't enough, I just found out that the guy they hired last week to do the same thing in Maury's group that I do in Roberto's makes $3,000 more than I do— even though he's right out of school with no experience! I just don't understand. I always get excellent evaluations. Am I doing a good job or not? If I am, I should get paid for it! Am I doing something wrong?

Maria,   indignantly: That's not fair! Three thousand dollars is a lot of money. If it was only $1,000 I would understand it. Does he have a family to support.?

Kristin: What if he does? I have children to support, too! I need a change. There's a new opening in Sales. Do you think I should apply for it? I'm a little concerned that it might be tough to be the only woman in the department.

Maria: It sounds interesting to me!

Kristin: I don't know how Ed would feel if I started traveling a lot. He'd have to cook and take care of his own shirts. It would be hard on the kids too, but it might be worth a try.

Maria: You've always done a lot for your family. I don't see how you do it all!

Kristin: To tell the truth, most of the time I feel like I'm just barely making it. Unfortunately, my child care arrangements are pretty shaky right now. I have a great person but she is threatening to leave because her husband doesn't want her to work anymore. I'm afraid that I won't be able to find a replacement who is as flexible and good as she is. If I have to find someone new, I'll probably have to pay more and I'm already paying the maximum we can afford.

APRIL

Maria, wearing a bright green dress: I wore my new dress today just to cheer myself up. My promotion is still up in the air. I can't believe what's happening at work. Bill is super critical of my work lately. I guess he doesn't want to be seen as granting me any special favors. Why else would he be so nasty and abrupt?

Kristin, in a beige spring suit: I hope you know what you're doing. Have you ever thought that maybe he's only pretending to help you toward a promotion?

Maria, sounding shaken: I don't even want to think about that! Earlier I would have said absolutely not, but lately he's been difficult. He even yelled at me, "Can't you get anything right?" I got so upset, I'm afraid I yelled back at him, because I was right and he was wrong. I'm afraid everyone on the floor heard us! But why should I take the blame? He's so loving when we're alone. All the time he tells me how much I've meant to him since his divorce. I was hoping it was the real thing.

Kristin: I'm still upset about my salary. I haven't decided what to do about it, but I know I need to do something.

Maria: You're right! You can't let that $3,000 difference in salary go by.

Kristin: I've decided to try for the job in sales, but I'm not really sure I want it. Ed isn't enthusiastic. He likes his comforts, and I do all I can for him and the kids. I'm so tired all the time.

Maria: It must be nice to be married and have a man around the house, but it seems like it's a lot more work for you.

Kristin: After I've worked all day, it really irritates me when he sits down and reads the newspaper while I'm trying to feed our two-year-old and get dinner for us. And then, of course, during dinner, I have to sympathize with Ed's problems. The extra money from the sales job would help us a lot.

Maria,   indignantly: That's not fair! Doesn't Ed realize that you work all day, too? He should do more around the house.

Kristin,   tiredly: I agree, but it doesn't seem to work out that way. I'm lucky that my child care arrangements are good for another month anyway. Ed says that, if I stayed home with the children, we could save all that child care money. He refuses to recognize the fact that it takes both our salaries to keep up our house payments.

MAY

Maria,   unhappily: Sorry I'm late. I just had to drag myself out today. You know, I really loved the guy! Even though I sensed there was a problem, I was devastated when Bill told me it was all over. He didn't help me get my promotion. In fact, he even suggested that I transfer out of his department or get a new job. He said that if I did it soon, he would give me a good recommendation. Otherwise, he could fire me for insubordination because I yelled back at him.

Kristin,   worriedly: I'm sorry it didn't work out for you and Bill, and the job. What a rotten situation.

Maria: We knew when we were getting involved that we were both mature adults. I guess it was my fault it didn't work out. When I told him how much I loved him, he hardly listened to me. He was so different last week. The worst part is that he is starting to date that attractive new receptionist. I just hate to think of the two of them together. I may not even keep the job I have!

Kristin,   sympathetically: Sounds like you should start looking right away. I hope you find a good job soon. Bill owes you a good recommendation. It's the least he can do.

Maria: You're right, I need to start looking.

Kristin: My situation has gotten more complicated, too. In addition to all my other problems, Roberto, my boss, suggested that I go to our national meeting with him. But, from the way he suggested it, I suspect that it would involve only one hotel room. The convention would be a wonderful opportunity to make professional contacts, but the price is too high.

Maria: It sounds tempting! Are you sure it means only one hotel room?

Kristin: I'm sure.

Maria: That's disgusting! I hope you let him know you weren't interested!

Kristin: I sure did, but it's a delicate situation. By the way, my friend Helen wants to come back to work now that her two children are in school. She was on the "fast-track" when she decided to take a few years off to raise her children. Now she's lost her contacts, and she's having a hard time getting started again. Her former boss has retired, and almost everyone else is new. Do you know of any jobs as an administrative assistant? It would be a real come-down for her, but at least it would get her back into the swim. She's really good!

Maria: I'd like to help, but I haven't heard of any openings. Most of those jobs seem to be filled from the secretarial staff. It is one of the few promotions for them. There are always a lot of good internal candidates. It's hard to come back after you've stopped working. Not only do you lose contacts, but your skills get rusty and out of date.

Kristin: Let me know if you hear of anything. I did explore that job possibility in Sales. In the interview, they asked me if I planned to have more children, and how my husband would feel if I had to be on the road a lot. They made it very clear that they did not want a woman in that job. It would have been quite a raise. I could have used the money, too.

Maria: That's really discouraging.

Kristin: The work itself is somewhat similar to what I do now. I was especially disappointed when they hired a football star right out of college. Have you noticed that, although we get top evaluations, we don't seem to get promotions or the higher paying jobs? We don't even get paid as much as the guys get for the same job!

JUNE

Maria,   in a discouraged tone: Well, I'm still looking for a new job. I've had several interviews, but no luck so far. I guess I don't need the kind of help that Bill is giving me. I haven't had the same questions that you did, but they're still bad. You haven't heard of any good leads in my area, have you?

Kristin,   very distressed: If I had a good lead, I would probably use it myself.

Maria: Isn't it illegal to ask women questions in job interviews that they don't ask men? Why do they have to know if I plan to get married soon? They had their nerve asking what kind of contraceptive I use. I know I don't want to work for that company. They're obviously sexist.

Kristin: I agree, it would be a terrible place to work. On a different note, I need some advice. I haven't told anyone yet, but my problem with Roberto is getting worse. He's been getting much more persistent and sexually demanding. He refuses to get the message that I'm not interested. What can I do? No one would believe that he's continually propositioning a happily married woman with two children.

Maria: Are you sure that you're not misunderstanding him?

Kristin: I'm sure! He's very clever. When I say "no," he says he's "just kidding." He makes me feel guilty—like I'm encouraging him—and I know that I'm not. He always waits until we're alone. I'm afraid he'll try to fire me if I keep on refusing to "cooperate." I'm beginning to dread coming to work every morning. I just don't know what he'll do next. I don't dare tell Ed.

Maria: You know, I've been thinking about your work problems. They all seemed to start after that project of yours that made so much money. I bet that the men in your section see you as a threat. Think about it for a minute. After your successful project, first came your dull work assignments, and then this sexual harassment. Do you think Roberto might be trying to control you and "put you back in your place?" It looks like a power play to me!

Kristin: I don't know why he's doing this to me.

Maria: Would he have given those jobs to any man? I doubt it!

Kristin, feeling desperate: I just don't know what to do.

ANALYSIS

Do these dialogues seem far-fetched? In fact, the situations just described happen every day. They do not usually all happen to the same person, and they may not have happened to you, but the odds are that at least some of them have happened to others in your organization or to one of your friends.

The ways that Maria and Kristin handled the situations could have been improved, and made a difference in the final outcomes, if they had been knowledgeable about the research on women in organizations that is included in this book.

Let us take a closer look at some of the specific issues. In the January episode, Maria is confusing her social and professional roles at work through her choice of clothing and her behavior on the job. She is emphasizing a traditional social role as a woman with her bright red

Confusing social and professional roles in an organization can lead to trouble.

dress and chunky gold jewelry, and by accepting the invitation to meet Bill, her boss, for a drink after work. Even though Bill mentioned that Maria might not get a promotion if she did not meet him, Maria chose to meet him and to ignore and deny the potential danger of sexual harassment. Bill may . . . or may not . . . have been joking. But joking about sexual harassment is like joking to the attendant at the airport metal detector that you might be carrying a bomb in your briefcase. If Maria wanted the promotion, it was crucial that she project a professional attitude and appearance on the job and toward the job during her interview with the Vice-President. By March, it became apparent that she had not convinced him to take her application seriously.

Katherine, who was promoted to Vice-President for Personnel and Employee Relations, illustrated to Maria that there is no longer any sex discrimination. However, Maria seemed unaware that all the other Vice-Presidents were men in line positions and eligible to move into the presidency. Katherine, with her outstanding performance, was in a staff position and could go no further.

Kristin initially believed that she had not experienced sex discrimination. Apparently, she was not aware that her heavy work load, including the boring routine assignments and being required to do her own clerical work, are common problems for women. Because women may be better organized and have some clerical skills, it is often expected that they will do their own clerical work, and also the jobs that no one else wants to do and that have little pay-off or prestige. Women are usually paid less than men, even, or especially, if they have to do their own clerical work in addition to their regular job assignments. Kristin's male colleagues, exempt from such expectations, appear to have plenty of time to go out to lunch together every day.

In the same conversation, Kristin unknowingly describes sex discrimination against Alice, who is in line for a promotion in the Accounting Department. Unfortunately, Alice does not break through the "glass ceiling" and is denied the promotion. This is an example of actual versus "perceived" job performance and capacity for authority and responsibility. Women like Alice, and other minorities, have to work harder and better than white men to get ahead. This

Women still have to work harder and better than men to get ahead.

is not fair, but it is reality. Even if she does everything right, a woman may still not advance in an organization if there is too much conscious or unconscious sex discrimination. Alice is "seen" as being "less competent" as an administrator than a younger man. Did you notice that even Maria questioned whether Alice, as a woman, would be good at giving orders or firing male subordinates? Because of the stereotypes, many women doubt their own or other women's abilities. And the continuing discriminatory treatment serves to further diminish their self-confidence. By March, with no progress on her promotion, Maria was beginning to doubt that she really deserved it.

Later in the conversation, Kristin, again unknowingly, described discrimination against herself. Roberto, her boss, responding to the gender stereotype that women are unaggressive and lack initiative, kept assigning her routine projects, thereby leaving her no time to develop her own initiatives. In addition, the heavy work load prevented her from going out to lunch with her colleagues, thereby keeping her out of the informal communication network, which diminished her access to the information she needed to keep on top of her job. Kristin is caught in a self-fulfilling prophecy.

In February, Kristin and Maria discuss a common problem of women in organizations, being ignored, unheard, interrupted, or put down when they speak in a group meeting. Kristin was not heard, then interrupted and ignored, when she presented a good idea. This occurs because women are erroneously perceived as less competent than they actually are, so their ideas are accorded less weight and less attention. In addition, women's speech styles evoke negative reactions. Maria told of how Marcia made a highly analytic presentation, backed by detailed evidence, and was then put down by being called "emotional." Many of the group members did not want to hear Marcia's negative conclusion, important as it was, and some of them may have felt threatened by her technical expertise. They effectively silenced her, and ignored her important information, by pinning the gender stereotype "emotional" on her. The fact that it was entirely unjustified was irrelevant. The fact that it is a gender stereotype gave it enough seeming credibility to nullify her presentation—and to provoke Marcia into becoming emotional. Marcia's angry denial, of course, then mistakenly seemed to "confirm" the accusation that her whole presentation was emotional.

Perceptual bias against women is both the cause and result of discrimination against women.

These incidents illustrate another important point. When women are discriminated against, in these and other ways, the organization loses the benefit of their ideas. Kristin's unit may have more costly problems and chaos in the computer transition because her ideas were never heard or considered. If Maria's organization bids on the contract and its production facilities can not meet the contract specifications, as Marcia explained, the organization will either suffer a major loss of credibility or be forced into costly production alterations.

The organization loses the benefit of their ideas when women are discriminated against.

By March, the problems discussed in January have escalated, and additional ones have surfaced. Maria is becoming more deeply involved with Bill, her boss. Whether he does or does not influence the decision on her promotion, it is dangerous for a woman to be perceived as trying to advance or gain favors through a personal or romantic relationship. Maria did nothing to dispel the sexual implication by her dress and ultimate involvement with her boss. If Maria got her promotion, there would always have been a question about why and how she got it, even though she was the most competent. Others would view the promotion as similar to nepotism, and she would be perceived as having been granted special treatment because of the relationship. Further, she would be tied to one person. When that person retired or left the company without her, or the relationship ended unexpectedly, she would find herself stranded and need to find another job. Maria is still interacting socially, not professionally.

Kristin, in addition to her dissatisfaction with her current job assignments, finds out that there is a $3,000 discrepancy between her salary and that of a newly hired male colleague. She identifies the mixed message of high job evaluations and the lack of appropriate financial rewards. Although salary compression may be a factor (because of inflation or a scarcity of applicants, entry pay for new hires may rise faster than annual increments for continuing employees), it is more likely that

The mixed message of high job evaluations without the appropriate financial rewards is commonly given to women.

gender stereotypes are operating and that her work is "seen" as less important and less difficult than what a man does. Kristin's salary inequity is a difficult problem. She needs to collect all the job descriptions and salaries of similar jobs to back up her request for a salary adjustment.

A second issue is whether changing jobs solves the problem of being viewed stereotypically. Sometimes it can help if there are several women already established in the new department, but too often the same problems emerge again and a woman ends up with less seniority and less pay in a new job. The issues must first be recognized for what they are and a plan made to counteract them. Often an educational process is needed, for women as well as men.

Before applying for the job in sales, Kristin needs to assess realistically whether she has the energy, skills, and interest for the required increased time and travel commitment. If she gets the job, being the only woman in the department will make it harder for her. Few, if any, exceptions will be made for a woman, regardless of any family problems. That would not be true for men, whose problems are inevitably perceived as "serious." She should be aware that many men in sales may believe that she should be home with her children, as most of their wives are, and not competing with them for "men's work."

As Kristin continues to be discouraged, tired and exhausted, it is clear that she is trying to do two jobs: run a perfect house and take care of her husband and children, as well as advance in her career. Fatigue is a serious problem for women who work, especially if they have preschool children. Child care is always a major concern, particularly when children become ill. It becomes obvious in April that Kristin's husband, Ed, is not supportive of her career, although he clearly enjoys the benefits of her salary. Kristin believes that he supports her working only if she also continues to do everything else for him and the children at home. Of course, Kristin is exhausted from trying to do it all. She has been unable to resolve her role conflicts between home and work. Uncertain arrangements for child care is another concern for Kristin, especially when Ed makes little contribution towards their care and expends little effort on their children. The work–home role conflict is a very real one for working women. It is important enough to identify it here, although we have not located any research on effective ways to get husbands and fathers to do their fair share of housework and child care. Thus, we will have little to say about this problem in the rest of the book, but note it here because it can be a serious problem.

In April, Maria is still not looking or acting like a professional. It becomes clear to everyone but Maria that her "office romance" is over, and that Bill is tiring of her and of their relationship. Not only will she not get promoted, she may lose her present job. It is common for bosses to blame their own mistakes on subordinates, especially subordinate women. Bill

A woman may pay a high price if she challenges the bosses' power, especially if she is right.

may have yelled at Maria deliberately to antagonize her. However, it can be very risky for a subordinate woman to respond emotionally, especially when others are within hearing distance. The challenge to his power is something that a boss will remember for a long time, and Maria may pay a high price for it, especially if she is right.

Bill, Maria's boss, used his power position and her gullibility to have a brief affair, giving her false hopes of a real relationship as well as false expectations of a promotion. As he tired of her, he quickly found another cooperative woman. His technique for getting rid of Maria was to deliberately prod her into insubordination. He ended up using both a carrot (a good evaluation for a different job) and a stick (firing her for insubordination). Maria is still blaming herself for the romance's ending. Bill does not feel that he owes Maria anything. He just wants to get rid of her.

After an office affair, a boss does not feel he owes her anything. He just wants to get rid of her.

Kristin's friend, Helen, who wants to return to work, is encountering the usual problems after dropping out of the work force for five years. Many young women expect to have a career, marriage, and family, taking time off when the children are small. It may be difficult to return to work for the reasons Maria described, loss of contacts and outdated job skills. In most career areas, it is very unusual for a woman to return to the same job level. Because Helen did not remain active in her professional organization and in contact with her colleagues, she lost many of the necessary contacts to reenter the work force.

In May, a serious problem of sexual harassment arose for Kristin. She was less naive than Maria and anticipated a compromising situation with Roberto, even though attending the convention would have helped her professionally. The sexual harassment worsened in June. Roberto, her boss, was smart enough to harass her when no one else was around. Any complaint Kristin made would be one person's word against another's. The stress for women is very high in such a situation. Kristin must continue to make clear to Roberto that she wants him to stop. Sexual harassment does not stop of its own accord, no matter how much women hope that it will. If Roberto continues to harass her, Kristin should report it to his boss or to a person designated to handle such issues, documenting it as well as she can.

Maria identifies what may be the cause of many of Kristin's problems. Earlier, Kristin had done an outstanding job on a project, but neglected to make her own boss "look good" in the process.

Roberto is asserting his power and authority over her with routine

---

The "damned if you do,
damned if you don't
dilemma" for a woman is
being undervalued if she
remains accommodating and
being punished if she does
not.

---

assignments, requiring that she
do her own clerical work, and sexual harassment. Kristin cannot
seem to win. She was penalized by
her boss for "not knowing her
place" and for being very successful by making a lot of money for
the organization. She is now being undervalued and not making
any progress by spending all her
time, and some overtime, on routine assignments. This professional
woman's problem of being undervalued if she remains polite and accommodating, and being punished if she does not, is known as the
"damned if you do, damned if you don't" dilemma.

In addition, if Kristin had known about the salary inequity, the
time to have requested a salary increase was when she saved the
company a great deal of money. However, she would have needed the
support of her boss to be successful.

Kristin's and Maria's job interviewing experiences are not unusual,
especially if a woman is seeking a position outside the limited stereotypical jobs for women. Legally, interviewers cannot ask questions of
women that they do not ask of men, but the questions are there in one
form or another and need to be addressed. It does not matter if a
woman is married or single. It is wise to anticipate the questions and
prepare your answers to issues such as marriage plans, family size,
ability to travel, unexpected overtime and weekend work. Maria could
indicate that her career has priority in her life and possibly avoid
having to make a direct answer to questions not directly related to the
position.

With a better understanding of the issues involved in both their
problems, Maria and Kristin could have identified the basic causes of
their difficulties. They would understand that many of the things that
happened were not their fault. Also, they would be aware that there
were a few things that they could have anticipated and they could have
designed better ways to handle them. Understanding the issues could
have made a difference in the final outcomes.

THE WIN–WIN SOLUTION

There is one strategy that is so important we will refer to it throughout
the book. The best general approach to any specific problem is the win-
win solution—devising a solution to the problem that brings gains, or a
"win," to both parties or to everyone involved (Pruitt & Lewis, 1975)

In a win–win strategy, everyone involved in the interaction benefits. Some may benefit more than others, but everyone "wins" something. It can include tradeoffs, status, recognition, power, money, or advancement. When the win–win strategy is incorporated in a proposal, a negotiation, or used to resolve a conflict, it usually gains support. The various benefits can be one of the most effective ways to create change. For example, if Kristin had included her boss as part of her earlier successful project, she would not be seen as a threat, and she would probably be enjoying his support instead of being penalized by overwork and sexual harassment.

> In a win–win strategy, everyone involved in the interaction benefits.

SUMMARY

Although a major change in the work force has been the greatly increased number of working women, the traditional male perspectives and values continue to govern organizations. Most men and women consider sex discrimination a thing of the past, but it is still quite common. It is very subtle and difficult to recognize. Women's work and communication is still being devalued by both men and women who are influenced by gender beliefs. It remains difficult for men and many women to interact with women in any way but the traditional stereotypical manner. The stereotypical beliefs and perceptions create a host of specific problems for working women. The best general strategy for dealing with problems is devising a win–win solution—a way to solve the problem that benefits everyone involved.

Specific solutions to these problems depend on the factors that cause them. The remainder of this book will describe what is known about these problems and its implications for solving them. We begin with the key issues of discriminatory perception, treatment, and evaluation of women. Although it seems preposterous, these processes continue to operate, although they are often difficult to detect or identify in the ongoing stream of work activity. In the next section we examine how, why, and when discriminatory processes operate, and their consequences for women, men, and organizations.

Section II
In the Mind's Eye:
How Women Are Seen
and Evaluated

Career progress and success depend primarily on the individual's ability, effort, and judgment—but not entirely. Career success can also be influenced, sometimes heavily influenced, by how work associates, especially supervisors, see you and think about you. As we saw in Chapter 1, women often blame themselves when things go wrong. This compounds the original problem by lowering the woman's self-confidence and making her doubt her ability. The two chapters in this section provide information that should make any woman think twice before blaming herself. They examine the mental processes that shape how women are seen and evaluated, and how they are treated as a result. Thus, they should also help women—and men—understand some of the hidden factors behind supervisors', co-workers' and subordinates' actions and decisions. These chapters are based primarily on research in psychology.

Chapter 2 begins with perception. It shows that "what we see" does not correspond exactly to "what is really there." Rather, it reflects an instant, automatic interpretation of what is really there, based on our previous knowledge, beliefs, and expectations about the situation and people involved. We "see" what we expect to see.

Unfortunately, what most people expect to see in a woman is the traditional gender stereotypes. Although we sincerely disavow the stereotypes consciously, they are still a part of everyone's store of "previous knowledge" about the world. Thus, they influence our perceptions and evaluations automatically, without our conscious awareness. As a result women are "seen" as less intelligent, less competent, and less "suited to authority" than they really are. Discriminatory judgments have been documented in virtually every area of organizational evaluation—hiring, salary, and promotion decisions; evaluation of intellectual products and performances; allocation of power, resources, and opportunity; and treatment in the face-to-face exchanges of daily work routines.

The outcomes of the discriminatory treatment create a self-fulfilling prophecy. The fact that women do not advance as fast or as far as men in the organization appears (erroneously) to "confirm" their lesser competence. Fortunately, the self-fulfilling prophecy can also work in reverse—to support women's perceived competence. The chapter concludes with some suggestions about how to turn this process to women's advantage.

Chapter 3 explains the mental processes that support and maintain the discriminatory effects of the gender stereotypes. First the stereotypes are organized together into a mental structure called the *gender schema*. The perceiver's gender schema is activated whenever the male–female category distinction arises, and it operates as a single unit, so a woman will be seen or assumed to be "emotional" with no evidence other than the fact that she is a woman.

The gender schema stereotypes operate as expectations. In addition to influencing perceptions and evaluations, they also influence behavior. One person's expectations, however false initially, lead the other to behave in a way that confirms them. This explains why women sometimes do behave in stereotypically "feminine" ways. The gender schema is also a matter of social consensus throughout society. Consensus, agreement about a matter of opinion, has the effect of making a belief appear "true," regardless of its objective validity. In the past, consensus about the stereotypes has disadvantaged women, but the consensus effect can also be used to validate women's ability, competence, and authority.

Other foibles of the human mind include the "fundamental attribution error"—seeing the characteristics of a person's behavior as caused by his or her internal dispositions, when in fact they were caused by external demands, such as the person's role status in the situation. In addition, people frequently lack awareness of the real determinants of their perceptions and judgments. Most importantly, all of these mental processes can operate without our conscious awareness of them. As a result, evaluators can sincerely, but ignorantly, claim fairness and objectivity, because they are genuinely unaware of their biases.

There is little hope of changing the way the human mind works. However, its products—the perception, evaluation, and decision results of the processes—can be changed by changing the contents of the "previous knowledge" on which the processes operate. The chapter concludes with some suggestions for changing the stereotypes.

The information in these two chapters has been an eye-opener and energizer for many women. Although the research results themselves are discouraging, remember that knowing what is happening is the first step to changing it.

2
Invisible Barriers: Gender Stereotypes and Discrimination

Remember Maria from Chapter 1? She believed she was not being discriminated against at work because of her sex, that her boss's evaluations of her were objective and fair. No doubt, her boss, Bill, would heartily agree. Most educated people now disavow prejudice or discrimination based on sex, and these disavowals are sincere. But despite their sincerity, for most people they are contrary to fact. The problem is that evaluation involves more interpretation than meets the eye—much of it unconscious.

> Evaluation involves more interpretation than meets the eye—much of it unconscious.

PERCEPTION REFLECTS PREVIOUS KNOWLEDGE

Imagine walking into a bank and seeing a man with a gun. If the man was wearing a police uniform, you would proceed with your errand and scarcely give him a second thought. But if he was wearing a ski mask and scruffy clothes, your reaction would be quite different. Our previous knowledge gives totally different meanings to the guns in these two situations. The experience we call "perception" gives meaning to a stimulus. The stimulus may be a person, object, event, or a record of credentials or performance. However, *what we see* depends on *what we know* about that stimulus in that situation. This is because we don't "see" with our eyes; we "see' with our brains. Our eyes are simply receptors of light waves. It is the brain that creates our conscious perception. This process of receiving and interpreting information is very fast and completely unconscious. Only the outcome, the result of the process, is conscious as our "perception" (Kuffler & Nicholls, 1976; Rock, 1983).

This is a difficult point to accept, because our experience is that we see the people and events around us accurately and immediately, as they really are. We *feel* that our perceptions faithfully represent reality. However, research on perception, cognition, behavior, and brain physiology consistently show that they do not (Campbell, 1967; Gazzaniga, 1985; Nauta, 1971; Nisbett & Ross, 1980). We are more likely to see what we already know is there, what we believe or expect to see in the situation.

These internal contributions to our own perceptions influence whether or not we perceive something, what characteristics of it we perceive, and which parts we fail to notice. They especially influence the meaning we attach to the stimulus and what we later recall about it (Erber & Fiske, 1984; Massad et al., 1979). The old adage proclaims that "seeing is believing." Research shows that the opposite is also true. Believing something makes seeing it more likely. This means that beliefs about women influence how evaluators see them. Characteristics of the stimulus also influence perception. A stimulus that is more intense (larger, brighter, louder, more distinctive) is more likely to be noticed than a less intense one (McArthur, 1981). "Perception" is an *interpretation* of the objective facts of reality.

The brain automatically selects relevant previous knowledge to guide and interpret conscious perceptions (Bargh, 1984). For example, before sitting down in a theater seat, we do not consciously consider whether or not it might bite us. Our *implicit knowledge* about the category of theater experiences, including theater seats, automatically provides the meanings that guide and interpret our conscious perceptions (Bruner, 1951; Marcel, 1982).

THE ROLE OF IMPLICIT KNOWLEDGE
IN CONSCIOUS PERCEPTION

Most of the information that shapes and guides conscious perception is implicit or tacit information, that is, previous knowledge about the world that we are not thinking about consciously, at the moment, but use unconsciously when the situation requires it. Specifically, it is information about common qualities or characteristics of *categories* of objects, events, and persons. For example, our store of implicit knowledge includes the facts that hamburgers might be edible, but chairs are not. Every adult has vast stores of implicit knowledge about "the nature" of men and women.

Much of this information can be made conscious, but it is *used unconsciously* to shape conscious perceptions and guide the focus of conscious attention (Lewicki, 1986). Being offered a hamburger makes you think consciously about the possibility of eating it, but being offered a chair raises no such considerations. Our implicit category knowledge also selects what kinds of evidence we will notice and what we will ignore. We might notice whether the hamburger has mustard or not, but consider the chair's comfort and location. Our previous knowledge also "fills in the gaps" in the actual evidence (Fiske & Taylor, 1984). For example, if we read that "Chris went to a restaurant, ordered steak, and was home by 9:00 p.m.," we assume that Chris ate steak for dinner—even though that fact was not included in the evidence. These same principles operate in our perceptions of people.

All perception is an approximation of reality. All evidence is more or less ambiguous. In the familiar routines of life, especially those involving simple, physical objects, we have learned that reality is and interpret the cues accordingly. When we see a magazine on a desk our eyes actually see a trapezoid, but our minds see a rectangle because we know that magazines are rectangular. In evaluating people, perception is also only approximate, and the evidence is complex as well as ambiguous (Bower, 1977; Calder, 1982). When the evidence becomes more complex, more loaded with bits of relevant information, we cannot absorb and process all of it, so we rely more and more on the categories and interpretations of our previous experience, and perception becomes less accurate (Bodenhausen & Lichtenstein, 1987).

We recognize this problem implicitly and therefore often have personnel evaluations, especially important ones, made by committees or groups. The idea is that misperceptions are idiosyncratic. Ordinarily, one person's misperceptions will be canceled out by the different interpretations of the others. Consensus, interpretations common to all members, usually provides reasonable accuracy. A problem arises only if all members' misperceptions are distorted in the *same* direction (Strasser & Titus, 1985). The fact that magicians can mystify an entire audience shows that misperceptions can be consensual. In personnel evaluations, gender stereotypes are a major source of consensual misperceptions.

GENDER STEREOTYPES AS IMPLICIT KNOWLEDGE

Gender stereotypes are common, culturewide beliefs about how men and women differ in personal qualities and characteristics. Stereotypic beliefs cause consensual misperception of work associates, job candidates, performances, and credentials (Deaux & Major, 1987; Hamilton,

1979; Nieva & Gutek, 1980). This occurs even though no one believes in stereotypes anymore, because there is a difference between our conscious beliefs and the store of implicit knowledge that our brains use automatically without our awareness (Bornstein et al., 1987). Although educated people sincerely disavow gender stereotypes when the topic is the focus of their conscious attention, the stereotypes still operate as implicit knowledge when attention is focused on other matters, such as evaluating someone's proposal at a staff meeting, or deciding which of several candidates is best qualified for a promotion (Hunt, 1987; Rasinski et al., 1985; Rothbart, 1981). Just as we see magazines as rectangular, we see women as "emotional." Stereotypes operate as both facts (descriptions) and values (prescriptions).

Stereotypes as Facts. Gender stereotypes are part of everyone's store of implicit knowledge. Imagine for a moment a scene in a hospital in which a doctor is giving instructions to a nurse about a patient's medications. In your imagined scene, what sex was the doctor? Which sex was the nurse? This is an example of automatic stereotypes filling in gaps in the evidence actually presented. The same kind of stereotyping is likely when you imagine a scene between a boss and a secretary. We all developed our previous experience about "what reality is" in a society and culture in which traditional gender stereotypes were assumed to be accurate descriptions of men and women. Women were loved and protected as wives, mothers, and sweethearts. At work, they were accepted in subordinate, nurturing, and service roles. But they were inconceivable as professional colleagues or in positions of authority over other adults (Caplow & McGee, 1958; Dubnos, 1985).

We all believed that women were inherently, by nature, different from men in abilities, interests, and mentality. Men and women were expected to differ in their interpersonal attitudes and behavior, especially toward each other, and were considered "suitable" for different kinds of occupations. Most people agreed that men were more intelligent, rational, objective, independent, aggressive, ambitious, and responsible. Men were the norm or standard (Deaux, 1976a). Women were seen as differing from this desirable standard in being less intelligent, and more subjective, intuitive, emotional, dependent, warm, sensitive to others, nurturant, and accommodating (Basow, 1986; Broverman et al., 1972; Williams & Best, 1982). Authority roles, at home and at work, required men. Women served as helpmates. Men were expected to be dominant, women deferent (Feldman-Summers & Kiesler, 1974).

The "masculine" attributes are *instrumental* or *agentic* traits, traits implying the ability to accomplish tasks. People have control over their abilities. We can use them or not as we choose in a given situation. The "feminine" traits are *expressive* or *communal,* the disposition to be sensitive and nurturing to others. Most people believe (erroneously) that we can not control our dispositions. Thus, women's "feminine" traits are seen as more inevitable than men's "masculine" traits. These stereotypic traits are the implicit knowledge that our brains use automatically, without our awareness, to guide our interactions with men and women, and to select, interpret, and remember information about them. Because we "see" what we believe (and therefore expect to see), a woman is seen as possessing the "feminine" traits and a man the "masculine" ones, whether they actually have them or not (Erber & Fiske, 1984).

> *Women are seen as possessing the "feminine" traits and men the "masculine" ones, whether they actually have them or not.*

Stereotypes as Values. These stereotypic gender expectations were not only *de*scriptive; they were also *pre*scriptive. We believed not only that men *were* naturally dominant and women submissive, but that men *should be* dominant and women submissive. A certain amount of "aggressiveness" was considered acceptable, even desirable, in men, but not in women. In short, the stereotypic traits were considered desirable as well as factual (Holter, 1971). Because they were desirable, we all tried hard to cultivate and display those considered appropriate to our sex and, equally important, suppress those considered inappropriate. As a result, the stereotypic differences in personality and behavior were real, albeit smaller than we liked to believe (Eagly, 1987). These stereotypes determine our implicit expectations for men and women, and thereby shape our perceptions of what each sex *can and should* do and what they *cannot or should not* do (Bem, 1981; Slusher & Anderson, 1987). The implicit demand for "feminine" behavior presents problems for women in organizations that will be discussed later in this chapter and in subsequent chapters.

> *People believe not only that men are naturally dominant and women submissive, but also that men should be dominant and women submissive.*

Gender in Occupational Stereotypes. Adding further to the impact of the gender stereotypes, there are also culturally consensual occupation stereotypes. For example, the appearance and personal characteristics we expect in top executives are different from those we expect in parking lot attendants. Unfortunately, the personal characteristics associated with most professional and managerial positions, that is, positions involving decision making and authority over other adults, match those of the "masculine" stereotype and do not match the "feminine" stereotype (Deaux & Lewis, 1984; Schein, 1973, 1975). Thus, a woman who does in fact possess the intelligence, leadership, and initiative required for an authority position will be "seen" as possessing less of these characteristics than a man who possesses no more of them than she.

Most crucially, a major stereotypic requirement of most high-level positions is simply "being a male"—regardless of ostensibly relevant personality traits (Glick et al., 1988; Kalin & Hodgins, 1984). Thus, even if a woman manages to demonstrate that she has the experience and personal traits required for a managerial position, she still will not meet the evaluator's automatic, unconscious image of the occupant of that position as well as a perhaps objectively less-qualified man (Futoran & Wyer, 1986).

GENDER DIFFERENCES: LEARNED OR BORN?

Until relatively recently most people (including most scientists) assumed that the stereotypic "masculine" and "feminine" traits were biologically inherent and sex-related. We now know that all of the traits, both "masculine" and "feminine," even those like aggressiveness that do have a biological basis, can be either enhanced or suppressed by training and life experience (Denenburg et al., 1966; Hyde & Linn, 1986).

Indeed, most of the stereotypic traits could be created solely by socialization, expectations, and practice. For example, (a) young boys and girls are given different kinds of toys. Boy's toys, like trucks, trains, and erector sets, encourage active, directive behavior and attitudes. Girl's toys, like dolls, toy stoves, and kitchen sets, encourage relational, caring, nurturant behavior and attitudes. (b) Little boys and girls are treated differently. A boy who falls and hurts his knee is encouraged not to cry. A similarly hurt little girl is cuddled, comforted, and allowed to cry. (c) In addition to such direct training, both children and adults also model or copy the behavior, mannerisms, attitudes, preferences, interests, and life goals of others of their own sex who seem to be liked, approved, or powerful (Bandura & Walters 1963; Mischel, 1970). (d) Finally, from childhood on, we all try actively to meet the social gender-coded expectations for our sex (Kohlberg, 1966).

Because we now recognize that the "sex" stereotypes are due less to biological sex than to social training, expectations, and modeling, we call them "gender" stereotypes. *Sex* refers to the biological category of "male or female." *Gender* refers to "masculine" or "feminine" characteristics resulting from social expectations, training, and experience. However, despite training, experience, and expectations, both men and women possess both the "masculine" and "feminine" traits, at least to some degree, and many possess both types of traits in virtually equal degrees (Bem, 1974). This mixing of both "masculine" and "feminine" traits in the same person is usually unnoticed or disregarded, because we notice what we expect, and we ignore, discount, or reinterpret what we do not expect. This means that anyone, of either sex, can, with practice, develop any of the traits he or she chooses (Yamada et al., 1983).

SUMMARY

The experience we call "perception" gives meaning to the objective facts of reality. The meanings are constructed in the brain, instantly, automatically, and without our awareness, from our previous knowledge about the world. We "see" what we believe or expect to see. Although most people now sincerely disavow gender stereotypes, they still operate as automatic "knowledge" when attention is focused on other topics. The "masculine" stereotypes imply competence and legitimate claim to authority; the "feminine" stereotypes imply lesser competence and subordinate status. These stereotypes select what evidence will be noticed, interpret the meaning of evidence that is noticed, and fill in the gaps when evidence is missing or forgotten. The stereotypes operate as facts—beliefs about the "nature" of men and women and what they can and cannot do—and also as values—beliefs about what men and women should and should not do. Although some personality traits have a biological basis, they can all be enhanced or suppressed by socialization training, social expectations, and practice.

PERCEPTUAL BIAS:
STEREOTYPES IN ACTION AND EVALUATION

Conscious beliefs about men and women are changing (McBroom, 1984), but stereotypes still operate as implicit knowledge (Basow, 1986). We are not aware of their influence on our perceptions because it is built into the evidence as we perceive it, but research can detect it. But first, a note of caution. Research results should be regarded as probabilities: "This is what happens in *most* cases—but not every case." For many of the results, the reader will undoubtedly know a real woman or man whose experience contradicts the research result. Such live examples are vivid and compelling. In our minds, they seem to outweigh the pale verbal statement of the research result. But this is an error. The research results are based on dozens, sometimes hundreds, of real people. Among them, there is usually a minority who were exceptions to the general result for the majority. The example you know just adds one more exception to the minority, but it does not change the finding that the majority acted as they did.

Some of the research studies are based on large samples of working managers and professionals. In others a standard procedure is to have a large number of evaluators judge a set of products, credentials, or candidates for quality, hiring, or promotion. A particular candidate (product or resumé) is identified as a man (or a man's work or record) for half of the evaluators, and the identical evidence is presented to the others as that of a woman. With this procedure, the perceived quality of identical evidence attributed to men versus women can then be compared precisely.

Intellectual Products. Evaluators in a critical reading exercise judged essays attributed to male authors as superior to the *identical* essays bearing female authorship (Goldberg, 1968; Paludi & Strayer, 1985). These evaluators were not discriminating intentionally. On the contrary, they sincerely "saw" the contents as more important, authoritative, and convincing when they believed the author was a male. Exactly the same result occurred when the products evaluated were paintings allegedly entered in an art contest (Pheterson et al., 1971). This is *perceptual bias:* We "see" what our implicit knowledge leads us to expect (Erber & Fiske, 1984). The stereotypes tell us that men are more intelligent and competent than women, so our brains interpret the actual evidence differently, depending on whether we "know" the author was a man or a woman. This means that evaluators discriminate against women—however unintentionally—in evaluating their performance in everyday work routines and their records of achievement in hiring, salary, and promotion decisions (Deaux & Emswiller, 1974).

> Evaluators sincerely "saw" the essays as more important, authoritative, and convincing when they believed the author was a man.

These product-judging experiments have been repeated dozens of times using different groups of people as evaluators and different kinds of products to be judged. Over half of them show promale bias. The others show no bias, or occasionally even profemale bias. Some of the no-bias results may reflect the increase in conscious egalitarianism.

However, another explanation for may of them involves the evaluators' expertise in the area and personal involvement with the judgment outcome (Fiske & Kinder, 1981). Most of the no-bias results come from studies in which the evaluators were of lower status or had less expertise than the authors of the products they were evaluating, for example, a random sample of inner-city "housewives" judging magazine articles by published authors. In contrast, most of the studies in which the evaluators had expertise relevant to the products, or were of higher status than the product authors, produced evaluations biased in favor of men. Obviously, in real-life organizations, the evaluators have higher status in the organization than those they are evaluating; they also have experience ("expertise") relevant to the judgments required, and they are personally involved in the judgment outcomes.

His and Her Salaries. Women receive lower salaries than men with the same qualifications receive for the same positions. The salary difference between men and women occurs not only at the initial entry level; it increases with increasing experience and status rank in the organization. Men receive higher salaries than women with the same job titles (Dipboye et al., 1977; Olson & Frieze, 1987; Salary Tables, 1982; Terborg & Ilgen, 1975).

Over the years from 1955 to 1983, full-time working women earned from 59 to 64 cents to every dollar earned by full-time working men. However, much of this difference in salary was due to a differen n occupations. Most women worked in low-paid "feminine" occupations, most men in higher paid "masculine" occupations. In 1982, entry-level salaries for women in a sample of managerial, business, and professional occupations averaged 98% of men's entry-level salaries in the same occupations, but decreased to 92% of male salaries at the higher levels of the same occupations (Blau & Ferber, 1985).

Economists using human capital theory (a theory of earnings as returns on investments in job training and experience) have looked for factors other than sex discrimination to explain the salary difference between men and women. These factors are years of education, years of work experience, job interruptions and part-time work, job area and industry, job level (e.g., line versus staff positions), marriage and children, family background, and personality traits. Olson and Frieze (1987) reviewed the research on these factors for men and women managers with MBA degrees and concluded that, indeed, men do have about 2 years' more work experience than women at the same job levels, and women have more work interruptions and periods of part-time work than men. Although some studies find no differences in job area and industry between men and women managers from the same business school, others find fewer women managers in production and engineering, metals, and investment banking, all areas with higher managerial salaries. Women managers are less likely than men to hold line positions, which are associated with better promotion prospects. Both marriage and children (especially three or more children) decrease women's salaries, partly, at least, because marriage often decreases women's geographic mobility.

It is sometimes argued that these factors represent individual choices, so women have no one but themselves to blame for their lower salaries. Yet differences in previous work experience, "choice" of job area and industry, and starting in a staff rather than line position could reflect discriminatory hiring practices rather than women's autonomous choices. Marriage and children are clearly individual choices. However, marriage and children do *not* decrease management salaries for men. Another factor, family background (having better educated parents with higher incomes), is associated with higher salaries for *men* managers. However, women managers come from higher socioeconomic backgrounds than men managers. Finally, men and women do not differ in years of education; and studies of men and women managers find *no* personality differences in work motivation, ambition, desire for success, recognition, or higher salaries, or knowledge about how to become successful as a manager. However, even when all of the real differences between men and women managers are taken into account, they "explain" only about half of the real difference in salaries (Blau & Ferber, 1985; Olson & Frieze, 1987). Gender discrimination in salaries remains alive and well.

Salary discrimination can be subtle and difficult to detect. For example, when a woman with 10 years of experience, and a man with 3 years, hold comparable positions, they may be paid the same because they are both doing the same job. However, in a reverse situation, when the man is senior and woman junior, he may be paid more because of his greater experience. As a result, men receive higher salaries, on the average, than women in comparable positions.

Hiring and Promotion. Promale perceptual bias also selects and interprets the evidence and fills in the gaps in evaluations of candidate resumés' for hiring decisions, and in evaluations of achievement records for promotion and salary decisions. For example, Fidell (1975) sent resumé summaries of eight psychologists to 147 chairpersons of psychology departments and asked them to give the rank at which each should be considered for hiring. Each candidate description bore a woman's name for half of the chairpersons and a man's name for the others. The average rank suggested for the candidates when they were identified as women was assistant professor, an entry rank without the job security of tenure. In contrast, the chairpersons saw the identical evidence attributed to men as meriting associate professorships, a higher rank usually associated with tenure and always associated with higher salaries.

As a result of the stereotypic expectations and the perceptual bias they cause, men are more likely to be hired for professional and managerial positions than equally qualified women (Arvey, 1979; Cohen & Bunker, 1975; Dipboye et al., 1975; Haefner, 1977; Powell & Posner, 1983; Rosen & Jerdee, 1974). Evaluators rate men's applications for such positions higher than identical applications from women on such qualities as acceptability, service potential, and longevity (Rosen et al., 1975; Gutek & Stevens, 1979).

Part of the sex difference in salaries, especially the increasing difference over years of employment, may be due to discriminatory promotion practices. It is still true in all business, industry, government and professional occupations that, as rank in the occupation increases, the percentage of women decreases (Blau & Ferber, 1985; National Research Council, 1981). This exclusion of women from the higher status positions is popularly called "the glass ceiling" (Morrison et al., 1987). The glass ceiling is a direct result of perceptual bias. Because women are "seen" as less competent than men, women are less likely to be promoted, or to be promoted more slowly than men with the same qualifications, experience, and performance levels (Nieva & Gutek, 1981). In fact, in one field study of working supervisors and subordinates, the women received higher performance evaluations than the men, but the men received more promotions than the women (Gupta et al., 1983).

The glass ceiling is perceptual bias in action.

Performance, Authority, and Leadership. Perceptual bias also distorts evaluations of performance, authority, and leadership. The same evidence that confers status or high competence evaluations on a man fails to bestow the same distinction on a woman (Frank, 1988). For example, being seated at the head of the table in a mixed-sex work group identified a man as the group's leader, but not a woman (Porter & Geis, 1981; Rhue et al., 1984). Competent men are judged to be more competent than women who are objectively equally competent (Deaux & Taynor,

Although the women received higher performance evaluations, the men received more promotions.

1973; Vaughn & Wittig, 1981). Men's leadership is judged better than identical leadership by women (Bartol & Butterfield, 1976; Dobbins et al., 1985). Men's responses to problem situations are seen as more "logical" than identical responses by women (Taynor & Deaux, 1975). These studies show that unconscious sex bias may influence the perceived quality of suggestions, opinions, project proposals, academic courses, leadership, and the handling of administrative responsibilities.

Again, there are some studies that show no promale bias in evaluations of leadership and competence (e.g., Goktepe & Schneier, 1988; Seifert & Miller, 1988). Most of these are very recent, suggesting that promale bias may in fact be decreasing. However, most of them also used college students, reputedly more liberal and egalitarian than their elders, as evaluators. Most importantly, the college student evaluators in these studies usually occupied the role of subordinates of the leader they were evaluating, not the leader's supervisor, the person who usually makes the evaluations that count in real organizations.

Opportunities, Resources, and Power. Rosen and Jerdee (1973, 1974) sent high-level bank administrators routine written requests ostensibly from junior branch executives. Requests for promotion and for financial support to attend a professional development conference were granted more often to men than to women presenting identical credentials and justifications. Men's requests to fire a subordinate they considered unsatisfactory were granted more often than the same request from a woman. Men are accorded not only more opportunities and resources, but also more power and autonomy on the job, than equally qualified women. Work done by women is not only devalued upon completion, it is given less organizational support from the beginning. This topic will be discussed in more detail in Section III.

Success, Failure, and Ability. Common explanations for why a person succeeded or failed at a task also produce negative expectations for women. Evaluators attribute men's successes to their ability, a stable, internal factor that is likely to continue into the future. They attribute men's mistakes and failures to unstable or external causes such as lack of effort, a difficult situation, or bad luck. Thus, men's failures can be discounted as "temporary." In contrast, people attribute women's successes to unstable or external causes, and their failures to "ability," specifically, *lack* of ability (Deaux, 1976a; Frieze et al., 1978). For example, if Jason, the purchasing accounts manager, frequently fails to complete his work, it would be typical to conclude that "the job is too heavy" and he needs an assistant. Note that this decision increases Jason's "supervisory responsibilities" and thus his salary. In contrast, if Megan, the sales accounts manager, frequently fails to complete her work, it would be concluded that she is incompetent. ("She can't handle the job"—and needs a less responsible, and lower paying, position.) Thus, men's successes confirm their merit, and their failures are discounted. In contrast, women's failures are perceived as confirming a lack of ability, and their successes are discounted. As a result, expectations of future performance are more positive and favorable for men than for women with identical performance records (Cash et al., 1977). Thus, men are more likely to be hired and promoted than equally qualified women.

Face-to-Face Interactions. The stereotypic expectations not only influence perceptions and judgments, they also influence people's behavior, how they treat men and women in face-to-face situations on the job. For example, Lott (1987) found that men physically distanced themselves from a woman work partner by turning their heads or bodies away from her, but did not distance themselves from men partners. This distancing would give the woman less informational feedback from her partner to use to coordinate her part of the team effort. In a study of problem solving in mixed-sex discussion groups, the researchers secretly gave one member of each group the correct solution beforehand with instructions that the solution could be proposed as his or her own idea, but that he or she could not reveal that it came from the experimenter. When a man had the solution, it was accepted and applauded. But when a woman offered the same correct solution, it was ignored or rejected (Altemeyer & Jones, 1974). In discussions generally, women's contributions are interrupted, overlooked, ignored, or "unheard" (Bunker & Seashore, 1975).

In another study of group discussions, both men and women group members responded to women's contributions with fewer facial expressions of approval and more expressions of disapproval than they gave to the *same* contributions from men. By assuming leadership and dominance, the women had violated others' unconscious stereotypic expectations (Butler & Geis, 1990). Such subtle, fleeting facial expressions can influence evaluations of the contribution. Because we do not recognize that the approving expressions are actually caused by the stereotypic expectations being confirmed, and the disapproving ones by their being violated, we misinterpret approval as "evidence" of a good contribution and disapproval as "evidence" of a poor one (Brown & Geis, 1984). These differences in the way men and women are treated can influence their performances as well as others' evaluations of them. This topic will be discussed further in Chapter 3. Women in small group discussions will be examined in Chapter 5.

AMBIGUITY, SEX TYPING OF JOB, AND COMPETENCE

Nieva and Gutek (1980) reviewed the research on sex discrimination in evaluation and concluded that the likelihood and amount of promale bias depends on three factors: First, promale bias increases when the situation is more ambiguous, and thus requires more inference or interpretation by evaluators. Recall that stereotypes influence interpretation automatically and unconsciously. More interpretation is required when the job criteria are vague, ambiguous, or highly complex, or when the evidence about the candidate is sparse or ambiguous. More inference is also required in hiring and promotion situations than for performance evaluations. In hiring and promotion decisions, the evaluator must infer the candidates' likely future performance in a new situation from evidence of their past performance in a different situation. It is here that evaluators' "ability" attributions for men's successes and "luck" attributions for women's can be especially powerful.

The second factor influencing the amount and prevalence of bias is the gender-role match or mismatch of the job or the behavior it requires. If the job is stereotypically masculine, women will be less likely to be hired than equally qualified men, and women's performances will be evaluated as poorer or less indicative of "ability" than identical performances by men. Most professional and managerial jobs are stereotypically masculine.

Finally, the likelihood of bias is also influenced by the performers' or candidates' level of competence. Evaluators rate competent men higher than equally competent women. On the other hand, incompetent women are rated higher and preferred more than equally incompetent men. Note that this seeming inconsistency actually reflects the gender stereotypes. In general, competence is preferred over incompetence. But "competence" is also a stereotypically "masculine" attribute, so it is expected and therefore seen in men. Incompetence is expected and accepted in women.

THE "DAMNED IF SHE DOES, DAMNED IF SHE DOESN'T" DILEMMA

Remember that stereotypes operate as values as well as facts. Not only are women believed incapable of assertiveness, they are also disapproved for it. Because stereotypes operate as values, professional and managerial women frequently find themselves in a "damned if you do, damned if you don't" dilemma. The problem is that women are *liked* when they conform to the stereotypic expectations for women, but many of these expectations are irrelevant to professional career success, or even detrimental to success (for example, the less intelligent, more emotional, and "sex object" stereotypes). When women are merely as competent as comparable men, they are ignored and undervalued (O'Leary, 1974). But when women are obviously more competent, they are often disliked, and some plausible-appearing reason is found for rejecting them. For example, they were excluded from task groups in favor of competent men, and often also in favor of *less* competent women (Hagen & Kahn, 1975).

Similarly, because women are expected to be accommodating to the needs and wishes of others, including their organization (Lubinski et al., 1983), they may be pressured more heavily and more often than men to accommodate. Thus, if they wish to preserve as much autonomy as men are accorded, they may have to refuse such requests more often and more forcefully. As a result, they may be seen as *less* cooperative or accommodating than the men.

Why don't women speak up and insist on being recognized or given fair treatment? Because when they do, they are likely to be perceived as cold, unfeminine, aggressive, abrasive, arrogant, or neurotic (e.g., Costrich et al., 1975; Denmark, 1979; Feather & Simon, 1975; Horner, 1972; Porter & Geis, 1981; Seyfried & Hendrick, 1972). A woman who oversteps the stereotypic expectations too far, in too many ways, will not only be disliked but can also incur hostility and reprisal (Alperson & Friedman, 1983; Butler & Geis, 1990). The professional woman's dilemma is often between being undervalued if she remains unassertive, deferent, and accommodating, and being punished if she does not.

> The professional woman's dilemma is between being undervalued if she acts "feminine," and being punished if she does not.

STEREOTYPE EFFECTS ON WOMEN'S PERFORMANCE

So far, we have emphasized the effects of implicit gender stereotypes on evaluators' perceptions, judgments, and treatment of women. However the stereotyped beliefs influence women as well as men. Women know, as well as men do, that women are assumed to be less competent and are expected to be deferent and accommodating, especially toward men. These beliefs influence women's performance.

Leadership. For example, in mixed-sex task discussions, women speak less than men and offer fewer contributions to the group's task (Kimble et al., 1981). Because leadership depends on amount of contributions, women have objectively shown less leadership than men (Nyquist & Spence, 1986; Schneier & Bartol, 1980; Sorentino & Boutillier, 1975). This is not due to a sex difference in intelligence or verbal skills. Women are as intelligent as men, get as good or better grades throughout school, and have as good or better verbal skills (Erkut, 1983; Maccoby & Jacklin, 1974).

Part of the sex difference in discussion performance may be due to a difference in task-relevant knowledge. Until recently, most of the discussion topics and problems used in such research were drawn from stereotypically "masculine" areas of knowledge and expertise. More recent research shows that, with stereotypically "feminine" topics, women contribute more than men (Wentworth & Anderson, 1984). These results also confirm that women do not lack discussion skills or initiative. However, most of the problems and discussion topics in the real world of managers and professionals are stereotypically "masculine." Even a discussion of recipes in a baking company would be "masculine" because of its financial implications for the company.

A major reason for the sex difference in discussion contributions is simply the set of social expectations that men should be dominant and women deferent, that "leadership" is a "masculine" behavior and prerogative. These social expectations have two effects, both serving to discourage women's contributions. First, they encourage women (who are as much influenced by them as men are) to inhibit their contributions and defer to men. Second, they lead men (and other women) in the group to treat women's contributions as unimportant or unwelcome, as noted previously in this chapter. Over time, this negative reception further discourages women from initiating contributions. These effects were illustrated in a study in which participants were paired on the basis of their individual dominance levels. The partners' task was to decide together which of them should be the leader for an allegedly following discussion. When two men or two women with unequal dominance levels were paired together, the dominant partner usually emerged as the leader. But when a dominant woman was paired with a nondominant man, it was usually the man who became the leader. The woman used her dominance to insure that social expectations would be met (Megargee, 1969). Leadership will be discussed in more detail in Chapter 6.

Self-Confidence. Women also show the effects of the "less competent" stereotype in their levels of self-confidence. Although women report as much self-esteem as men in response to general questions about self-worth, they report lower confidence of succeeding on specific tasks and problems and in male-dominated occupations (Bridges, 1988; Erkut, 1983; Maccoby & Jacklin, 1974). One problem of low confidence is living with unpleasant feelings and anxiety. Another is that lower confidence actually decreases performance quality (Lenney & Gold, 1982). Again, this sex difference may be due to the use of stereotypically "masculine" tasks and problems, or to cues that the performance situation is competitive (Lenney, 1977). However, it could also represent the effect of the stereotypes that men are more intelligent and competent than women (Vollmer, 1986). Women's explanations for the causes of their successes and failures also reflect the stereotypes. Women themselves attribute their successes to luck or an easy task, and their failures to "lack of ability" (Bar Tal & Frieze, 1977). These beliefs could explain women's lack of self-confidence in their ability to succeed at any new task or problem.

However, this research on leadership and confidence should be interpreted with caution. The results come from random unselected samples of men and women, mostly university students. They indicate that the *average* women differs from the *average* man in these ways. However, those women who enter professional or managerial careers differ considerably from the average women (Moore & Rickel, 1980). In fact studies of actual, working managers and professionals indicate that men and women in similar positions do the same things in the same ways with the same frequency and achieve the same results (Instone et al., 1983; Pyke & Kahil, 1983). The final word on sex differences in performances is not yet available.

Career Aspirations. Until recently, few women were preparing or applying for professional and managerial positions (Blau & Ferber, 1985). Many women rejected the lengthy training programs required for such positions in order to remain free to follow a potential or existing husband when he moved across the country for his training or job. Women also rejected such occupations because the time and commitment they required would interfere with domestic responsibilities. Finally, many women assumed (realistically) that, even with training, they were unlikely to be hired. They therefore prepared instead for stereotypically "feminine" occupations. Although salaries were low, they were sure of a job, and the skills were immediately transferable to their husband's changing locations. The specific reasons are many, but they all come down to the social expectations of cultural gender beliefs—expectations that a woman should follow her husband where his career took them, that women's first responsibility was to home and family, and that women were "unsuited" for authority positions. These more conscious social expectations are now changing. Since about 1970, more and more women have been preparing and applying for professional and managerial positions (Fiorentine, 1988; National Center for Education Statistics, 1982).

Although most women still assume responsibility for most home and family duties, there is more talk of sharing them, and perhaps more actual sharing. (If so, it has yet to be documented by published research.) More women are securing management positions (Blau & Ferber, 1985). The problem now is advancing above the "glass ceiling" of the gender stereotypes that keeps most women in the lower ranks.

The evidence clearly shows widespread perceptual bias and discrimination against women in the work place. In addition, the stereotypes may lower women's own self-confidence and the quality of their performance. These conditions must certainly cause confusion, frustration, and discouragement for working women. However, despite the inequities and frustrations, research also shows that work is good for women. Married women who hold full-time jobs have higher self-esteem, better mental health, less depression, and report feeling less lonely, more competent as homemakers, more happy and satisfied with their marriages, and more attractive to men, than married women who are exclusively homemakers (Birnbaum, 1975; Gove, 1972). This is not to imply that women like or want the inequities. Rather, they endure them in order to enjoy the real rewards and benefits of work.

Outside employment is good for women despite the frustrations and inequities.

SUMMARY

Stereotypes causes discriminatory treatment of women. Because we "see" what we believe or expect to see, women's work is "seen" as less valuable than identical work by men. This is *perceptual bias.* Women are paid lower salaries than those of men holding the same positions. Women are less likely to be hired for professional and managerial positions than men with identical qualifications, and even if they are hired, they are less likely to be promoted. Women are not granted the power, authority, or organizational resources that supervisors automatically accord men in the same position. Because the stereotypes devalue women's intellectual competence, others do not listen to women's ideas. Thus, it is difficult for women to contribute enough to emerge as leaders, and when they are appointed as leaders, their leadership is judged as less effective than identical leadership by men. Women's successes are attributed to luck, men's to ability; women's failures are attributed to lack of ability, men's to bad luck. This means that expectations for a woman's future performance are lower than expectations for a man with an identical performance record. The stereotypes influence face-to-face interaction as well as formal evaluations.

Perceptual bias is greater when the evidence is more ambiguous, when the job is stereotypically masculine, and when the candidates are highly competent. Professional and managerial women often face a "damned if you do, damned if you don't" dilemma. Women are expected (unconsciously) to conform to the "feminine" stereotypes, but such behavior does not match conscious norms for managerial behavior, and is often detrimental to career success.

The stereotypes influence women as well as their evaluators. Women are less likely to contribute to mixed-sex group discussions and are therefore less likely to become leaders. Women have less self-confidence in their ability to succeed at new tasks, especially stereotypically "masculine" tasks. Until recently women have had lower career aspirations than men, but this is rapidly changing. In spite of the frustrations and inequities caused by perceptual bias, women who work outside the home are healthier, happier, and more satisfied with their marriages and their personal attractiveness than women who are exclusively homemakers.

So far we have considered how implicit, cultural stereotypes operate unconsciously to influence supervisors' perception, evaluation, and treatment of women, and women's performance levels and their perceptions of themselves. Next we turn to the questions of what keeps the discriminatory system going, despite our best intentions, and how it can be changed.

STEREOTYPES, SEX, STATUS, AND ROLE MODELS: A SELF-FULFILLING PROPHECY

Stereotypes and Sex. Because a person's sex, being male or female, is a biological category, we tend to assume automatically that the stereotypic traits associated with sex also have a biological basis—

People mistakenly assume that men are rational because they are male, and that women are emotional because they are female.

that men are rational and ambitious because they are male, and that women are emotional and dependent because they are female (Campbell, 1967). The sex differences in behavior are real, but most of them have no biological basis (Maccoby & Jacklin, 1974).

This does not mean that the traits themselves have no biological basis. Indeed, some do (Reinisch et al., 1987). However, the biological dispositions for both the "masculine" and "feminine" traits occur in both sexes. Thus, members of the same sex differ more from one another on most traits than the average of that sex differs from the average of the opposite sex. Women differ more among themselves in intelligence, rationality, and competence (and men differ more among themselves) than the average woman differs from the average man. Why, then, do our beliefs in sex differences, and actual behavorial differences, continue to prevail?

One answer is socialization. As discussed previously, from infancy on, males are trained to be "masculine" and females "feminine." However, training and practice cannot be the whole answer. Childhood behaviors and attitudes disappear in adulthood unless they continue to be rewarded. Socialization explains *how we learn* the gender roles, but not why they continue to persist in adulthood.

Stereotypes, Sex, and Status. The continuing source of rewards for gender-role behavior and expectations must lie in adult activities. One clue to that source of rewards is the difference in the roles traditionally assigned to men and women.

Given the minimum ability requirements, most people behave according to the demands and expectations of the roles they occupy. "Personality" (including the biologically based traits) has *less* influence than role demands on the way people behave (Baumeister et al., 1988; Dovidio et al., 1988). Remember that most people actually possess both the "masculine" and the "feminine" traits, at least to some degree (Bem, 1974). Thus, when the need arises they can express whichever of the traits are required. In fact, people come to take on, as their own, the characteristics of the roles they perform (Fazio et al., 1981). Thus, for most of us, our individual personality traits represent an interaction, a mixture, of our own inherent dispositions and the characteristics of the attitudes and behavior required by the social roles we choose and are assigned by society (Eagly, 1987). This suggests that we should look for the basis of the "masculine" and "feminine" traits not in individuals' sex, but rather in the social roles they occupy in groups and organizations (Hoffman & Hurst, 1990). The traditional roles of men and women differ most consistently in status level. High-status roles require dominance, ambition, and independence (Ickes & Knowles, 1982). In organizations of all types throughout our society, most high-status roles are occupied by men (Basow, 1986; Kanter, 1977). Thus, only (or primarily) men are seen displaying these high-status behavorial or "personality" traits.

> The "personality" traits traditionally labeled as "masculine" and "feminine" may simply be the result of high- versus low-status role demands.

In contrast, low-status subordinate roles require sensitivity, responsiveness, deference, and accommodation to the superior's style and wishes (Ickes & Knowles, 1982). Most of the women we encounter in most organizations hold lower status roles. Even in the family, although most husbands and wives consider themselves personally as equals, the wife *role* is often subordinate to the husband role (Scanzoni, 1982). As a result, virtually all women are seen displaying these low-status behavioral traits. In short, the stereotypic "personality" traits traditionally labeled as "masculine" or "feminine" may simply be the *result* of high- versus low-status role demands.

Because advancement and status are assigned preferentially to men, only men are observed displaying the high-status behavioral traits. Accordingly, these high-status traits *appear* to us to be "masculine." Because virtually all women are seen in low-status roles, the low-status traits appear "characteristically feminine" (Thompson, 1981; Winter & Uleman, 1984). Role status determines not only the role occupants' behavior, but also others' expectations for them, and thus how they are treated. People who are treated as less important or valuable come to behave accordingly, and also to think of themselves as less important, competent, or valuable. The effects of others' expectations will be discussed further in Chapter 3.

Research has begun to document the impact of role status on the perceived personality traits of the role occupants. In one study (Geis et al., 1984) viewers watched replicas of three TV commercials showing unequal-status relationships between a man and a woman. In one set of replicas, both actors treated the man as the important, high-status partner in the relationship, treating his wishes, needs, and preferences as the only concern in the situation. Neither made any reference to wishes or preferences the woman might have had. In the other set of replicas, the *same* man and woman switched roles in the same scenario, the woman this time playing the high-status role of the important person, and the man the low-status helpmate role. Viewers described the men in the first set as "rational, independent, dominant, ambitious leaders," and the women as "emotional, dependent, submissive, contented followers." When men and women were seen in the traditional unequal status interactions, they were also seen as possessing the traditional "masculine" and "feminine" personality traits. However, when viewers saw the reversed-role scenarios, they described the *women* as "rational, independent, dominant, ambitious leaders" and the *men* as "emotional, dependent, submissive, contented followers." The stereotypic "personality traits" depended on the actors' role status, *not* on their sex or their real personalities. Similar results have been reported by Deaux and Lewis (1984), Eagly and Steffen (1984), Linimon, Barron, and Falbo (1984), and Hoffman and Hurst (1990).

Why don't we recognize that the "masculine" and "feminine" traits are created by high- versus low-status role demands? Because we all habitually commit "the fundamental attribution error" (Ross, 1977)—mistakenly attributing the characteristics of the person's behavior to his or her internal "personality traits" when in fact they were caused by situational factors such as role demands or expectations. We fall into this error so easily and so often because the person is physically visible and the focus of our attention, and the situational role demands are not physically visible and are usually not the focus of conscious attention. (This error will be discussed in more detail in Chapter 3.) In the case of the stereotypic gender traits, we take this error process one step further. Because virtually all women are seen in low-status roles and only men are seen in high-status roles, we compound the initial error by further assuming that the "personality dispositions" are not only inherent, but are also biologically linked to sex (Campbell, 1967).

In short, our stereotypes, reflecting our implicit cultural belief system, tell us that sex, being male or female, determines which personality characteristics we will inevitably possess, and that those personality traits then determine which occupations and status levels are "suitable" for us. In contrast, research shows that our sex actually determines social expectations for "suitable" jobs, roles, and statuses, and these "sex-appropriate" jobs, roles, and statuses then determine which particular "personality traits" we will develop.

In the past, this process has worked to make men and women appear to have different sets of personality traits—the traditional gender stereotypes. However, the *same* process can also work to eliminate the stereotypes. If the stereotypical traits are created by the unequal status of men and women, then they should be broken when men and women occupy high- and low-status roles in equal numbers. As noted earlier, women are now entering high-status careers in increasing numbers. Although they are still a minority in such careers, if the process continues, the sex-based expectations and stereotypic personality differences should continue to diminish. In these circumstances, women's femininity would be guaranteed by their biological sex— being female—*not* by their personality characteristics. Thus, women could be tough, objective, and decisive, or sensitive and nurturant, as the situation required, without fearing a "loss of their femininity." And the same would be true for men.

FEMALE AUTHORITY ROLE MODELS

As women increasingly enter high-status careers, they serve as role models, not only for those who see and know them, but also for the general cultural consensus about what is possible and acceptable for women. A *role model* is someone who, by holding a particular role or position, demonstrates to observers how that role or position can be performed.

Female Authority Models and Gender Stereotypes. In carrying out their responsibilities, role models also display the behavioral characteristics ("personality traits") required by the role. Research suggests that the visible presence of many women in authority positions would indeed serve to break the gender stereotypes. The emphasis here is on the "many." If there is only one woman in the unit with an authority position, and she disconfirms all of the stereotypes by her intelligence, competence and ambition, she can be discounted as an exception. She may also be defeated by the effects of tokenism (see Chapter 3) and the "damned if she does, damned is she doesn't" dilemma, discussed previously. However, when many different women disconfirm different stereotypic attributes, they create a visible majority or consensus effect (see Chapter 3), and those who see or deal with them change their stereotypic "personality" assumptions (Weber & Crocker, 1983).

Female Authority Models and Women's Careers. So far, in our society, most authority role models have been men. This has led observers not only to attribute the stereotypic personality traits to men and women, but also to assume that only men could perform adequately in authority roles. The observers, of course, include both young men and women in the process of forming their career choices, and also the mature generation of organizational managers evaluating subordinates' performances and deciding whom to hire and promote. In a social environment of male authority models, women have lower career aspirations and demonstrate poorer assertiveness skills than men of equal ability; fewer women take intellectual initiatives, and fewer choose high-status careers; and evaluators are unable to recognize women's achievements even when they are objectively equal to men's (Campbell & Fairey, 1985; Geis et al., 1985; Goldstein, 1979; Tidball, 1973).

Visible female authority figures increase young women's career aspirations, their behavioral skills of self-confidence and independence of judgment, their leadership initiatives—and evaluators' ability to recognize their contributions (Douvan, 1976; Geis et al., 1984; Jennings et al., 1980; Selkow, 1984; Tidball, 1973). When discussion group participants had been exposed to only male authority figures, the usual condition of contemporary society, the men and women group members contributed equally. But, acting as evaluators after the discussion, they both followed the stereotypes and rated the men higher than the women in "leadership," the usual outcome in contemporary society. In contrast, when the group members had previously seen a variety of accepted female authorities, men and women again contributed equally, and in addition, they also evaluated the men and women in their group as equally high in leadership (Geis et al., 1985). The authority role model effect is not specific to women. It has also been found for Blacks (Cohen et al., 1976).

In our society, men have traditionally been the "producers" and "achievers." Because women have not shown these accomplishments, we assumed they were inherently incapable of them. But if you stop to think about it for a minute, you will realize that men's achievements and recognition have always occurred in a social environment of many male authority role models—fathers in the home, professors at college, bosses on the job, and presidents, judges, and congressmen running the country. It would appear that when women are given the same role model advantages that men have always enjoyed, they produce the same achievements and receive the same recognition.

> When women have the same-sex authority models that men have always enjoyed, they produce the same achievements and receive the same recognition.

Role Models and Social Support. The difference between a successful woman role model and defeat by the effects of stereotypes and discriminatory treatment may be a matter of social support in the workplace. The automatic assumptions of gender stereotypes have always led work associates to accept male authorities' assignments and support their suggestions, proposals, and efforts, but fail to accord the same acceptance and support to female authorities (Lockheed & Hall, 1976). It has been this differential treatment of women that has produced the negative consequences for them discussed throughout this chapter. When supervisors and co-workers give women the same acceptance and support that men have always received, the women are evaluated as high as equally competent men in leadership, quality of ideas, hiring desirability, salary deserved, and promotability (Brown & Geis, 1984; Isaacs, 1981).

Role Models, Acceptance, and Familiarity. The visible presence of many accepted female authority models appears to have a broad impact on both women's behavior and evaluators' judgments of women. The reason for this impact may be as simple as ordinary familiarity. We like or come to accept what is familiar, and feel uncomfortable with what is strange, unfamiliar, or unpredictable. For example, Zajonc (1968) had evaluators watch a long series of photographs of different people's faces. Afterwards, they reported liking the people whose photographs had been shown more frequently in the series than those shown only once—regardless of which particular faces were included in the "more frequent" set. This familiarity effect might be especially powerful in situations that can affect our own future outcomes, such as in choosing a career or in hiring or promoting someone in our organization.

When virtually all authority figures have always been men, a woman who acts dominant or assumes authority seems strange and unpredictable. We lose our sense of control over our own outcomes. This tends to be unpleasant and threatening (Brooks, 1982; Voudouris et al., 1985). Women do not consider high-status careers or advancement because there is no evidence, no female authority role models, to show how a woman could handle the responsibilities or be accepted in such a position. Supervisors do not hire or promote women to authority positions for the same reason, and subordinates do not want to work for a woman boss. In contrast, the presence of many female authority figures makes them familiar, and therefore predictable and acceptable. Young women can see how other women like themselves do in fact handle the responsibilities and enjoy the challenges (and rewards) of high-status positions. High-level decision makers can see the same evidence, then recognize women's achievements, and therefore recruit, hire, and promote them without fear of the unknown.

THE SELF-FULFILLING PROPHECY: STEREOTYPES AND SOCIAL STRUCTURE

A *self-fulfilling prophecy* is an initially false belief that, by itself, causes exactly the behavior that then makes the belief come true (Jones, 1977; Merton, 1948). Automatic, implicit gender stereotypes create exactly such self-fulfilling prophecies in three ways. First, as noted previously, stereotypes operate as expectations. Research shows that one person's expectations about another, however false initially, cause that person to treat the other in a way that leads the other to respond in accord with those expectations. For example, if Mark, Natalie's supervisor, believes (erroneously) that Natalie lacks initiative, he will treat her in a way that causes her to show little initiative. For example, he might constantly suggest projects for her to pursue, leaving her no time to develop and pursue her own ideas. Thus his initial (actually false) expectation is "confirmed." The effects of expectations will be discussed in more detail in Chapter 3.

Second, stereotypes also cause self-fulfilling prophecies because they cause perceptual bias, as noted previously. Because the stereotypes select what parts of the evidence supervisors notice, and interpret those parts they do attend to, the supervisors, unaware of this influence, "see" men's work as superior to identical work by women. As a result, they are more likely to hire and advance men into authority positions, and hold women in subordinate roles. As this pattern continues over time, it becomes obvious to everyone that women are not advancing as fast or as high as men in the organization. Then, because we all believe that evaluations and promotion decisions are fair and objective, we can only conclude (erroneously) that men are actually more competent and qualified than women.

Finally, because women are held in subordinate roles that require the dependent, deferent, nurturant behavior that is stereotypically called "feminine," the stereotypes are in fact "confirmed" by the women's actual behavior. Thus, the initially false stereotypes create the very behaviors (discriminatory treatment, evaluations, hiring, and promotion decisions) that then appear to confirm that the stereotypic beliefs were true all along. In short, the stereotypes cause discriminatory treatment, and the unequal treatment outcomes then perpetuate the stereotypes. Note that the circular causal process of the self-fulfilling prophecy depends on the initial perceivers' *igno-*

> Stereotypes cause discriminatory treatment, and the results of the unequal treatment then perpetuate the stereotypes.

rance. If perceivers knew that their initial beliefs and expectations were in fact false, the process would not occur. Thus, one way to counteract the circle of negative self-fulfilling prophecies about women is to educate all perceivers, men and women alike, about the falsity and negative effects of stereotypes, conscious and unconscious, and their role in creating self-fulfilling prophecies.

Another way to counteract negative self-fulfilling prophecies is to create positive ones, preferably based on initial beliefs and expectations that are, in fact, true. Fortunately, this process can also work in reverse (Geis et al., 1984, 1985; Jennings et al., 1980). If organizations' sexually unequal status structure becomes more equal, stereotypic behavior will diminish, thus disconfirming the stereotypes and reducing the resulting discriminatory treatment. The difficult parts of this solution are (a) getting enough women initially hired or promoted into authority positions, (b) insuring that they have the same power that men holding similar positions have, and (c) giving them the support of their supervisors, peers, and subordinates that is automatically accorded to men. Affirmative action programs were designed to address the first difficulty, although actual compliance is still problematic in many organizations. *The power and support problems remain critical*, and will be discussed further in Chapters 4 and 6.

Self-fulfilling prophecies also operate in the social exchanges of daily work. We intend to treat men and women the same in the ordinary routines of work, but in fact we do not. The unequal treatment of men and women can often be seen in mixed-sex discussions, especially in staff meetings and work groups. Men talk more than women in such situations. They also interrupt women more than women interrupt men (Zimmerman & West, 1975). Interruptions by women appear aggressive and are not permitted; men's interruptions are accepted, unnoticed. Others turn their attention away from the woman who was speaking and toward the man who interrupted her, so the woman stops talking. Even when women and not interrupted, they are ignored or "unheard" (Bunker & Seashore, 1975). And when they are heard, their arguments are challenged more often than men's (Sterling & Owen, 1982).

The basis for this unequal treatment is the false automatic implicit "knowledge" provided by the stereotypes that men are more intelligent and competent than women, and therefore that what they have to say is more important than what a woman might have to say. Consider, for example, a disagreement between a man and a woman in a group meeting. In such a situation, the man may do 80% or 90% of the talking. After the meeting, the group members will not recall the difference in interruptions, speaking times, attention, or challenges, but they will recall that the woman "failed" to make a convincing argument for her position (Altemeyer & Jones, 1974). In fact, they have unconsciously and unintentionally facilitated the man and suppressed the woman. Notice the self-fulfilling prophecy. The stereotypic beliefs create unequal treatment of men and women in the group. As a result of the unequal treatment, the men will in fact produce more "good' (i.e., accepted) ideas than the women, thereby seemingly confirming the initial stereotypes.

Again, this process can also work in reverse. If just a few other group members begin listening to the woman, supporting her ideas, and objecting to the interruptions, the consensus effect of their actions will create the "equal opportunity" for women that everyone sincerely endorses consciously.

SUMMARY

All perception is interpretation based on previous experience. Most of the old information the brain uses to interpret new information does not register at all in conscious awareness. Stereotypes of men and women, now scientifically discredited and consciously disavowed, fall in this category. They remain active and automatic, although unconscious and unintentional, because they still dominate contemporary social structure and daily routine. The stereotypes of men are those traits associated with legitimate claim to authority, high status, salary, and prestige. Stereotypes of women imply subordinate positions and deferent behavior. These implicit stereotypes provide the meanings that guide our conscious attention, construct our interpretation, and fill in gaps in the actual evidence. Because we "see" what we expect to see, the stereotypes create perceptual bias and sex discrimination in how men and women are treated in face-to-face interactions at work, and in organizational evaluations, including those involving recruitment, hiring, performance, salary, and advancement decisions.

Perceptual gender bias has been scientifically demonstrated in hiring, promotion, and salaries; in evaluations of intellectual products, credentials, and performances; and also operates in informal daily routines. The resulting discrepancy in opportunity means that a given level of ability and effort in a woman will yield less evidence of progress than the identical level in a man. Gender bias in evaluations means that the same performance and productivity yields lower salaries and less advancement for women than for men. Gender bias increases when the evidence requires more interpretation by the evaluator, when the job is stereotypically "masculine," and when the performers are highly competent. Gender bias occurs in every type of organization, and it increases with increasing status level in the organization.

Many organizations advertise their equal opportunity policies, but each specific opportunity depends on recognition of previous achievements. If women's achievements do not receive the same recognition as identical achievements by men, then women are not receiving the "equal opportunity" being advertised.

Contemporary social structure, both in and outside of organizations, is still unequal with respect to sex. Virtually all authority positions are occupied by men; virtually all women occupy subordinate, lower status positions. This unequal social structure has two major results: (a) The visible presence of same-sex authority role models raises that sex's career aspirations and also evaluators' ability to recognize that sex's achievements. (b) Authority positions require the behavorial traits socially labeled "masculine;" subordinate positions require those labeled "feminine." Because people behave according to the requirements of the roles and positions they occupy, the unequal social structure creates a self-fulfilling prophecy. Evaluators' implicit stereotypes hold women in subordinate positions, where they then display exactly the kind of behavior that seemingly "confirms" their "possession" of those traits. Similarly, the stereotypes serve to advance men to positions that require them to confirm their "masculine" traits.

There is some evidence that perceptual gender bias and discrimination may be diminishing. As more women seek and obtain professional and managerial positions, and succeed in them (despite discriminatory treatment) they will disconfirm the old stereotypes in the only way they can be disconfirmed effectively—by the actual behavior and success of the women. The self-fulfilling prophecy can work both ways. The visible presence of many female authority role models in our own organization, and the knowledge that there are many more in other organizations across the country, can change perceived personality traits, increase women's career ambitions, self-confidence, independence of judgment, and leadership initiatives—and can also increase evaluators' ability to recognize women's contributions. If present trends continue, the way may become gradually easier for each new generation of women.

3
Tricks of Mind:
The Gender Schema
and Other Foibles

The previous chapter reviewed gender stereotypes and their effects on how supervisors and other associates perceive, treat, and evaluate women at work. The personality and "occupational suitability" stereotypes cause discriminatory treatment in hiring, salary, work evaluation, and promotion, and the results of the discriminatory treatment then seemingly "confirm" that the stereotypes were true all along. This chapter will examine the cognitive processes that keep this self-fulfilling prophecy system going. The stereotypes achieve their power over both evaluators and performers (a) because of the schematic nature of human information processing, (b) because they operate as social expectations, and (c) because they are consensual in society.

THE SOCIAL GENDER SCHEMA

Our vast store of implicit knowledge about the world does not exist as fragmented "bits and pieces" jumbled in our memories. Rather, the knowledge is organized into bundles or structures of related items called *schemas* (Taylor & Crocker, 1981). A schema is a mental representation of a category of objects, events, or persons and their typical characteristics. The characteristics and their relationships give the meaning of the category. For example, most people have schemas for categories such as "theatre experiences," "fast food restaurants," "animal pets," and so on. Our beliefs and information about people are also organized into schemas. The most basic category distinction about adults is their sex.

Which category schema we use to interpret information about a person depends on situational cues and the various categories' availability in our minds at the time (Tversky & Kahneman, 1973). We are most likely to use the category that we have used most frequently and most recently in the past (Higgins & King, 1981). The male–female category distinction is one of the earliest learned, and one that we use in almost every activity and social exchange of our daily lives. The sex of a person is the item of information about them that we notice first, fastest, and most automatically (Klatzky et al., 1982; Smith & Miller, 1983). People's sex makes a difference in how they behave and how others see them and treat them in virtually every aspect of their lives (Bem, 1985). Thus our gender schema is likely to be most available and most automatically used.

STEREOTYPES AS GENDER SCHEMA ATTRIBUTES

The information organized in a schema consists of *attributes*, the typical characteristics or qualities of the category members. For example, our fast food restaurant schema might have attributes like "fast," "limited menu," "unwholesome food," and so on. Similarly, our gender schema contains the "typical attributes" of men and women. These attributes include all of the gender stereotypes discussed in Chapter 2 (Taylor & Crocker, 1981). Because a schema's attributes are grouped together in our minds and interconnected with each other as well as with the category label, when the category label is activated, all of its attributes are also activated (Fiske, 1982). This means that as soon as we notice that someone is a woman, all of the stereotypic attributes of the category "women" are also activated. This activation, and the resulting use of the attributes in interpreting information about the woman, can all occur unconsciously (Tsujimoto, 1978).

The attributes of the gender schema have functional, causal, evaluative, and relational implications (Fiske & Taylor, 1984). Functional implications tell what category members do and don't do (and should and should not do). For example, one functional implication of the gender schema attributes is that men can be counted on to take the initiative and pursue a task goal aggressively, and women cannot. Another functional implication is that women will give higher priority to their home responsibilities than to their job, but men will give first priority to their job. Another is that women respond to pressure or emergencies by becoming emotional and "losing their heads," men by calm rationality.

Causal implications tell what causes category members' behavior and outcomes. For example, the "male competence" and "female incompetence" attributes of the gender schema imply that men's successes are caused by their ability, but women's successes must be due to "good luck," an easy task, or even cheating (Feather & Simon, 1975). Evaluative implications tell how good or bad category members are for the purposes the evaluator has in mind. The gender schema attributes imply that men are better than women for positions of authority and decision making, and that women are good for subordinate positions and routine tasks.

Relational implications tell how category members relate to one another, and to other objects and events. For example, the gender schema attributes imply that women should defer to men because they are more intelligent and should therefore be dominant over women. Another relational implication is that women should accommodate to the needs or wishes of men (or the needs of their organization), but that men's needs should be accommodated by others, including their organization.

Of course, educated people know that not all of the stereotypic attributes are true of all women. That is, we know it consciously, when someone asks us and we think about it consciously. But when our conscious attention is focused on other matters, the rest of our mind functions on "automatic" (Bargh, 1984). Because the stereotypes are organized together and related to each other as well as to the "male-female" category label, they all operate together,

Simply knowing a person's sex automatically triggers our gender schema, which interprets all of our information about that person.

sometimes despite conscious knowledge to the contrary. Simply knowing a person's sex automatically triggers our gender schema, which then serves to interpret all of the information we have about that person, and most of the interpreting occurs without our conscious awareness. Like the stereotypes they contain, gender schemas operate as *expectations*. They not only *describe* beliefs about how women differ from men in abilities, attitudes, interests, and goals, but also *prescribe* how women *should* differ from men.

TYPES OF SCHEMAS

Within our broad-category schemas, we also have subschemas. For example, the gender schema is actually a powerful subschema within our general "people" schema. We may also have subschemas for "extroverts," "career women" (a subschema within the gender subschema), or "socialites," and so on. Schemas can nest within each other, each category level containing smaller, more specific categories within it. Several types of schema and subschema systems have been identified (Fiske & Taylor, 1984). The type most relevant to this book is called *role schemas*, which encode our beliefs and expectations for broad social categories of people based on age, race, sex, or occupation. Both the gender and occupation stereotype systems discussed in Chapter 2 are role schemas.

Event schemas or *scripts* (Schank & Abelson, 1977) contain our implicit knowledge of the actions and behavior required in particular situations, and their sequence in the situation. For example, our event schema for "eating in a restaurant" involves not only the role schemas for "customer" and "waiter," but also the event schemas for being seated, the waiter bringing the menu, ordering, eating, paying the bill, and leaving. Event schemas are important, because many of them are gender-coded. The "appropriate" and expected behavior differs for men and women in the same situation. For example, the dominance–deference attributes of the gender schema make it appear appropriate and expected for a man to assume leadership in a mixed-sex work group, but inappropriate for a woman to do the same.

The *self-schema* contains our implicit knowledge about ourselves, our abilities (and weaknesses), preferences, goals, values, interests, and other characteristics. Self-schemas are important because they define our self-confidence, efforts, and aspirations. Not surprisingly, the stereotypic gender attributes are substantial components of most people's self-schemas (Bem, 1981; Spence, 1985). Other types of schemas are *person schemas* or *prototypes* such as "extrovert," "athlete," "sharp operator," and so on; *object schemas* for things like TV sets, elephants, and fast food; and *procedural schemas* that have no content but contain the rules for our internal processing of information.

SCHEMAS SELECT EVIDENCE, INTERPRET ITS MEANING, AND FILL IN ITS GAPS

Our gender schemas influence what we "see" and ultimately what we "know" about a person. The general rule is that evidence that is consistent with the schema will be selectively noticed, more easily stored in memory, more cognitively available for recall, preferentially recalled, and seen as more relevant and informative than evidence that is inconsistent with the schema or irrelevant to it (Darley & Gross, 1983; Rothbart et al., 1979; Snyder & Cantor, 1980; Zadney & Gerard, 1974).

Evidence about a person is always complex, and evidence about each of several people (e.g., candidates for a position) is even more complex.

No evaluator can absorb and remember all of the details. Thus, evaluators' schemas select which parts of the evidence will be noticed and which parts will be unnoticed (Bodenhausen, 1988). Their gender schemas lead them to notice evidence of men's competence but "miss" the same evidence about a woman. On the other side of the coin, information casting doubt on a candidate's suitability for the position will be noticed about a woman but unnoticed about a man. Researchers (e.g., Levine & Murphy, 1943) have long known that it is easier for people to learn and remember facts supporting what they already believe than facts supporting a contrary opinion. The more recent work indicates that some contrary facts may not be learned or remembered because they were not even noticed in the first place.

A second function of schemas is to interpret the meaning of the information that is noticed. Usually this involves making it consistent with the schema attributes (Bodenhausen & Lichtenstein, 1987). For example, evaluators might interpret information that Laura previously "managed the design department at Revco for three years" in terms of Revco's small size, the relative simplicity of its design requirements, and the excellent direction and support of Laura's supervisor there. They might interpret the identical information about Lawrence in terms of Revco's recent vigorous growth, Lawrence's several very quick promotions, and his "obvious" competence.

The third function of schemas is that they fill in any gaps in the actual evidence with schema-consistent "information" (Bellezza & Bower, 1981; Stangor, 1988). In the example given in Chapter 2, we assumed Chris ate steak for dinner, given the information that she went to a restaurant and ordered steak. (This is part of our restaurant event schema: Customers usually eat what they order.) Gender schemas "fill in the gaps" differently for information about men and women. In the Laura and Lawrence example above, the evaluators might "remember" that Lawrence was looking for a new job because he had outgrown Revco and was ready for more challenge and responsibility. However, they might recall the identical application from Laura as indicating that she was perhaps having some problems at Revco and simply needed to get out of there. Similarly, they might recall Lawrence's application as showing evidence of "leadership" (although the word had never occurred in either his application or reference letters), because it is an attribute of the "masculine" gender schema, but they would recall no such "evidence" in Laura's application. Schemas can lead us to "re-

> Schemas can lead us to "remember" facts that did not exist and "not to remember" facts that did exist.

member" facts that did not exist and "not to remember" facts that did exist (Cantor & Mischel, 1979; Moscovici, 1983).

Schemas in Perceiving, Interpreting, and Recalling Information. We process information in three stages, and all three of them are influenced by gender schemas. First, we must *encode* (perceive or absorb) the information from the evidence available. It is at this first encoding stage that selective attention to gender schema-consistent information is most likely to operate (Bodenhausen, 1988).

However, the evidence itself usually does not directly answer the question, so the evaluator proceeds to the second stage, *inference* (i.e., interpretation). What do the various bits of evidence *mean?* Does the statement in a letter that "Susan pushes hard for what she believes in" mean that Susan won't give up easily even in the face of obstacles? Or does it mean that Susan pushes hard *only* on those (perhaps rare) occasions when the project is one of her own devising? It is at this inference stage that gender schemas interpret the evidence and fill in the gaps, changing its meaning, depending on whether the applicant is a man or a woman (Taylor et al., 1978). In fact, inferences often occur spontaneously as the evidence is being encoded, so that evidence and inferences are mixed together and become indistinguishable (Smith & Miller, 1983). Thus, evaluators cannot tell which parts of their "information" about a candidate were actually contained in the evidence and which were their own inferences and interpretations. This means that gender schema stereotypes and implications get encoded, stored, and then recalled as "facts."

The final stage of information processing is memory or *recall.* When it comes time to make the final hiring, salary, or promotion decision, what will the evaluator recall about the candidate? First, evaluators are more likely to remember their own inferences or the labels ("go-getter," "team player," "weak sister," etc.) they have attached to a candidate than they are to remember the actual information on which their inferences and labels were based (Fiske & Pavelchack, 1986). Second, they are more likely to recall information that is consistent with their gender schemas than information that is irrelevant or inconsistent (Cohen, 1981; Kulik, 1983). Some research shows that dramatically inconsistent information is recalled as well as or better than consistent information (Hastie, 1981). However, dramatic information in real life

Overall impressions and conclusions can remain consistent with the stereotypes, despite well-remembered disconfirming evidence.

work situations is rare. Even if it occurs, the evaluator may consciously or unconsciously interpret it during the inference process to change its meaning, reduce its relevance, or exclude it as "an exception." In addition, overall impressions and conclusions can remain consistent with the schema despite well-remembered disconfirming evidence (Dreben et al., 1979; Kulik, 1983; Ross et al., 1975).

EXPECTATION STATES AND STATUS CHARACTERISTICS THEORY

The other major theory of sex effects on performance and evaluation is the sociological theory of expectation states and its branch of status characteristics theory (Berger & Zelditch, 1985). This theory proposes that people's behavior, perceptions and judgments, about themselves and others, are determined by their expectations for the situation and the people involved. Expectations for high-status people differ from those for low-status people, and women as a group have lower status in society than men as a group. These "diffuse status characteristics" and expectations are carried into job, task, and social exchange situations *unless* specific, relevant information negates them. Thus, low-status persons, including women, are not expected or permitted to make high-status contributions, or to receive high-status rewards, regardless of their contributions. In general, the explanations of this theory are consistent with those of the psychological schema theory described above. Both theories refer to expectations (called *schemas* in schema theory) of individuals. Both theories locate the source of individuals' stereotypic expectations in the social consensus of society. Both assume that the expectations can operate unconsciously. Both have voluminous research support documenting the impact of the expectations on those who hold them and on those about whom they are held.

SUMMARY

Gender stereotypes remain powerful influences on the perception, evaluation, and treatment of women because they form a gender schema. The gender schema is an organized mental structure of all of the stereotypic characteristics and behavioral rules that operates as a unit that is activated whenever the male–female category is activated. It is the gender schema that provides the meanings the brain uses automatically and without our conscious awareness to interpret information about a woman. The gender schema has implications for what men and women can and cannot do (and should and should not do), for what causes their successes and failures, for how good or bad they are for various tasks and positions, and for how they do and should relate to each other. The gender schema selects what evidence will be noticed, interprets the evidence that is noticed, and fills in any gaps when the evidence is ambiguous, missing, or forgotten. In general, information and assumptions consistent with the schema meaning will be noticed, believed, and remembered.

THE POWER OF SOCIAL EXPECTATIONS

Chapter 2 outlined how stereotypic beliefs and discriminatory treatment create self-fulfilling prophecies. The beliefs, often initially false and used unconsciously, cause discriminatory treatment, and the behavioral or advancement outcomes of the treatment then seemingly "confirm" that the (initially false) beliefs were true all along. This process occurs because the gender schema and its stereotypic attributes operate as social expectations. Such expectations influence not only attitudes, perceptions, and judgments, but also the behavior of those who hold them and those about whom they are held.

Expectations influence the behavior of those who hold them and those about whom they are held.

For example, Rosenthal (1974) told elementary classroom teachers of a new kind of intelligence test for their pupils that would predict "intellectual blooming," the readiness of a child to make significant intellectual advances. Actually, the researchers gave the children an ordinary academic achievement test. They then selected about one-third of the children in each class completely at random, without regard to their actual test scores, and reported their names to their teachers as those who were ready to "bloom." At the end of the school year, the children who had been arbitrarily identified as "bloomers" had indeed made greater gains than their classmates. Although the teachers claimed that they treated all children alike, and pushed each one as far as he or she could go, their (initially false) expectations influenced the children's actual accomplishments and created a self-fulfilling prophecy. In addition, children who were *not* identified as "bloomers" but made large gains (presumably because they were actually very bright) were rated by their teachers as "maladjusted" and difficult to work with. Men may have been more successful than women in the past, and those few women who did succeed may have been seen as unhappy and maladjusted simply because the gender stereotypes led to expectations of greater intellectual achievements in boys and men than in girls and women. Effects of some stereotypic gender expectations have been documented. Snyder, Tanke, and Berscheid (1977) tested the belief that beautiful women are warm, sociable, and responsive toward men by having men and women hold a get-acquainted telephone conversation. Each partner was asked to provide some personal information to be delivered to the other. The experimenter took a polaroid photo of the man, allegedly for his partner, but did not actually deliver it to her. Photos were not mentioned to the woman. The man, however, received a photo allegedly of his partner (actually selected by the experimenter from a set prepared previously) showing either a very beautiful woman or an unattractive one. Each partner's part of the ensuing telephone conversation was then recorded on separate tapes. Later, evaluators listening to the women's tapes judged those women whose partners believed them to be beautiful as showing more warmth, responsiveness, and sociability than those whose partners believed them to be unattractive. The men's expectations led the women to behave in a way that "confirmed" them.

> The women whose partners falsely believed them to be beautiful were actually warmer, more responsive, and more sociable.

Expectations also work on men (Snyder & Swann, 1978). Two men were assigned to play a competitive game involving a "noise weapon" that would interrupt the opponent's concentration and lower his score. Before the game, the experimenter privately informed one partner (falsely) that his opponent was very aggressive. This first partner was then given the noise weapon for the first round of the game. Expecting a heavy attack from his opponent later, he used the weapon liberally. The second partner, taken aback at the unexpected assault, duly reciprocated when he had the weapon in round two. After several rounds, the first man was replaced by a third man. With this new partner, who had never behaved aggressively toward him, the second man continued his heavy use of the weapon. The first man's expectations had made him actually aggressive.

The same principle also operates on the job (Word, Zanna, & Cooper, 1974). People interviewed Black or White job applicants using a standard interview outline. Both interviewers and applicants were videotaped on separate tapes. Later, evaluators watching the applicant tapes judged the Black applicants to be less qualified than the Whites. Then a new group of applicants, this time all White, responded to the interviewer videotapes. Those responding to an interviewer who had

originally been talking with a Black applicant were judged less qualified than those whose interviewer had been talking with a White.
These results show that the original Black applicants had appeared
less qualified because the interviewers' stereotypic expectations led
them to treat the applicant in a way that elicited responses confirming
their expectations. If interviewers assume that women are less competent, they may lead female applicants to actually appear less competent.

   In another study (Skrypnek & Snyder, 1982), a man and a woman
who could not see each other negotiated a division of tasks. Some men
were led to believe that their partner was a man, others that their
partner was a woman. The women whose partners believed they were
women chose more feminine tasks for themselves than women whose
partners believed they were men. This finding suggests that women,
whose work associates of course know their sex, may collaborate with
others' stereotyped expectations for them by choosing more "feminine"
and routine tasks for themselves. Similarly, when women job applicants learned that a job interviewer held either traditional or liberated
gender values, they changed their physical appearance and nonverbal
style to match the interviewer's alleged values (von Baeyer et al.,
1981). These studies illustrate how other people's stereotypic expectations can influence a woman's performance, even when the woman
herself knows they are not true of her.

   People subtly communicate their expectations to each other by verbal and nonverbal cues, and by overt actions (Harris & Rosenthal,
1985). There are conditions that reduce the power of other people's
expectations, but they do not seem to offer much hope for the workplace.

   When we are aware that others hold false expectations about us, we
can resist their influence and disconfirm them (Hilton & Darley, 1985).
The problem here is keeping constant, conscious vigilance for false
expectations at the same time that ongoing work discussions also
require the focus of conscious attention. Similarly, the expectations of
someone who does not control our important rewards and punishments
have less influence than those of someone who does (Zanna & Pack,
1975). But work supervisors and associates do control important rewards and punishments. Finally, expectations are less powerful when
those who hold them are less certain about them (Swann & Ely, 1984).
But gender expectations are often held with confidence and certainty
because they are consensual in society (Swann, 1984). At work, resisting the effects of others' false expectations would seem problematic, at
best.

In these studies one person's expectations influenced another's behavior, attitudes, or outcomes over the course of a few minutes to an entire school year. The moral of this story is that people's behaviors and outcomes depend not only on their own ability and effort, but also on how they are treated by others. And how they are treated depends on others' expectations for them (Wood & Karten, 1986). In the case of gender stereotypes, the expectations are held not by just one other person, but by virtually everyone we encounter in our daily lives, including family, friends, and work associates. They are presented as social reality in movies, TV, and magazines. In addition, they operate from the moment we are born to the day we die. They are inescapable, because they are basic assumptions throughout our society.

Summary. Gender stereotypes operate as expectations. One person's expectations, however false initially, about the characteristics, intentions, or abilities of another create self-fulfilling prophecies. The one holding the expectation treats the other in a way that causes the other to fulfill the initially false expectation. Remember from Chapter 1, when Marcia was falsely called emotional, it made her angry, so she became emotional. This principle explains why women do often behave in accord with the stereotypic "feminine" expectations. They are treated in a way that virtually forces such responses. What is remarkable is that so many women persist, excel, and succeed, despite work associates' negative expectations.

THE POWER OF SOCIAL CONSENSUS

When there is a physical criterion for deciding some issue (e.g., a thermometer for deciding what the temperature is, a counter for deciding how many widgets an assembly line worker produced that day), we usually use it. However, for many issues of human concern, including evaluation of oneself and others, credentials, and complex performances, there is no physical criterion or at best an ambiguous one. Which of the two candidates would be best as president of the country? How good are Morgan's managerial skills? How much are Randolph's decisions actually influenced by reason versus emotion? For such issues we use social consensus—agreement among the people (or a majority of the people, or the most important people) most relevant to the issue. Once the consensus is known, that particular opinion acquires the value of being "the truth," simply *because* it is the consensus, regardless of whether it is objectively correct or not (Festinger, 1954).

The truth value of consensus defines social reality. Once the consensus is known and recognized as consensual, disputing it appears "wrong," "ridiculous," "embarrassing," or "unrealistic." In fact, most of us accept the social consensus on most issues. And even when we privately disagree with society, we are still influenced by the social consensus, consciously or unconsciously. If you doubt this, think of entering a crowded elevator and singing "The Star Spangled Banner" in your loudest voice. (Or think of wearing your bathing suit, or your bathrobe, to work on Monday.) These behaviors are not against the law. They are outrageous and "unthinkable" simply because they are contrary to the social consensus of what is "appropriate" for the situation. The gender stereotypes achieve their power over everyone's automatic assumptions, values, attitudes and behavior because they are consensual in our society, and we know they are. If social consensus defines women as "weak and emotional," it is almost impossible not to believe it, at some level, even if we know consciously that it is not true.

Social consensus defines individual opinions. Sherif (1935) had evaluators make repeated estimates of how far a point of light appeared to move in a dark room. Tested alone, individuals differ in their estimates. Some perceive distances averaging as little as 2 or 3 inches; others reliably estimate 10–12 inches. After being tested alone, the same evaluators were again tested in groups of two or three persons. Over the course of the session, in which they heard each others' estimates, they converged on a common estimate, for example, 5–6 inches. They had been explicitly instructed to make up their minds for each trial before any of the others answered for that trial, and they reported that they had been careful to follow this instruction and remain independent of the others. In fact, their perceptions of reality had been influenced. These results illustrate how consensus can change a private belief or perception the individual has already formed previously.

In the same study, other evaluators were tested first in small groups and then a week later in individual sessions. They formed a group consensus rapidly in the first session, and then retained the consensual judgment as their own personal estimate in the later private sessions. Having once learned "the truth" about an ambiguous phenomenon shapes our later perceptions of other events in the same category. This part of the study illustrates the situation of first experiencing an opinion as a consensus, for example, being born into a society in which consensus on an issue already exists, as in the case of gender stereotypes.

Asch (1956) had evaluators judge which of three comparison lines matched a criterion line in length over a set of 20 judgment trials. In this study, there was an objective correct answer for each trial, and the perceptual judgment was easy. When evaluators were tested alone, they made virtually no errors. However, when they were tested in a group, and the others all gave a unanimous wrong answer (following previous secret instructions from the experimenter), a third of them agreed with the false majority, and two-thirds of them agreed at least once over the 12 repetitions of the situation. Social consensus can be more powerful than the objective evidence of physical reality.

Social consensus can be more powerful than the objective evidence of physical reality.

The studies above demonstrated consensus effects on physical length judgments. Other researchers (e.g., Festinger, 1954; Suls & Miller, 1977) have had groups discuss various opinion issues. First, each group member gives his or her private opinion about the issue on a questionnaire. Then they discuss the issue. On subsequent private opinion measures after the discussion, they report the group consensus as their own private opinion. They also report more confidence that their opinion is correct.

Social consensus "validates" the truth of an opinion.

Consensus has the effect of appearing to validate the truth of an opinion simply by defining what the consensual opinion is. For example, if a woman presents an important new idea, the group members may focus their discussion exclusively on minor procedural ambiguities or weaknesses and totally ignore the substantive main point and its implications. After the presentation, what will be remembered is the verbalized consensus that the proposal was "weak and full of holes." When Marie Curie presented her discovery of radium to the French Academy of Science, the distinguished scientists gathered for the occasion probed only for flaws in her methodology and completely ignored the substance and implications of her discovery.

Consensus on specific issues emerges from discussion. But when consensus on an issue is already prevalent throughout society, as in the case of gender stereotypes, we don't need a discussion to learn what the consensus is. We already know it. The consensus shapes our interpretation of the objective facts of reality (Allen & Wilder, 1980). The consensus effect is stronger and people are less aware of being influenced, when the evidence about the issue is more ambiguous and on issues more relevant or important to the group. Evidence about individuals' possessing or not possessing the stereotypic gender traits is usually highly ambiguous, as is evidence about managerial skills and ability. And hiring and promotion decisions are important to the group in organizations. Thus, in these areas consensus prevails, and individuals are "seen" or assumed to possess the personality and behavioral traits and abilities (or disabilities) ascribed to them by the socially consensual gender schema (Spence & Helmreich, 1978).

It is because consensus defines "the truth" that stereotypes operate as values as well as facts. If most people agree that women are passive, emotional, and nurturant, then passivity, emotionality, and nurturance become hallmarks of "femininity." As a result, these characteristics become normative and valued for women, because displaying them both defines and validates their "true femininity." Similarly, the consensual observation that authorities have always been men creates the schema that authorities *should be* men. Thus do consensual descriptions of "what is" become normative prescriptions for "what *should be*."

The Consensus Effect Can Work Both Ways. In the past the consensus effect has worked to seemingly "confirm" women's stereotypic personality, ability, and interest traits and "validate" discriminatory treatment in day-to-day work routines as well as in hiring, salary, and promotion decisions. However, the consensus effect can also be used to break the stereotypes and reduce discriminatory treatment. Chapter 2 discussed evidence that multiple female authority role models could change perceptions of stereotypic personality traits, increase women's achievement skills of self-confidence and independence of judgment, raise their career aspirations, and increase evaluators' recognition of their leadership. The multiple female authority role models created a consensus effect that both defined and validated the changed perceptions, evaluations, and behavior. The Asch (1956) study noted above revealed that the number of people needed to create a consensus effect and influence perceptions and judgments is just three people. This suggests that the number of female authority role models needed for constructive change in a group is at least three. (More might be needed in larger groups of 20 or more.)

Chapter 2 also suggested that the consensus effect could be used to reduce the discriminatory treatment of women in discussion groups. Again, the "rule of three" applies. The number of group members who need to show facial expressions of approval in response to a woman's contributions, or speak up and insist that the woman be heard and object to others' interrupting her, is three.

Summary. Consensus is agreement about a matter of opinion. When most of those who are relevant or important agree about something, that particular opinion is perceived as "the truth"—regardless

of whether it is objectively correct or not. The gender schema is powerful in our society because it is consensual. The consensus effect is
powerful, especially when it operates outside of our conscious awareness, as it usually does. However, it is a double-edged sword. In the
past it has served to define women as less competent and validate their
subordinate status at work. In the future it can just as effectively be
used to confirm women's competence and validate high status positions, behavior and salaries for them in organizations. In small groups,
just three people, all supporting the same point (or person) can create a
consensus effect.

OTHER MENTAL LOOPHOLES

Perceptual gender bias and discrimination are documented in research
studies by comparing evaluations of matched credentials, products, or
performances, or by comparing the actual career advancement or salaries of matched professionals or managers as discussed in Chapter 2.
But when discriminatory bias occurs in natural settings, each particular incident is "invisible." This is partly because there is usually no
matched comparison available in the particular situation, but evaluators might not recognize a match even if one were available. In addition to the gender schema itself with its powers of social expectations
and social consensus, there are other quirks of human perception and
mental processes that perpetuate sex discrimination and keep it invisible to both the perpetrators and victims of it, as well as to other
observers in the organization. The human mind processes information
to produce perceptions that "work" (i.e., work well enough to suit the
perceiver's immediate needs), and to produce them rapidly and efficiently, not necessarily accurately.

The Perceptual Bias Process is Unconscious. Although we form
some conclusions on the basis of conscious facts, values, and emotions,
we also form conclusions on the basis of facts, values, and emotions
that are not consciously recognized or even consciously accessible (Gazzaniga, 1985; Lewicki, 1985). The stereotypic gender assumptions
probably operate unconsciously in most cases. In addition, the discrimination is usually unintentional. Because the evidence is interpreted
in neural processing *before* it registers as a conscious perception, evaluators genuinely "see" men's and women's evidence differently; they
interpret it in terms of different sets of implicit meanings, so the
"evidence" *as they perceive it* is in fact different (Brewer, 1979;
McArthur & Baron, 1983). All of the processes discussed in this chap-

ter can operate outside of conscious awareness. The result is that men are more likely to be advanced than equally qualified women.

The Fundamental Attribution Error. "Attribution" is the explanation we give for the causes of people's actions and behavior. When we explain our own actions, we usually attribute them to opportunities and constraints in the situation: "I was late for work this morning because my car wouldn't start." But when we explain other people's actions, we usually attribute them to the person's internal personality disposition: "Sarah was late to work this morning because she is disorganized" (Jones & Nisbett, 1972). We make the same distinction between ourselves and others when we explain the characteristics of behavior, for example, acting dominant or submissive toward others. We see people (correctly) as the "cause" of their actions, but incorrectly ignore the fact that they "caused" their actions in response to the situation they were in at the time.

We make this error because we attribute causality to what we are attending to, consciously, in the situation. When we act dominant, we are focusing on those characteristics of the situation that call for dominance. But when we see another person acting dominant or submissive, it is the person who is visibly, physically present and the focus of our attention. The situational demands for us, as observers, are either disregarded background or may even be unknown. At least, they are not physically visible. Thus, we attribute the characteristics of the behavior to some force or disposition in the person. When we see Theresa habitually waiting for Thomas's directions, we assume that Theresa is passive and submissive by nature, and that Thomas is active and dominant, and fail to consider the situational constraints, such as role and status relationships, that could have caused their behavior. This principle is called the *fundamental attribution error* (Ross, 1977).

> When we see Theresa habitually waiting for directions, we assume that Theresa is passive, but this could be wrong.

Thus, if women are more often in situations and roles requiring sensitivity and deference to others, and men are more often in situations and roles requiring decisiveness and dominance, these characteristics of their behavior will be seen (erroneously) as caused by their internal dispositions or "personality traits" (Eagly, 1987). Because the sex segregation of occupations has, until recently, kept virtually all women in nurturing and subordinate roles and restricted authority roles to men only, we compounded the initial error and assumed, not only that the behavioral characteristics were "internal personality dispositions," but also that they were biologically rooted in sex.

Further, this tendency to attribute characteristics of behavior to personality dispositions is stronger when we are explaining a woman's behavior than a man's (Hansen & O'Leary, 1983). Remember from Chapter 2 that the "masculine" traits are instrumental, agentic, or ability traits under the control of their possessor. In contrast, the "feminine" traits are expressive and communal, and thus are seen (erroneously) as dispositional and therefore as less controllable by those who possess them. This means that we attribute women's actions to their sex, specifically to the stereotypic traits implicitly assumed to be biologically inherent in their sex, even when we attribute identical actions by men to situational requirements. For example, when a woman speaks vehemently, we tend to assume that it is "because she's a woman." ("Women are overly emotional.") But when a man speaks vehemently, it is "because the situation is important." Ironically, women may speak vehemently *because* they are ignored when they speak calmly.

The fundamental attribution error explains why certain particular "personality traits" have been socially labeled as "masculine" and others have been labeled as "feminine" in our society. There appears little hope that we will ever learn to avoid committing this error. Even understanding it thoroughly does not prevent our making it. However, we *can* change the particular traits that are consensually attributed to men and women by changing the unequal role and status structure of families and work places.

Causes of Decisions Versus Reasons for Decisions. Personnel decisions are always based on facts—the evidence. However, information about people is complex, with many facts varying in importance and implications. The particular facts that we perceive as the reasons for the decision may not be the facts that actually caused the decision (Nisbett & Wilson, 1977; Quattrone & Tversky, 1984; Zuckerman & Evans, 1984). For example, Nisbett and Bellows (1977) gave different groups of evaluators different versions of a woman's resume and job interview. Those who learned that she had been a little nervous and spilled a cup of coffee on the interviewer's desk later reported liking her more than those not given this information. Another item of information, that she had high grades in school, was unrelated to liking. But when the

> *The particular facts that we perceive as the reasons for the decision may not be the facts that actually determined it.*

evaluators who received both items of information were later asked why they liked her, the reason they gave was her school grades. They were unaware that the real cause of their liking her was the coffee-spilling incident. When people are unaware of the actual causes of their judgments or decisions, they provide an explanation that is socially plausible (Gazzaniga, 1985; Miller, 1984; Nisbett & Ross, 1980).

Legitimate reasons can usually be found for each decision. For example, a man may be promoted or given a raise "*because* of his success in bringing in new business," despite his constant budget overruns. A woman may be denied promotion or given a smaller raise despite her success in bringing in new business, "*because* of her constant budget overruns." Similarly, who gets hired for the new entry-level management position—Adam, with glowing recommendations from a second-rate school; or Janice, with perfunctory recommendations from a nationally top-rated school? Because Adam and Janice also differ on other criteria—relevant interests and ambition, specific courses they have taken, relevant summer work experience, outgoing friendliness, etc., there will always be ample "evidence" to support the final decision. Meanwhile, the actual cause of the decision, the implicit gender schema that interpreted the evidence, remains unrecognized (Winter & Uleman, 1984).

The Natural Metamorphosis of Rules and Criteria. Automatic stereotypic assumptions influence evaluators' perception of the rules and criteria, as well as their perception of the candidates. For example, they may selectively invoke or interpret the rules, or selectively weight the criteria, to facilitate a man's advancement (Drory & Ben-Porat, 1980; Schriesheim et al., 1979), but apply them more literally to a woman. She cannot claim discrimination, because the rules and criteria that officially apply to everyone were not violated in her case. Ironically, this could be a result of evaluators' sincere efforts to avoid stereotyping. Traditional stereotypes included chivalry norms, "making allowances" for "the weaker sex." The more stringent (actually, less lenient) evaluations of women could represent supervisors' efforts to resist the chivalry impulse.

The "Established Fact" Effect of Nonverbal Innuendo. Part of the basis of discriminatory sex bias often lies obscured in many incidental impressions preceding the formal evaluation. In daily interactions as well as in advancement evaluations, we notice actions and events made salient by the stereotypes (Cantor & Mischel, 1977). Recall from Chapter 2, for example, that discussion group members often showed disapproving facial expressions in response to a woman's assertive contribution, and that such expressions of disapproval are (erroneously) interpreted by others as "evidence" that the contribution was poor in quality. Vocal intonations can also convey a put down. The connotative impressions such incidents create are seldom questioned, because the cues (the disapproving facial expressions or intonations) are fleeting, have no verbal content, and occur in the context of attention to other matters (e.g., in work groups or staff meetings). Although the specific incidents are soon forgotten, the evaluative impressions they create accumulate over time (Fiske et al., 1983; Schul & Burnstein, 1983). Then the accumulated impressions influence the interpretation of whatever evidence is presented for formal evaluation (Brown & Geis, 1984).

Tokenism: When Men are Colleagues and Women are "Female." Stereotyping and perceptual distortions fall particularly on women who are the only one of their sex in the group, or one of a small minority (Kanter, 1977; Lord et al., 1984). This is because a woman is distinctive in a group of men, and it is her sex that makes her distinctive. This distinctiveness constantly activates work associates' gender schemas and thus increases stereotypic assumptions, treatment, and perceptual bias. When one of the men misses a meeting or fails to contribute, no one notices, because "men" were present and contributed. But when the group's lone woman is absent or silent, everyone notices. Similarly, because she is a woman, the men (unconsciously acting on the "women are less competent" stereotype) may offer to help her with simple tasks for which she does not need help. If she accepts the help, wishing not to appear aloof, she "confirms" the "less competent" stereotype. If she refuses the help, she may indeed be seen as aloof and arrogant, so they do *not* offer help later when she really does need it. This is another example of the "damned if you do, damned if you don't" dilemma discussed in Chapter 2.

> When the group's lone woman is absent or silent, everyone notices.

Another frailty of human perception and cognition also affects women in the minority in their groups. We tend to associate frequent events with majority group members and infrequent events with minority group members, even if the actual rate of both types of events is the same for both subgroups (Hamilton & Gifford, 1976; McArthur & Friedman, 1980). In most groups adequate performance is the rule, mistakes and failures infrequent. Thus, if the men and women in the group actually err at the same low rates, failures will be perceived as more characteristic of women, the minority subgroup.

WHAT CAN WE DO? PROCESS VERSUS OUTCOME

There is probably little hope of changing the way people process information about the world in general or about women in particular. Understanding the "fundamental attribution error" does not prevent one from making it. Nor can understanding schemas, and the gender schema in particular, eliminate schematic thinking or the unconscious, automatic use of schemas in perception and evaluation. Similarly, there is little hope of eliminating the effects of social expectations, consensus, or tokenism, or the automatic, unconscious use of implicit knowledge and subsequent rationalization. However, all is not lost. Although we cannot change the processes, we can change their results, the outcomes of the processes. We can make them work *for* women, or at least not against them.

> Although we cannot change human mental processes, we can change their outcomes.

If the "personality," occupation and status stereotypes depend on the present sexually unequal status structure of society, then equalizing the roles and status of men and women will break the stereotypes. As more and more women enter high-level careers, and succeed in them, despite discrimination, the visible evidence of their behavior and success will create a consensus effect. Most people will then agree that women are suited for high-status careers and succeed in them. Ideally, there should be approximately equal numbers of men and women at each status level of the organization, but remember that consensus effects can be created by as few as three people. Similarly, expectation effects on decisions about women and on how women are treated will not disappear, but *what* is expected of women will change from incompetence to competence. Consequently, what is noticed, inferred, and remembered about their qualifications and performance will change in the same way. Evaluations and hiring, salary, and promotion decisions will still be made on the basis of implicit knowledge, often used unconsciously, but the *content* of that implicit knowledge will no longer disadvantage women.

What can we do to hasten this more equitable world? The research suggests the following: (a) Work to get more women into high-status positions in our own organizations. No one can change society as a whole, but everyone can influence the particular groups in which she or he participates. When most particular groups have changed, society will have changed. Influencing one's group is something that cannot be done overnight or (usually) by a single individual. It usually requires a network of allies and progress must be measured over years, not weeks or months. (b) Support women at all status levels by granting them the same power and authority that we currently accord men at the same level, and encourage others to do so, too. (c) Reduce the negative consensus effect. Avoid disparaging women publicly, either verbally or nonverbally. (d) Create a positive consensus effect. Support women by recognizing and accepting their authority, listening to their ideas and suggestions and insisting that others do also, and giving them public credit for their actual contributions and accomplishments. The more "most women" succeed, the better the chances for each individual woman.

SUMMARY

Discrimination against women in evaluations, hiring, salary, and promotions is created and maintained by the way the human mind processes information about people. Information about people in organizations is perceived and interpreted in terms of *meanings* provided by our cultural gender schema. The *gender schema* is a mental structure of implicit knowledge about the categories of men and women. This "knowledge" consists of all of the personality, ability, interest, and occupational gender stereotypes of our culture. People are more likely to notice and recall information that is consistent with the schema than information that is inconsistent or irrelevant. The gender schema interprets the meaning of information that is noticed and fills in the gaps when actual evidence is missing, unnoticed, or forgotten.

Schemas operate as *expectations*. In addition to shaping perceptions, interpretations, and memory, a person's expectations about another also influence how he or she treats the other, which in turn influences how the other will respond. People who are treated as if they were intelligent, competent, incompetent, socially responsive, or hostile are led to behave in a way that "confirms" the initially false expectation, creating a self-fulfilling prophecy. The gender schema is powerful because it is *consensual* throughout society. When there is no physical criterion (for "personality" traits or managerial competence, for example), social consensus defines social reality and the consensual opinion is perceived as "the truth." Social consensus defines and validates individual beliefs, particularly those implicit beliefs of the gender schema that we use without awareness.

The *fundamental attribution error* involves attributing the characteristics of a person's behavior (such as acting dominant or submissive) to his or her internal personality disposition, when in fact those characteristics were actually caused by situational factors such as the person's role or status relationship in the situation. Because women have historically occupied subordinate roles that require little initiative but much deference, dependence, and nurturance, and only men occupied high-status roles requiring initiative, dominance, and decisiveness, these behavioral characteristics were attributed to their biological dispositions and continue to operate as stereotypes in contemporary society.

The facts people see as the *reasons* for their decisions, judgments, or actions may not be the facts that actually *caused* them. When people are unaware of the actual cause of their action (as they often are), it is easy to find a socially plausible explanation to offer as its cause without awareness of the substitution. Thus, evaluators can always sincerely offer plausible and legitimate reasons for their hiring, salary, and promotion decisions.

All of these processes work to selectively emphasize and reinterpret the *rules and criteria* for decisions as well as the qualifications or performance of the candidates. A major problem in evaluating men is the leniency effect, that is, rating all men too high. Evaluations of women appear not to suffer from this problem. The processes that devalue women and their performance also occur in daily routines as well as in formal evaluations. They often take the form of subtle *nonverbal behaviors* such as disapproving facial expressions or denigrating vocal intonations directed either at the woman directly, or used to convey negative connotations in conversations about her. Although such incidents are subtle and fleeting, their impact accumulates to influence subsequent formal evaluations. All of the processes are increased by *tokenism*. A woman who is the only woman in her status group, or one of only a few women, is perceived and treated more stereotypically than she would be in a group containing more women. Rare events, such as mistakes and failures in most groups, are also perceived and recalled as more characteristic of those in the minority.

There is little hope of changing the way the human mind works. The best hope for equality for women is changing not the processes, but their products. That means changing the contents of the implicit beliefs and "information" on which the processes operate. As roles and status in families and work places become more equal, more interchangeably male or female, women's behavior, required by the high status roles, and their success in those roles, in spite of discrimination, will disconfirm the old stereotypes. With implicit knowledge and assumptions that are egalitarian, the human mind will still suffer from the tricks and foibles outlined in this chapter, but they will no longer operate to disadvantage women.

Section III
Communication and Power: Who, What, Why, Where, and When

All work in organizations involves and depends upon communication, and communication both creates and reflects the power positions of organizational members. Effective performance and career success depend upon communication and power.

Communication, Power, and Paradoxes for Women, Chapter 4, covers the role of communication in organizations. Without communication, no social collaboration is possible: Communication makes organizing possible. The exercise of power and decision making are two crucial aspects of organizations, and both are discussed with respect to gender. Generally women appear to exercise less power and less influence on decision making than do men in comparable positions.

Chapter 5, *Working in Small Groups: Process, Power and Perils*, discusses communication in small task-oriented groups. Much of the work done in organizations is accomplished through such groups, so it is important to understand how such groups operate. Men tend to be perceived as more task-oriented and participate more than women do in mixed-sex groups. The task, the sex composition of the group, and whether or not a leader is designated influence how such groups operate.

The focus of Chapter 6, *Leadership: Myth and Reality*, is on the paradoxes of leadership for women. The old mythology of gender stereotypes makes it difficult for women to act as leaders and even more difficult for them to be recognized or accepted as leaders. In reality, however, women appear to make excellent leaders, and research suggests that they are, in fact, becoming more accepted as leaders.

Finally, Chapter 7, *The Many Facets of Managerial Style*, deals with managerial communication, primarily focusing on communication between superiors and subordinates. Subordinates generally evaluate female managers as having less power than male managers, and thus are less satisfied with them. Women appear to closely supervise subordinates and offer them support, whereas men delegate from a distance. Both women's and men's managerial styles are valuable in different organizational contexts, although the male model is expected and rewarded.

4
Communication, Power, and Paradoxes For Women

Organizations influence every aspect of an individual's life. Schools, churches, businesses, governmental agencies—all are organizations that profoundly affect our everyday lives. In order to be effective organizational members, we need to be aware of the nature of organizations. However, understanding organizations should not be limited to understanding just one's own job, but should also incorporate a general understanding of the entire organization. Such knowledge will aid one's career development and advancement, and help women cope with perceptual bias.

Organizational reality differs for women and men. Unconscious bias in perception and evaluation of women's work, sex-segregation of occupations, and the application of different standards for performance and evaluation have created different organizational realities for women and men. These differences apply, in varying degrees, to all organizations. For example, you personally may have experienced relatively little perceptual bias, but other co-workers may have experienced much more. Because our society, in general, has different standards and expectations for women and men, it is highly unlikely that organizations would not reflect these dual values.

Organizational reality differs for women and men.

This chapter discusses the nature of organizations and the importance of communication in organizations. Without communication no organizations could exist. Communication allows us to share ideas with one another and to coordinate our activities. Communication is also the process through which we form impressions of others and carry out organizational responsibilities. Effective commu-

Men's communication style is the dominant organizational communication style.

nication is critical for organizations and for organizational members. However, in this area too, we will find men's communication more highly valued than women's.

A general understanding of organizations and organizational communication, coupled with an awareness of perceptual bias in treatment and evaluation, can help women recognize barriers to their advancement. Once these barriers are recognized and understood, strategies can be developed to counteract them.

COMMUNICATION IN ORGANIZATIONS

All organizational processes depend upon communication because communication enables us to cooperate with one another and to coordinate organizational activities. Just as organizations vary, so do their communicative practices.

Communication is an organized, standardized, culturally patterned system of behavior that makes possible human relationships (Scheflen, 1974). Communication behavior is standardized: There are norms for acceptable communication, like being polite and making comments relevant. But it is also unique: Each individual has his or her own individual communication style. Norms for appropriate communicative behavior are culturally governed—what is polite in the United States may be an insult in India. Communication is also interpretive; people draw inferences about one another from what is said. The sequence of communication also influences the interpretation of messages (Haslett, 1987). Finally, communication is both verbal and nonverbal. Verbal communication may be either oral or written, either face-to-face or mediated, for example, by phone, tape-recording, or videotape. Nonverbal communication includes eye gaze, facial expressions, gestures, posture, movement, use of space, smell, and artifacts such as clothing or jewelry.

An organization can be viewed as a group that shares agreed-upon values and standards of interpretation. Communication enables us to share meanings with others, and the corporate culture provides meanings that are agreed upon by the group. The process of organizing, then, is fundamentally a communicative process. Communication creates organizations and organizational structures subsequently direct communication: Both processes simultaneously influence one another.

Formal and Informal Communication Networks. Organizations contain both formal and informal communication networks. Formal lines of communication follow the official hierarchy in an organization and their messages are officially endorsed by the organization. Informal communication cuts across an organization's structure and hierarchy, both laterally and vertically, and is not officially endorsed by the organization. Formal communication reveals the official position of the organization or of key organizational members, whereas the informal communication network often "interprets" what is meant by specific formal messages. The two systems complement one another and serve as ways to check the accuracy of information.

Formal lines of communication follow the designated lines of leadership and authority in an organization. Formal messages may vary from notes on bulletin boards to memos sent to department heads. The communication generally flows from the top down, from superiors to subordinates, and each message addresses a specific, limited topic. At any point in the formal network, individuals may act as "gatekeepers" of the information and prevent the message from being passed along further. One's status is important in the formal communication network because an organizational member with higher status tends to control, initiate, and terminate interactions. Finally, messages in the formal network are generally recorded and retained. In brief, messages in the formal communication network tend to flow from the top down, have restricted topics, and are recorded.

In contrast, the informal network of communication is multidirectional, cutting across the entire organization. Topics are unrestricted and message content is not officially endorsed by the organization. Informal communication is generally private, shared in face-to-face contact or over the telephone. Hierarchy or status does not necessarily influence the informal communication network. Individuals in the informal network may also serve as gatekeepers at any point. Finally, the content of the informal network is often an interpretation of formal policies and actions as well as gossip.

Both communication networks are important. The informal network should be viewed as an important source of information, especially because it aids organizational members in making sense of their everyday activities. Frequently, women are excluded from all-male informal networks and are denied important organizational information. This problem will be discussed more thoroughly later in this chapter. Formal communication is important because these messages represent the duties, tasks, and positions of the organization.

As we have seen, communication is vital to all aspects of organizational life. However, an organization's structure shapes both its activities and its communication. Thus, we need to appreciate the structural aspects of organizations as well, especially their impact on organizational communication.

Although organizations vary considerably in size, complexity, products, services, and many other dimensions, nevertheless we can specify general characteristics that define organizations. Organizations are groups of individuals who join together to pursue a goal. The most basic organizational goal is survival. Organizations are characterized by the need for skilled personnel, by job specialization, and by interdependence among organizational members. In addition, organizations typically have a hierarchy that outlines leadership functions and responsibilities. Although belonging to an organization is a matter of choice (as opposed to, for example, belonging to a family), most organizations have membership or entry requirements, like a specialized skill or degree. Finally, organizations have names; norms for behavior, such as standard operating procedures; and boundaries, both internal, separating one unit of the organization from another, and external, separating the organization as a whole from the rest of society.

ORGANIZATIONAL CULTURES

Although all organizations share these characteristics, they also differ from one another significantly. Even though people may work in the same industry or on similar products or services, the practices and policies of their different companies may vary substantially. Understanding the general nature of organizations is important, but even more important is understanding the organizational rules and values that operate in your particular company.

Researchers have explored organizational differences through the idea of organizational culture, the unique way in which a company does its work (Deal & Kennedy, 1982). Strong organizational cultures have myths, heroes, symbols, and clear, cohesive values that are very important to its members.

An organization's culture also defines the way in which the members make sense of their work activities. An organization's culture can be identified (Pacanowsky & O'Donnell-Trujillo, 1983) by its:

1. Relevant constructs—organizational concepts and units that describe the operating procedures. In a university, for example, "faculty," "students," and "alumni" would be relevant constructs.
2. Vocabulary—how members describe and talk about their organization and their work. For example, members refer to some organizations in terms of sports or military metaphors, like being a "team player," for example.
3. Facts—how the organization really works as opposed to what might be formally stated or required.

4. Expectations—what is appropriate and likely organizational behavior.
5. Strategies—plans and actions for accomplishing organizational goals.
6. Myths and oral history—highlights of the past and current events in the organization. For example, myths might focus upon an important leader.
7. Rites and rituals—ceremonies that emphasize what is important to the organization. For example, graduation is an important culminating experience for high school and college; a marketing convention might be an important ceremonial event for a sales organization.

Values must be added to this list. The most important part of an organization's culture is its values. Values control and guide the organization's activities. They provide guidelines for employee behavior and reflect the philosophy of the organization. Frequently, corporate heroes are those members who typify the values of the organization, those who achieve outstanding success in an important area of the organization.

Individuals need to be able to assess an organization's culture so as to judge the fit between their own values and the values of the organization. Understanding an organization's culture enables members to be successful because they understand how success is judged in that organization.

What type of organizational culture might you encounter? Two factors determine an organization's culture: The degree of risk faced by the organization, and the speed of feedback an organization receives about its activities (Deal & Kennedy, 1982). A *tough guy, macho culture* is a high-risk, quick-feedback organization, such as police work, venture capital or advertising. A *work hard, play hard culture* has low risk with quick feedback. Real estate, sales, and computer companies exemplify this type of organization. A third cultural type, the *bet your company culture*, has high risk and slow feedback. Architectural companies and capital-goods companies illustrate this type of organization. And last, a *process culture* is a low-risk, slow-feedback type of organization, such as insurance or banking. These cultural types are broad categories, and some organizations may not fall cleanly within only one category. In fact, different parts of a single organization may have different cultures.

Culture also traditionally refers to the values and way of life of a social group, like a country, region or tribe. Organizations exist within the culture of the country in which they operate. U.S. firms operating overseas must deal with both the native culture of North America and the cultural customs of the countries in which they do business. Increasingly, the U.S. is itself becoming more culturally diverse and within our borders, organizations need to deal with important subcultural differences between ethnic and racial groups. It is estimated that, by the year 2000, 85% of individuals entering the workplace will be women or minorities. Cultural diversity affects every aspect of personal and professional life; thus, understanding of and sensitivity to cultural diversity is an important issue. Although we cannot discuss cultural diversity in great depth in this book, we can pinpoint some different value orientations that influence organizations.

Each culture or subculture makes basic judgments on values, and these values influence the actions of individuals and groups. These basic value dimensions are (Schein, 1985):

1. *The nature of humankind*—are people basically good or evil? This decision determines the degree of trust and openness between individuals, for example.
2. *Time orientation*—are individuals oriented to the past, present, or future? These values influence such things as planning and resource allocation.
3. *Human relationships*—how do people govern their relationships with one another? Do they emphasize obligation, reciprocity, kinship, individualism, or some other theme? Such practices would determine legal codes and moral practices in a culture and obviously constrain corporate activities as well. Note that many cultures, including that of the U.S., answer this question differently for women than for men. Women are expected to give first priority to kinship values, their family. Men are expected to be individualistic and give first priority to their work.
4. *Relationships between humankind and the environment*—are humans in control of, subject to, or in harmony with the forces of nature? A philosophy that views human society as being in control of nature reflects a scientifically oriented culture.
5. *The nature of human activity*—are individuals relatively active or passive? This issue affects such matters as work practices and initiative. Again, answers for men and women differ. Men are expected to be more active, women more passive.
6. *The nature of reality*—are humans controlled by fate, or are they in control of their own lives? Such values affect people's beliefs about their own activities and outcomes.

As you can see, these values also influence one another. For example, beliefs about human activity and reality are likely to shape what people decide to do in a given situation. An awareness of cultural differences will enable us to interpret activities in another culture which might be inexplicable or unusual from our own cultural viewpoint. Knowing these differences can also free us from blindly assuming that our own organizational practices are the most acceptable and desirable. Finally, sensitivity to cultural differences opens up our own thinking about organizations, and how they might work effectively.

With this brief overview of organizations and their communication systems, we next turn to a discussion of some critical organizational issues. These issues are power, barriers to power such as discriminatory practices, and networking. Understanding the dynamics of power, networking, and using information are important for survival and success in an organization.

CRITICAL ORGANIZATIONAL ISSUES

POWER

Conflict and cooperation are key processes in organizations, and both are directly affected by power. Often, power determines how conflict is resolved and how cooperation is achieved. When compared to their male colleagues, women are less powerful generally. A number of factors contribute to this discrepancy. Among them are women's early socialization to accommodate others; the negative evaluation of women's work; lesser power given women than men in comparable positions; slower promotion of women in organizations; pay and treatment inequities; and women's exclusion from networks of information and opportunity (Benokraitis & Feagin, 1986).

Power resolves conflict and determines cooperation.

Power is a difficult concept to understand because it operates in many ways and on multiple levels. Power relationships are developed and maintained by communication, and communication provides a vehicle for the exercise of power (Frost, 1987). Thus, power and communication mutually and simultaneously influence one another.

A general definition of *power* might be the ability to compel another person to do what he or she would otherwise not do. In other words, power enables one to control the actions and choices of others. Power may be manifested overtly in open arguments over which particular policy to pursue, or exercised covertly, as when an organizational member chooses not to mention a particular problem because people generally do not talk about it.

Power can be viewed in a variety of ways, each perspective revealing an important aspect of power in organizations. The *resource dependency* perspective focuses on control over critical resources. Power is created by dependency, as when two parties are motivated to achieve certain goals and these goals cannot be met without the other party. For example, an organization is dependent upon an outside supplier if that supplier is the only source of needed materials. Similarly, individuals achieve power within the organization when others must depend on them for needed products, information, or assent. A *sociohistorical* perspective examines the social, historical context in which organizations develop. If a social setting favors scientific analysis, then technology can develop and flourish. A *political* perspective examines the competing interests among different units in an organization, or competition among companies in the marketplace. This view acknowledges the differing goals of subunits of an organization. Organizational control may be negotiated over time by competing interests. Finally, a *functionalist* perspective emphasizes the structural aspects of power as defined by the hierarchy in an organization. Power becomes defined by job responsibilities and privileges inherent in a given position.

The multifaceted nature of organizational power is reflected in these alternative perspectives. Each perspective highlights different aspects of power and different uses of power in organizations. Taken together, these views suggest that power is dynamic and changing: As an organization matures over time, the basis of power will change as well. Power also operates at both the systemic level, the organizational hierarchy, and the individual level, as a function of individual knowledge, ability, charisma, etc. Each of the different dimensions of power may be active at different times in different organizations. For example, crises will often involve political maneuvering for power among competing interest groups, whereas mature, stable organizations may have substantial power vested in the organization's structure.

Power is complex because it is both open and hidden. The overt use of power can be seen in the discussion of key issues and in whose opinions are finally accepted. However, the most important aspect of power is the power holder's ability to set limits for others and establish guidelines for action. These organizational guidelines are tacit, implicit understandings about how things are done in a

Understanding power involves recognizing both covert and overt aspects of power.

particular department or organization. These tacit understandings enable organizational members to make sense of organizational activities. An accurate understanding of power must include the covert, hidden aspects of power as well as its overt instances (Bacharach & Baratz, 1962; Conrad, 1983; Frost, 1987).

Power exists on both macro- and microlevels of an organization. Macrolevel sources of power would be societal sources, such as those derived from the structure of an organization. In contrast, microlevel sources of power primarily reflect individual sources of power and their exercise, for example, individual knowledge or expertise in an important area, or control over needed resources. When power is legitimized or institutionalized, that power source has become an authority for that context or relationship.

So far, this analysis has emphasized the structural aspects of power. However, individuals have power as well. If an individual has an important job and does it well, then she or her commands a commensurate degree of power. Power is also accorded those who can convince others that their task is critical (Pfeffer, 1981).

Three critical elements for personal power are one's organizational position, ability to perform the task, and ability to persuade others about the importance of the task.

Individual Use of Power. Using power involves relationships, dependency, and sanctioning. First, using power is relational because power involves interaction with others. Second, power implies dependency in a relationship. The more dependent one is on a particular relationship, the less power one has in that relationship. The degree of participants' dependency is a function of their other available alternatives for action, and the costs and rewards of each alternative. The fewer one's acceptable alternatives, the more dependent one is on the present relationship. Sanctioning, the action component of power, refers to specific actions. A negative sanction, for example, would be a punishment of some sort, such as a pay reduction. It is also important to remember that the potential to use power—rather than its actual use—may be enough to influence the actions of others (Bacharach & Lawler, 1980).

> *Potential power may be as influential as actual power.*

Although authority and influence are both sources of power, they differ from one another. Authority is power granted by virtue of one's organizational position: An authority's decisions are those that others must follow if they are to remain members of the organization. Subordinates legitimize this authority by their acceptance of it. Power is relational because the use of power must be matched, at some point, by others' acceptance of that power. In contrast, influence affects decisions, but does not impose them. Authority is directed toward subordinates, but influence is multidirectional. Individuals with authority attempt to control others, but they also have influence attempts directed at them. Generally, the higher the status of an individual, the greater his or her authority. There is a tension between authority and influence: Subordinates try to reduce superiors' authority, and superiors try to reduce influence attempts by subordinates (Bacharach & Lawler, 1980).

Many sources of power exist in organizations. There are coercive sources such as punishments. Other sources include rewards, expertise, legitimacy (authority), referent sources like friendship or charisma, and information (knowledge about the organization and how it works, or about a particular task). These sources of power can reside in one's position, personal characteristics, expertise, or opportunity. Power is limited by the number of people involved, the scope of activities controlled, and its legitimacy, the extent to which organizational members accept the rationale behind the authority.

In summary, power is an important dimension of organizations, influencing the flow of information, communication, and decision making. Power can be defined in terms of organizational structure, such as authority or control over scarce resources, as well as in personal terms, such as charisma or expertise. Within any organization, there are multiple sources of power, and these sources may change as the organization itself changes.

A number of studies have explored differences between men and women in their exercise of power. Generally, men and women appear to use different types and sources of power, although both exercise power.

Sex Differences in Using Power. Societal gender stereotypes, discussed in Chapters 2 and 3, also operate in organizations. Men exercise power and make decisions, whereas women provide support. Furthermore, isolated women in male groups are usually stereotyped in one of four ways: Women are viewed as mother (the nurturing caretaker), pet (the cheerleader on the sidelines), sex object, or "iron maiden." In any of these roles, it is difficult to demonstrate independent, critical, on-task behaviors and to develop any real power (Kanter, 1977).

Women are rewarded for gender stereotyped behaviors; however, they are negatively evaluated when they do not display appropriate behaviors (Fairhurst, 1986; Putnam & Fairhurst, 1985). This paradox—that social expectations for women often conflict with expectations for appropriate task behavior—is a major conflict for women on the job. While actual behaviors of men and women may be similar in a given situation, evaluation of these behaviors will differ. Gender stereotypes thus make the exercise of organizational power problematic for women.

Both men and women appear to have an equal need for power. The claim that women fear success or fear failure apparently does not apply to managerial women. Studies have shown that both women and men strive for power; in fact, women score higher on the use of power for the good of the group. According to two different personality tests, women managers had significantly higher achievement and power needs than managerial men (Chusmir, 1983). Managerial women may be highly motivated to succeed and influence others because they have had more obstacles, such as societal pressures and gender-role conflicts, to overcome in pursuing their managerial careers. Or it may be that only the most motivated women choose managerial careers.

The need for power can be divided into two different components, personalized and socialized power. Socialized power is directed toward the good of the group or organization. It reflects planning, mixed outcomes, and concern for colleagues. In contrast, personalized power focuses on personal advantage and opposing others to get such power. This conceptualization of power is based on McClelland's (1954) work on need for achievement, affiliation, and power. Women managers scored higher on the organizationally valued socialized power and did not differ from managerial men in their desire for personal power. However, socialized power was related to job satisfaction for men, but not for women (Chusmir & Parker, 1984). This finding suggests that most women managers have high needs for socialized power, but that only some of them are satisfied with their jobs.

Although men and women do not differ in their need for power, nevertheless different expectations create different power strategies for men and women. Generally, individuals are most highly evaluated when they use strategies consistent with gender role expectations. Because the use of expert power by women would imply gender-role inconsistent claims of expertise and competence, men are perceived as more effective when they use expert power, but women are perceived as more effective when they use reward power (Wiley & Eskilson, 1982). However, reward power is considered unreliable because managers need to check for compliance. There are also limits on the rewards a manager can dispense.

Status characteristics, like sex, influence the relationship between the power strategy used and managerial evaluations (Wiley & Eskilson, 1982). The use of indirect information, referent (relationship) power, nagging, and helplessness is associated with women, whereas the use of coercion, legitimate power, direct information, rewards, and expertise is associated with men (Johnson, 1976). Differences in how men and women exercise power may result from their early socialization, when men are encouraged to be competitive and aggressive, and women are encouraged to be supportive and nurturant (Hennig & Jardim, 1977). However, the differences may also reflect the ongoing pressure of implicit gender role expectations operating directly in the immediate situation (see Chapter 3).

Because of differing expectations, women and men use different types and sources of power.

When women use power strategies that are stereotypically "masculine," they tend to be viewed more negatively and as less effective. Women using power strategies associated with men (like expertise), and those who behaved more dominantly as leaders were rated as less effective (Haccoun, Haccoun, & Sallay, 1978). Women who used a dominant style were less influential than women using a considerate, problem-solving approach. They were also rated as less effective when evaluated by an all-male group (Watson, 1988). These differences in the evaluation and acceptance of men's and women's use of power reflect the prevailing gender stereotypes that characterize women as not only less competent than men, but also subordinate in status to men. Women's use of power, especially direct or expert power or dominance, violates the prescriptive stereotypic expectations and thus elicits negative reactions. It should be noted that the problem here is not in the women themselves but in others' biased expectations.

Women are disapproved of when they use "masculine" strategies.

Given the negative reactions to their use of power, it is not surprising that women have learned to modify their behavior accordingly. In an organizational simulation, men and women in equivalent positions used different strategies to influence subordinates. Although these differences were weak, women tended to use fewer different influence strategies, but those few were highly coercive. In contrast, men used more different influence strategies, gave more rewards, and used fewer coercive strategies. The women had significantly less self-confidence, and this was linked to both their higher use of coercive strategies and their use of fewer influence strategies in general. Both men and women were more confident when they were supervising same-sex subordinates (Instone et al., 1983).

Men and women also differ in their responses to powerlessness. In one study, *powerlessness* was defined as the degree to which workers were dependent on others to complete a task. Powerless women used more acquiescent strategies than powerless men. Acquiescent strategies were those in which the low-power individual accepted the power imbalance and decided that nothing else could be done in the situation. However, one's power position made more difference than one's sex in this study. Individuals in high-power jobs, both men and women, were more likely to search for alternatives in completing the task or resolving the problem. Thus, relative job dependency had a greater influence than sex on the use of acquiescent strategies (Mainiero, 1986).

Minorities (tokens) in small group settings (e.g., a single woman or minority in a small group of white men) may have more power than might be readily apparent (Fairhurst & Snavely, 1983). Tokens tend to be socially isolated, confronted with unique standards and expectations, and trapped in roles. However, these effects can be modified by power (the potential to define and alter another's behavior). Power can accrue to tokens by their longevity, attractiveness, and location (Mechanic, 1962). As Fairhurst and Snavely point out, tokens must offset the power of the majority through the number and importance of their own power base, their ability to influence decision making, or their individual power skills, like risk taking and self-confidence.

> Tokens may possess important sources of power.

In brief, the exercise of power by women is problematic. First, women are likely to be sex-segregated in the workplace and to hold relatively low-status, low-power positions. For those whose positions allow exercise of power, its use appears to be limited by stereotypical expectations of masculine and feminine behavior. Those women exercising gender-role-inappropriate power (e.g., power sources associated with men) are viewed as less effective and are less liked by their subordinates. However, even individuals in low-power positions have some power and can work to enhance it. Experience (having long tenure in the organization and thus having substantial knowledge about it), being interpersonally skilled, and having extensive knowledge about the task are all important bases of power. *Any* power can be enhanced and used to further one's career advancement.

BARRIERS TO POWER

The interrelationships of power, gender, and communication in organizations are complex. Two barriers to power—perceptual bias and structural limitations—will be discussed in more detail. These barriers limit women's performance and affect evaluations of their work.

Perceptual Bias in the Evaluation of Women's Work. Perceptual bias, explained in Chapters 2 and 3, operates as a barrier to power and effectiveness for women. One's ability to perform a given task is influenced by others' perceptions of the skills required and whether or not those skills are gender-stereotyped (Eagly, 1987). The traditional division of labor between the sexes, with women doing a disproportionate share of domestic activities and men primarily working in paid occupations, creates the stereotypes of women being communal (nurturant, expressive and warm) and of men being agentic (aggressive, independent, and instrumental). These expectations are also passed along to children and subsequently affect their behavior.

The perception of one's performance is related to (1) whether or not the task itself is perceived as being masculine or feminine, (2) the evaluator's conscious and unconscious gender attitudes and beliefs, and (3) whether or not the employee is male or female. Jobs usually held by women are evaluated more negatively and perceived as less demanding than jobs typically held by males. Interestingly, even when job descriptions are manipulated experimentally, jobs alleged to be occupied primarily by women are judged to be easier—regardless of the actual skills or behavior they require (Deaux, 1984).

Expectations and attributions about men and women are also related to gender-role stereotypes. Men are viewed as competent, and women as warm and expressive. In addition, men are viewed as more independent and competitive, whereas women are judged to be warmer and more emotional (Deaux & Lewis, 1984). However, such judgments are relative rather than absolute. People do not view women as totally emotional, but as more emotional than men. Gender stereotypes also influence occupational beliefs concerning the traits needed for particular jobs and the relative suitability of women or men for certain jobs (Mellon, Crano, & Schmitt, 1982). A sample of over 800 male managers rated women lower than men on aptitudes, skills and knowledge, temperament, work habits and attitudes, and motivation and job interest (Rosen & Jerdee, 1978). Again, the problem is in the eye of the beholder. As noted in Chapter 2, men and women managers do not actually differ on these dimensions.

When gender-based expectancies do not differ for a task, there will

be no differences in attributions. In making judgments, gender information is used relative to other sources of relevant information
(Deaux, 1984). In the absence of
other information, gender stereotypes appear to prevail. A field
study of middle managers found
no differences in male and female
managers' perceived effective-

> In the absence of other
> information, gender
> stereotypes often prevail.

ness. The authors suggested that this finding reflected specific information available about managers concerning past behavior and performance, and thus stereotyped expectations did not affect the ratings as
strongly (Tsui & Gutek, 1984). However, other research shows that
stereotypes influence judgments regardless of other relevant information that contradicts them (Fiske & Pavelchak, 1986).

Given the male-dominated model of organizations and effective organizational behavior, generally women are not "seen" as having the
necessary skills for effective performance—regardless of their actual
skills and talents. Because they are not seen as having these skills,
women may not be given an opportunity to develop them or use them
(Eagly, 1987). While there will obviously be exceptions, in the main,
studies have documented that women are negatively evaluated when
they display skills such as expertise or dominance that are viewed as
gender inappropriate.

Finally, to be effective, one has to be acknowledged as a powerful
person or as holding a powerful position. Again, for women this will be
counter to gender-role expectations and thus more difficult to achieve
than for men of comparable competence. In addition, the well-
documented tendency of women to blame themselves for their failures
and credit their successes to external factors like luck, while men do
the reverse, makes it difficult for women themselves to acknowledge
the value of their own contributions and convey this impression to
others.

Remember that the important result of perceptual bias is that it
creates self-fulfilling prophecies. (1) Because women are perceived as
less competent, they are given fewer and poorer opportunities, and
therefore may actually achieve less. (2) Because they are perceived as
less competent, their actual achievements are then further devalued
and given less recognition and reward than the same achievements by
men. The lesser recognition and rewards, then, erroneously seem to
"confirm" the false initial perception of lesser competence.

Structural Barriers to Power. One's power in organizations is
directly influenced by one's position within the organizational hier-

archy. Women primarily occupy positions of low power and thus learn patterns of powerless behavior (Kanter, 1977). A number of reasons have been given to explain women's relative powerlessness. First, given the sex segregation in the workplace, women are not likely to be in powerful organizational positions. Although more women are entering the workforce, they are doing so primarily in the clerical ranks (98% female); women hold less than 40% of managerial positions, primarily at the lower managerial levels. Second, for women who do work in managerial positions, their performance may be constrained and evaluated by gender-role spillover, which typically undervalues women's achievements. In gender-role spillover, women are expected to fulfill the same nurturant, supportive roles in organizations that they are expected to do for the family. Women have less status and less influence than their male counterparts in similar positions (Stewart & Gudykunst, 1986). "Without jobs that offer opportunities to gain visibility and influence, women are unable to gain access to the sources of structural power and remain caught in the cycle of powerlessness" (Mainiero, 1986, p. 634). Generally, most power sources are less accessible for women than men. This is a consequence of both past and present patterns of sex segregation in the workplace, and the gender-role expectations that derive from those patterns.

Organizational members must understand both the behavioral and structural dimensions of power. Behavioral strategies address issues like beliefs and expectations, role conflict and ambiguity, and motivation. In contrast, structural strategies address hierarchical issues, such as the lack of women in upper-level management. Behavioral strategies are actions that individuals can take to achieve change, whereas structural strategies need to be pursued on an organizational or group level.

Structural sources of power depend on the centrality of one's position (such as being in a line position rather than a staff position); one's ability to control uncertainty (like possessing skills that enable the organization to better control its environment); and one's access to and control over resources. Centrality in an organization is determined by the degree of organizational centralization (is power relatively centralized or decentralized); whether the position is a line or staff position; and the organizational chain of command and its division of labor. The more central one's organizational position, the more power one has (Smith & Grenier, 1982).

Because women do not frequently occupy central positions, they need to analyze their own organization carefully and determine its most central positions in order to create opportunities to work with these colleagues and thus advance their upward mobility. To cope with uncertainty, women must assess the risks associated with specific actions. Structural sources of discrimination require one to analyze such issues as the hierarchy in the organization and sex segregation within the organization. Structural bias is systemic bias and thus requires group action for change to occur. Knowing that a bias is structural in nature helps identify appropriate responses to it.

In addition to organizational and peer discrimination, women may also limit themselves by their own expectations and self-evaluations. As recently as the 1970s men evaluated themselves as managers more favorably than did women. The men also rated themselves as more intelligent and as having greater ability than did the women managers (Deaux, 1979). Women experience role conflict when they are treated on the basis of gender expectations rather than as professionals (Chusmir & Koberg, 1986). This greater internal conflict would appear, at a minimum, to make job performance much more stressful for women.

Role conflict also creates barriers to effective performance for women. Women reported family demands for time, and the loss of potential family income, limited their ability to seek additional training (Rosen & Jerdee, 1978). Conflict may also arise from a woman's self-perception of her role and her role as perceived by others (Terborg, 1977). Female managers with high job stress, as measured by pay inequity, perceived sex discrimination, lack of support from their boss, and underutilization of their skills, were more depressed and anxious, less satisfied with their jobs, and had greater intent to leave than those with lower job stress (Greenglass, 1985). Such stresses could cause *anyone*, man or woman, to feel depressed, anxious, or dissatisfied, and to wish to leave the job. However, studies also show that jobs are a greater source of satisfaction and self-esteem for women than their families are, and that families are a greater source of stress than jobs are. This stress is due, in part, to the disproportionate burden of family work that women do (Wilkie, 1988). A recent survey reported in *USA Today* (June 9, 1989) revealed that women who were planning to leave their jobs were doing so because of lack of opportunity for advancement, not because of a desire to devote themselves to homemaking. Corporations do not appear to recognize dual role pressures, and thus women have little support in resolving such stresses.

Inequities in on-the-job work will create barriers to effective performance. Mary Rowe (1977) argues that microinequities on the job directed at women or minorities (e.g., having one's work typed last,

> Role conflicts create stress as well as inhibit job performance.

regardless of when it was turned in, being left off vacation lists or being last to be scheduled, etc.) create substantive job barriers over time. While each incident in itself may be very small, taken together such microinequities accumulate to create an extra burden for a worker. Sexual harassment will also create stress on the job, both psychologically and economically, and thus provide more barriers to advancement.

One major message of the research on power is that when women use the little power they have available to them, they will be more accepted and successful if they restrict themselves to the power strategies stereotypically considered "appropriate" for women, such as indirect power, helplessness, nagging, and appeals to friendship and cooperation, and avoid such "masculine" strategies as legitimate authority, expertise, or dominance. This represents organizational reality, but it may not be the optimal solution for some—or for the organization. A better solution, we believe, would be for women (and men) to use the *most effective* power strategies for the situation and people involved, regardless of whether they have traditionally been considered "masculine," "feminine," or neutral—*and* for women's associates, male and female alike, to learn to accept and appreciate these behaviors from women as they presently do from men. This solution is more difficult, because it involves changing stereotypic expectations for men and women, but we believe it would enhance both men's and women's job performance, and thus the organization's effectiveness. It is also the only solution compatible with our current conscious ideals of equal opportunity.

So far, we have discussed two major organizational issues—power and its exercise, and discriminatory barriers. Next we turn to the issue of networking. Networking enhances one's power, facilitates effective job performance, and provides a key to promotional opportunities. We will also discuss mentoring as a specific type of networking.

NETWORKING

Networking refers to the development and use of contacts to further one's career. Network members provide each other with valuable information, future contacts, and referrals (Burke, 1984). Networking is more difficult for women, because they may frequently be excluded from the "old boy network" (Harriman, 1985). Because networking implies perceived similarity as well as trust, it is difficult for female-male networking to occur. In addition, the limited numbers of women in managerial and upper managerial positions makes it difficult to establish a women's network. Making the situation even more complicated, some women in positions of relative power and influence may sabotage other women's careers for fear of losing their own power (Kanter, 1977).

On the basis of interviews with individuals who were identified as having helped another's career or personal development, several different types of networking were identified. *Informational peers* provided information to their network associates, whereas *collegial peers* provided friendship and career strategizing. The third type, *special peers*, provided friendship, emotional support, and feedback. Informational peer contacts were most frequent, followed by collegial, then special peer contacts. Peers in larger organizations had a wider network, and women maintained contact with their network peers more than did men (Burke, 1984).

Mentoring. Networking is dispersed over a wide number of people, but mentoring is a one-to-one relationship in which an older, more established individual facilitates the career of a more junior employee. Mentors provide both career and personal assistance. With respect to careers, mentors serve as sponsors, fight battles for their proteges, provide them with inside information and increased visibility, and give them a way to bypass the hierarchy. Personally, mentors provide support, counseling, and friendship (Harriman, 1985; Moore, 1986).

Mentoring also enhances proteges' perception of their power. Mentored individuals (proteges) reported having more organizational policy influence, more access to important people, and more access to resources in their organizations than did nonproteges. Having a mentor may be especially important for entry-level women. Low-level women's perceived influence on organizational policy was significantly less than that of low-level men, and also less than both high-level men and women (Fagenson, 1988). Mentors also help proteges develop closer ties to the organization and integrate them into the corporate culture. Because proteges have status at varied organizational levels, they may serve as communication links between hierarchical levels of the organization.

Networking should be a fundamental part of one's career. Networks can be private, personal networks as well as public, professional ones. DeWine (1986a) suggests a number of networking principles: Make every contact count; track and follow-up on contacts; integrate networking into your daily routine; analyze your own skills and talents, and market them. Effective networking is built on trust and reciprocity of support.

A trend toward establishing designated mentorships in organizations may open up the benefits of mentoring to women on a more widespread scale. However, cross-sex mentorship will still be problematic because of the issues of trust and lack of perceived similarity. Finally, not everyone may be a good mentor, and to "institutionalize" mentorship might make mentoring, which is a very personal relationship, much less effective (Burke, 1984).

SUMMARY

Organizational life, especially success, is considerably more problematic for women than for their male counterparts. This is particularly so in the areas of communication and the closely related issues of power and networking. In order to be an effective organizational member, one needs to understand the nature of organizations, their structures and different cultures. In addition, one needs to understand communicative processes in organizations because communication is the basis of an organization's existence and all of its activity. Informal lines of communication, such as the grapevine or networking, are as critical to organizational members as the more formal, hierarchical communication systems.

Power determines organizational decision making and thus is a key organizational function. In general, power strategies are most effective when they are consistent with gender-role expectations. These expectations characterize men as instrumental, direct, and focused on the task, and characterize women as more supportive and indirect. When men and women have equivalent organizational positions, women are accorded less status and power. When women act in gender inappropriate ways (e.g., being domineering), they are more negatively judged than their male counterparts for whom the same behavior is gender role consistent. Finally, because women have less access to organizational power through sex segregation of occupations and gender-biased perceptions, subordinates may be more dissatisfied with women as superiors. These expectations place paradoxical demands on women: Women are expected to behave in gender-inappropriate ways to fit the male organizational model, yet such behavior is negatively evaluated. This is the "damned if you do, damned if you don't" problem.

In order to succeed in organizations, both women and men must be aware of organizational environments and expectations. Being knowledgeable about the conflicting expectations for women enables women to evaluate the situation more clearly and to take appropriate actions. Whatever action one takes must be judged against the risks and stress involved. Being aware of some of this complexity, we believe, enables one to deal more effectively with it.

What are some strategies to help address some of the issues discussed in this chapter? Here are six suggestions.

1. Communicate! Pay attention to the formal network messages, but participate in the informal network as well. If you are a junior member, try to develop a mentoring relationship with someone more senior, preferably someone of your own sex. Remember communication is the medium through which power is developed and used.

   Informal communication is as important as formal communication.

2. Be visible. Draw attention, when appropriate, to your contributions. Take credit for your work and competence. Create opportunities to talk positively about your own work and that of your department. But do so without excess.

3. Be aware of your organization's power structure, sources, positions, and individuals. You can use them to enhance your effectiveness and further your career.

4. Empower yourself. Assume power until you are explicitly told that a task or responsibility is outside your job responsibility. Form coalitions to extend your power through the exchange of information. Remember, information is power—never give it away.

   Communication is the medium through which power is developed and used.

5. Choose your power strategies carefully. "Feminine" strategies have been more acceptable for women in the past, but some of them fail to build reliable power bases for the future. Consider the potential costs and rewards of the alternative strategies.

6. Be aware of the "damned if you do, damned if you don't" demands in the workplace. Accurately assessing the situation is the first step in doing something about it.

7. Assess an issue first, then act. Analyze an issue or problem at work from all participants' viewpoints. You will then have a good handle on the risks and benefits involved, and can plan appropriate action. Pick the battles you want to fight, rarely does one have the time or energy to tackle them all.

In the next chapter, we discuss communication in small task groups. Because a significant part of organizational work is done in small groups, it is important to understand their dynamics and how gender issues may surface in small group interaction.

5
Working in Small Groups: Process, Power, and Perils

Organizations do much of their work in task forces or project groups, small groups of five to seven members. In fact, an organization itself may be viewed as a group of groups. An understanding of how these groups function will enable people to participate more effectively and to analyze their small group interactions more accurately.

A *group* is also a collection of people with interconnected, repetitive communicative behaviors. Within small groups individuals perceive one another as individuals as opposed to larger groups where individuals may be identified only as "a member" of this or that category or faction. Small groups, therefore, have (1) *norms*—shared expectations and patterns of behavior; (2) *roles*—specific functions, carried out by specific behaviors and obligations; (3) *goals*—specific purposes to be accomplished; and (4) *interdependence*—goals and behaviors of group members that are interconnected and depend upon one another (Bales, 1950; Fisher, 1974).

Groups in organizations can be temporary and ad hoc, assembled to perform a specific task or project, or relatively permanent, such as a manager and his or her subordinates. Although all small groups have the above characteristics, *task groups* in organizations have unique characteristics. They are also influenced by (1) their relationships with other organizational units; (2) the organization's hierarchical structure, the organizational level at which the group functions; and (3) multigroup memberships. Members may belong to several groups and thus have divided loyalties and commitments. Task groups' interrelatedness with one another depends upon three factors: The degree to which their tasks and goals overlap, frequent communication with one another, and a commonly controlled fate (Putnam, 1988).

Groups within the organization are connected by a liaison person, or *link pin*, who has overlapping membership in different groups and shares information from group to group. Link pins thus play the important role of providing a communication network across an organization. Some individuals, such as public relations specialists, serve as link pins between an organization and its external environment.

SMALL GROUP DYNAMICS

Dynamic refers to processes of change over time. Group activity changes over time, both in longer term intervals called *developmental stages*, and also in the shorter term intervals of ongoing communication within a single group meeting. In order to understand how small groups work, we need to look at their input, process, and output. *Input variables* include characteristics of the group, such as the ability of group members, and task characteristics, such as task difficulty or complexity. *Process variables* reflect the amount and type of communication that occurs during the group's interaction. *Output variables* include productivity, accuracy, quality, and speed, and also socioemotional factors, such as group morale and satisfaction (Pavitt & Curtis, 1990).

Developmental Stages. Most groups pass through consistent patterns or phases in working on their problems. Which phase a group is in is an important characteristic of the group because it controls group activities. Several alternative models of group development have been proposed. Both stage models and multiphase models provide useful insights into group processes. These models help identify where groups are in their work and can enable the members to facilitate group progress.

Some scholars have proposed three-stage models. First, there is an *orientation* stage, in which group members develop a common understanding and definition of their task. Second, an *evaluation* stage takes place, in which members come to agree upon criteria for selecting a good decision or solution. Finally, in the third or *control* stage, group members come up with the best solution (Bales, 1950). Four-stage models include: *orientation, conflict* over alternatives, *emergence* of a proposed solution and, finally, *decision*, a reinforcement or commitment to the solution (Fisher, 1974).

Recently, multiphase models have been proposed. These models suggest that groups cycle through periods of relative inertia and intensive work. These group cycles reflect the members' sensitivity to deadlines and time pressures. A major transition from inertia to concentrated work occurs roughly at the midpoint of the group's time deadline. This transition uses the work in the first half of the cycle to build new directions for completing the task during the second half of the group's work. Thus, group activity is governed by the pace of the group's work and attention to time factors, rather than the universal stages proposed by earlier research (Gersick, 1988).

Although these models focus primarily on tasks, researchers have not neglected the socioemotional dimensions of groups; its cohesiveness, identification, and the personal needs of group members for approval and recognition. It is necessary for groups to maintain good working relationships with one another (the socioemotional dimension) in order to solve their assigned task (the task dimension).

Some models of group development have focused on the relationship between a group's task activities and its socioemotional processes. Groups may develop concurrent "tracks" or phases of task and socioemotional development (Poole, 1983). These models focus on the task and socioemotional dimensions as they co-occur simultaneously.

Phase I   Socioemotional dimension—sets standards for appropriate behavior.
Task dimension—defines the task and operating procedures.

Phase II Socioemotional dimension—conflicts within the group emerge.
Task dimension—conflict develops around individuals, and between different individual perspectives on the task.

Phase III Socioemotional dimension—creates group cohesiveness and a structure for social interaction.
Task dimension—exchange of opinions concerning alternative solutions.

Phase IV Socioemotional dimension—use of social structure to resolve interpersonal problems.
Task dimension—an agreed-upon solution emerges and the group expresses commitment to it (Tuckman, 1965).

Such models see groups as trying to maintain a balance between instrumental, task requirements and the integrative demands of socioemotional or relationship needs (Bales, 1950).

Communication: Task Demands and Emotional Needs. Within a single group meeting, members' communication addresses both task and socioemotional needs. Task comments include answering and asking questions, and offering and asking for opinions, information and suggestions. In contrast, socioemotional comments include supportive statements, such as showing solidarity, giving help, displaying approval and showing agreement or understanding as well as negative statements, such as disagreeing, showing hostility, or displaying tension (Bales, 1950, 1953). In groups with satisfied members, more positive than negative statements are made. Most of the talk in groups is task oriented, and the most frequent verbal activity is giving opinions. One study found that 25% of the group's talk concerned initiating and developing ideas; 25% clarified and substantiated ideas; and another 25% evaluated ideas. Usually about two-thirds to three-quarters of the talk addresses task issues, and about one-quarter deals with socioemotional issues (Scheidel & Crowell, 1964; Piliavin & Martin, 1978).

However, many of the earlier studies did not assess who said what. In fact, different speakers have different impacts. We will discuss differences between men and women as group members below; leaders' contributions and problems are addressed in Chapter 6.

Group Structure. A group's structure also influences how it operates. Smaller groups of three or four members can often work faster than larger ones of six or more members, but they can also be less accurate. Each additional group member adds an additional body of knowledge and ideas to the group, but also an additional source of individual interests and emotional needs that take up the group's time. Groups may also operate differently depending on their type of leadership. In "leaderless" groups, leadership emerges as the various members provide it through their contributions. The sex composition of the group is also an element of its structure. We will discuss this topic later.

> Each group member contributes knowledge to the group but presents emotional needs as well.

Within organizations a structure may be imposed on a small group. At a minimum, organizations form and disband small groups. A designated leader or an assigned task are other examples of imposed structures. In groups where all group members are of approximately equal status and have a diffuse communication network, usually there is better task performance and more group satisfaction. When compared to cooperative groups, competitive groups initiate more, disagree more, inform more, and agree more (Baird, 1976). In a group having a definite hierarchical structure, like a military group, information is spread very quickly and efficiently. Such centralized group networks have less overt conflict because group members communicate little with one another. Centralized groups perform best on tasks that require exchange rather than manipulation of information. Power relationships are often clearer in such groups, with group members in centralized positions serving as leaders and being the most satisfied group members (Pavitt & Curtis, 1990).

Group Cohesiveness. When the members are attracted to one another or to the group overall, they form cohesive groups. Cohesiveness may also broadly characterize the overall integration of the group or the degree to which group members feel like part of a team. Group cohesiveness is greater when group members like and identify with one another, and when the group is better able to meet its members' needs. In more cohesive groups, the members make more attempts to influence each other, and accept more influence from others. Also, the more cohesive the group, the more risk-taking, such as expressing individual idiosyncrasies or group norm-breaking, is allowed (Stokes, 1983). All other things being equal, the more cohesive the group, the more effective it is.

Because much organizational work is done in small task groups, understanding group processes is important for all organizational members. This knowledge will facilitate your own participation in groups as well as the overall performance of the group. Effective groups take care of the socioemotional needs of group members in addition to completing the assigned task. Communication plays a critical role in how well small-group members function on both task and socioemotional dimensions. Analyzing group interaction reveals that the predominant amount of talk is directed at various task dimensions such as initiating and evaluating ideas. There are important differences between men and women in small group communication, and it is to these differences we now turn.

SEX DIFFERENCES IN SMALL GROUP COMMUNICATION

Contribution Differences. Men's and women's communicative behavior varies with the gender role demands of the situation as well as the individual characteristics of participants. Both sexes, in both same-sex and mixed-sex groups, behave in accordance with traditional stereotypes: Men are more task oriented and instrumental, whereas women are more interpersonally oriented and nurturant (Aries, 1977; Piliavin & Martin, 1978).

Men and women behave in accordance with traditional sex-role stereotypes in small groups.

In a study of a mixed-sex informal committee meeting, when the interaction is hierarchically structured, men tend to dominate. However, women participated equally with men when the interaction was collaborative (Edelsky, 1981).

Participation in small groups also varies with the sex composition of the group. In same-sex groups, women share interaction relatively equally among group members, tend to develop and pursue a single topic cooperatively, discuss topics of intimacy and interpersonal relationships, support others' remarks, and give more attention to socioemotional issues than men do in all male groups. Men in all-male groups establish a relatively stable dominance hierarchy and discuss a range of general, nonintimate topics, which a few men dominate. They express competition and leadership, and their talk focuses on competition and status. In all same-sex groups, task talk increases over time and socioemotional talk decreases (Aries, 1977; Carli, 1982; Piliavin & Martin, 1978). However, a more recent study of same-sex groups found no differences between men and women in rates of participation, cooperation, and interaction style (Yamada et al., 1983).

Mixed-sex groups fall between these two extremes of all-male or all-female groups. In mixed-sex groups, both men and women tend to accommodate to each others' style. Men become less dominating, and women less supportive, than they are in same sex groups. However, sex differences persist. Participation in mixed-sex groups also seems to be guided by sex role expectations. In mixed-sex groups,

> In mixed-sex groups, male and female communication styles begin to converge.

men talk more, initiate more topics, make more contributions than women do, and receive more comments from others. Women increase their communication with men but not with other women. Men's talk becomes more personal and less competitive, but they still express more dominance and competition than women do, and women still express more concern for others and more affection. Men are more vocally assertive and more influential than women, and they are perceived as more dominant than women. This may partially reflect women's more uncertain speech forms. Women use tag questions ("It's a nice day, isn't it?") rather than the direct forms ("It's a nice day.") more in mixed-sex than in same-sex groups (McMillan, Clifton, McGrath, & Gale, 1977). However, women who speak up first in a group are viewed as more assertive than women who speak second.

Structured rather than open-ended discussion facilitates men's vocal assertiveness and their emergence as leaders. Men yield to others less in mixed-sex groups than in all-male groups because they yield to women less than they yield to men. Women yield more in mixed-sex groups because they also yield to women less than to men. However, greater knowledge and interest in the topic decreases susceptibility to persuasive remarks made by others. Men predominately give and ask for opinions, focusing on task contributions, whereas women tend to be friendly and agree, providing the socioemotional contributions. However, this division of labor depends on the topic's gender characteristics. When the topic is related to the interests and knowledge of one sex more than the other, the "favored" sex displays more task behavior (Aries, 1977; Bernard, 1972; Carli, 1982; Kimble et al., 1981; Lockheed & Hall, 1976; Piliavin & Martin, 1978; Strodtbeck & Mann, 1956).

These differences suggest that men and women may perform better on different kinds of tasks. Women may perform best in tasks that require discussion, negotiation, or creative, integrative solutions, whereas men may be best suited for group tasks that require a high volume of ideas (Wood, Polek, & Aiken, 1985).

Two explanations have been proposed for the relative power and influence imbalance between men and women in small groups. Expectation States theory (Berger & Zelditch, 1985), described in Chapter 3, proposes that because men are accorded higher status than women in the broader society, they will also be accorded more power and status in groups. This is another way of saying that high status and authority are parts of the masculine stereotype. Dozens of studies have supported the expectation states explanation. Some researchers have suggested that it may be necessary for an authority to intervene in groups so that the initial status difference does not control the structure and power of the group (Lockheed & Hall, 1976). This suggestion was tested. In mixed-sex groups, when an experimenter asked a male to speak more, gender role stereotypic behavior increased: The women talked even less. However, when the experimenter asked a woman to speak more, stereotypic behavior decreased for both male and female group members (Piliavin & Martin, 1978). This finding illustrates the importance of authority support for women's contributions.

Other researchers suggest that sex differences in group participation may also stem from the traditional instrumental role of men, and the expressive role of women, in the broader society. These roles would predict that women would be more easily influenced than men (Eagly & Wood, 1985). In addition, because men are often given higher status, they are perceived as more independent, assertive, and self-confident. Consequently, men's comments tend to be given more weight than women's. In contrast, women's communal orientation may commit them to preserving group harmony and enhancing positive feelings among group members. Women's focus on group harmony and interpersonal accord may thus make them more easily influenced (Eagly, 1987).

These general findings are limited by the diverse ways in which communication was measured in the various studies, and by whether or not participants' responses were made in private or in public. When responses are known publicly, there is additional pressure to respond consistently with gender-role expectations. In brief, both gender-role expectations and occupational positions tend to emphasize women's communal behaviors, rather than agentic or instrumental behaviors.

In considering these findings on sex differences in group participation, the reader must keep in mind that the organizational culture and the status of group members in the organization also influence group behavior. For example, a female group leader may behave in a more task-oriented fashion than if she were not in a position of authority. For men, of course, no contradictory expectations are present because male gender-role expectations are consistent with task-oriented behaviors. This is one of the profound paradoxes for women in organizations: There is conflict, rather than agreement, between task-oriented behaviors and gender-role expectations for women. In other words, one is "damned if you do, damned if you don't" (see Chapter 2).

> *Group behavior is partly determined by an organization's culture and group members' status.*

The paradox of conflicting gender and professional expectations for women can be viewed as a cultural "double-bind." If a woman acts as an effective group participant by offering substantive, task-oriented contributions, she is seen as exhibiting masculine traits and viewed as "unfeminine." On the other hand, if she displays culturally preferred behaviors, such as being nurturant, she is judged as unsuitable for managerial responsibilities. Such double-binds not only exist with regard to expectations for group participation, they can also be found in contradictory messages sent to women. Such messages have dual meanings that contradict one another (see the dialogue in Chapter 1). For example, if a manager tells his subordinate to manage her time wisely and then asks her to perform trivial tasks which do not facilitate her career advancement, he is sending a contradictory message. The manager is saying, in essence, "Think of your own career advancement first while

> *For women, gender-role expectations and task-oriented behaviors conflict with one another.*

you work on my special projects which will get you nowhere" (Putnam, 1983, p. 45).

As we have seen, organizations are dominated by so-called "masculine" values and characteristics. Because small task-oriented groups are a basic work unit in organizations, groups are also dominated by "masculine" values and characteristics. Women are perceived as being expressive or communal. Although these characteristics fulfill genuine and crucial socioemotional needs of the group, they are not officially recognized or valued in groups or organizations. In contrast, men are viewed as instrumental or agentic, qualities that are recognized and valued. Thus, women tend to play supportive roles in groups, and men tend to assume leadership roles, irrespective of their individual competencies. As discussed in Chapters 2 and 3, what you believe and expect is what you see, and when women behave in a way consistent with gender-role expectations, their behavior is devalued by groups and by organizations generally.

Women tend to be supportive in groups, while men tend to assume leadership.

In contrast, when women behave in instrumental or agentic ways, valued by groups and organizations, but not viewed as appropriate for women, they are also negatively evaluated. Some of the stress caused for women by this "double-bind" may be lightened by understanding that their behavior is not at fault, but that they are trapped in a dilemma. Recognizing the male bias in tasks and expectations may also relieve contradictory demands, especially if colleagues can be made aware of these contradictory expectations. Chapters 8 and 9 propose some strategies for dealing with "double-bind" situations.

Working in groups involves dealing with leadership, handling conflict, making decisions as a group, and both giving and receiving feedback. We now turn to a discussion of three of these important group processes, conflict, decision making, and feedback. Leadership is addressed in the next chapter. For each process, we will discuss potential gender differences and their implications for the workplace.

CONFLICT

Conflict and cooperation are built into organizations because of their hierarchies, diverse goals, and the division of labor within organizations. Conflict occurs when there is interdependence, when there

Conflict is unavoidable, but it can increase involvement and satisfaction, and enhance decision making.

are scarce rewards, and when there are incompatible goals (Hocker & Wilmot, 1985; Thomas, 1976). Conflicts vary in intensity and duration, and they may be positive as well as negative. Conflict can be positive in that it increases involvement in the group and ultimately results in better decision making and more satisfaction (Pavitt & Curtis, 1990). On the other hand, conflict, if not contained, may destroy the organization. Conflict is time consuming and can delay the resolution of a problem.

Communication and conflict are intimately interrelated because conflict emerges through communication, and only through communication can it be resolved. Through communication, people define opposing positions on an issue; develop alliances and oppositional relationships with others involved in the conflict; develop strategies and tactics to influence one another; propose alternative solutions, and finally reach agreement or resolution (Putnam & Poole, 1987). To accomplish both organizational and personal objectives, we must be sensitive to conflict issues as well as communication styles in dealing with conflicts.

Conflict can occur at different levels in an organization. Conflict can occur between equal-status colleagues or between superiors and their subordinates. Bargaining and negotiation to resolve the conflict may involve individuals, groups, or entire organizations. Groups may have conflict within organizations, such as departments competing for scarce resources. Finally, there is conflict between organizations. Individuals need to assess at what levels conflict is occurring because different strategies may be needed depending upon the context of the conflict.

Within any given conflict, tactics for dealing with it will vary according to the issues, participants, relationships, and contextual factors involved. Issues may vary in terms of how many people are affected, the complexity of the issue, and resources available for resolving it. Because individuals vary in their ability to tolerate conflict and in their styles of coping with conflict, different situations may create conflict for some people whereas others in the same situation would not be in conflict with one another. Relationships between the disputing parties also influence how conflict is handled. For example, people who like one another will make more of an attempt to resolve a conflict than those who do not (Putnam, 1983). Goals and outcomes also vary across conflicts. Your goals will influence your choice of conflict strategies. Goals may be changing an individual or changing a relationship, increasing some benefit, obtaining permission to do something, or defending a right (Canary, Cunningham, & Cody, 1988).

Strategies for resolving conflicts can be distributive, integrative, individualistic, or avoidant. *Distributive* strategies are basically competitive. Individuals or alliances seek to obtain as much for themselves as possible relative to what others obtain. This is the strategy of seeking one's own advantage at the expense of others. *Integrative* strategies are basically cooperative. They seek the maximum benefit for all of those involved, even if that means slightly lesser benefits to particular individuals, including themselves. *Individualistic* strategies seek the individual's own gain without regard to the gains or losses of others involved in the conflict. *Avoidant* strategies are attempts to avoid, ignore, or deny the conflict.

Integrative tactics may include disclosure and mutual efforts, whereas distributive tactics may include displaying anger, ridiculing by sarcasm, or being critical. Avoidance strategies may include shifting the topic, with a joke for example, or denying that any conflict exists (Canary et al., 1988). Although one might suppose that men and women would differ in their preferences among these strategies, apparently they do not. When men and women were placed in a conflict situation and forced to choose among the strategies, approximately equal proportions of both sexes chose each of them (Kuhlman, Brown, & Teta, in press). However, other studies have found sex differences, to be discussed later in this section.

Some responses, like giving explanations for an action, may help avoid or deescalate the conflict (Bies, 1988; Bies, Shapiro, & Cummings, 1988). In some situations, third-party intervention may be necessary to achieve a resolution. For example, both labor disputes and divorce settlement may require mediation. Conflicts may involve adjudication, negotiation, mediation, and conciliation. In complex organizations or for complex problems, conflict may also involve litigation. For example, women have achieved more equitable salaries in some organizations through class-action suits.

Individuals may also have preferred styles for handling conflicts. Some people are typically argumentative, while others are usually accommodating. Understanding individual differences in handling conflict helps us deal more effectively with the conflict. We can anticipate how others may react and thus can plan our strategies accordingly. Five basic individual styles for managing conflict have been suggested (Blake & Mouton, 1964):

Identify others' conflict style in order to handle conflict effectively.

1. *Competitive* style—being dominant, aggressive, and controlling; frequently most concerned about one's own needs.
2. *Accommodative* style—being friendly and unassertive.
3. *Avoidance* style—withdrawing or appearing indifferent to the situation or the individuals involved.
4. *Compromising* style—being assertive yet cooperative and demonstrating a willingness to make trade-offs.
5. *Collaborative* style—seeking to solve problems and to meet the needs of everyone in the group.

In the workplace, co-workers used the following strategies to influence their peers: Reason, friendliness, bargaining, assertiveness, forming coalitions, and appeal to a higher authority (Kipnis & Schmidt, 1982). These styles may be appropriate in different situations or for different individuals. Using conflict productively depends on understanding your own conflict style and that of other group members, as well as the ability to understand different points of view.

Conflict is a daily part of individual and organizational life. With practice, skill in handling conflict effectively can be learned. First, we need to assess the factors discussed above in conflicts we experience. Then, based on our assessments, we need to select our goals and strategies carefully. Although these factors are general and apply across many situations, gender expectations also influence conflict resolution. Although the research on gender influences in conflict resolution is mixed (Conrad, 1985), nevertheless stereotypical expectations seem to play a role in how we handle disputes and, even more importantly, in how we *are expected* to handle disputes.

Sex Differences in Handling and Resolving Conflicts. Conflict may be particularly complex for women in organizations because they may be regarded as status inconsistent individuals. Status inconsistency occurs when an individual is high on one dimension of social status, such as job position or expertise, but low on another, such as being a woman. If a mutually acceptable relationship cannot be negotiated between a status-inconsistent person and another colleague, there is greater potential for conflict (Fairhurst & Snavely, 1983). Conflict occurs because the participants cannot decide or agree on which of the woman's conflicting statuses will govern their interaction (Fleishman & Marwell, 1977). This problem may underlie men's inability, in some situations, to take women seriously.

Although results are mixed, men and women appear to differ in their approaches to resolving conflict. In organizations, women deal with conflict by minimizing differences, emphasizing similarities, and

In resolving conflict, women emphasize group goals whereas men favor individual goals.

smoothing over problems (Putnam, 1983). Women appear to follow communal goals and strategies, whereas men pursue instrumental goals emphasizing individual interests. Because of their more communal orientation, women are more likely to use strategies that maintain positive relationships (Cody, Canary, & Smith, in press). However, both sexes respond positively to compromise as a conflict management strategy. Female supervisors appear to talk openly with their subordinates about disagreements, whereas male managers tend to withdraw from conflict situations.

One study suggested that both sexes may feel more confident and possess a larger repertoire of coping strategies when they operate from their familiar, traditional positions of status inequality. When men and women were assigned to traditional positions of status inequality, with the man in the high-status position and the woman in the lower status position, or to nontraditional status relationships, both the men and the women rated themselves as being more influential in negotiations in the traditional relationships. When the men were dependent on a lower status person to make an important decision, they perceived themselves as lacking influence and tried to avoid conflict with the subordinate (Thompson, 1981). These results for women show the effects of familiarity and practice. Occupying the subordinate status position is not a real advantage for anyone, man or woman.

"The results of the conflict studies seem consistent with the idea that the [traditional] 'feminine' role requires avoiding the kinds of behavior associated with competitive status enhancement or dominance, rather than with a low level of interest in the task or with a high motivation for equality, harmony or 'helping' others" (Meeker & Weitzel-O'Neill, 1977, p. 100). Women appear to avoid conflict when it involves competition or dominance rather than being motivated by a desire to nurture others.

Women avoid conflict when it involves competition or dominance.

Bargaining and Negotiation. In a number of early conflict experiments, women took more extreme bargaining positions than men did, but also responded more positively to cooperative strategies (Tedeschi, Schlenker, & Bonoma, 1973). These sex differences were attributed to women's tendency to be more affiliative and dependent. As a result, women were less likely to exhibit such behaviors as coordinating or directing that researchers thought necessary to achieve cooperation in conflict tasks (Terhune, 1973).

Women have been found to prefer more passive bargaining approaches such as low-key approaches and supportive tactics than men do. Both sexes value reason in persuading others, but women depended on this strategy more than men did (De Wine et al., 1982). In a simulation of bargaining, same-sex negotiator pairs used attacking statements more than mixed-sex pairs did. Male negotiators used argument by analogy, whereas their female partners used examples and cause-effect reasoning (Putnam & Jones, 1982). Another study of same-sex bargaining pairs found that men were less likely than women to reach an equitable settlement. The women focused on understanding each other's feelings whereas the men used anger and logical arguments in the dispute (Putnam, 1983).

The perception of women's behavior in conflict situations is influenced by expectations reflecting gender stereotypes. Although, objectively, men and women used equally controlling negotiation tactics, the women were perceived as less controlling than the men. In fact, men and women used "intense structuring" (directive) behaviors equally in dealing with the dispute (Burrell, Donohue, & Allen, 1988).

> Despite the same behavior, women and men are perceived and evaluated differently.

This finding suggests that women learned to use the directive behaviors over the time period since the older research of the early 1970s. Most importantly, the discrepancy between behavior and perception is consistent with other major findings showing that, even when behaviors do not differ as a function of sex, perceptions and evaluations of them will. Inconsistencies in the research results suggest that these sex and gender effects may be mitigated by length of time in the organization (Putnam & Jones, 1982), expertise, or interpersonal relationships. Such factors may serve as alternative bases of power.

Again, we urge readers to remember that the research results reflect reality as it exists and has existed in the recent past. They do not indicate the status perceptions or conflict resolution strategies that would be optimal for the personal satisfaction or growth and development of individual women (or men) or other group members, or for group productivity and decision quality. It would appear that both competitive and collaborative strategies can bring benefits to both individuals and to the group, and that both men and women can learn and combine both of them.

In summary, conflict is an inescapable part of organizational life and needs to be managed constructively. Men and women appear to handle conflict similarly in some ways and differently in other ways, with men preferring more competitive, direct strategies and women preferring more collaborative, supportive strategies. How men and women deal with conflict, and approach its resolution, seems consistent with stereotypical gender expectations.

Conflict may frequently occur around decision making. There may be conflict over who makes decisions, as well as over the decision itself. Because decision making is vital to organizational functioning and is often the assigned task of a work group, it is appropriate to examine the nature of decision making more closely.

DECISION MAKING

Group decision making often creates group polarization. Polarization occurs when group decisions become more extreme than they would be if the same individuals voted privately on the issue. When group members tend to favor a particular decision for the particular reasons they know, hearing other, additional arguments in favor of that decision from other group members ultimately results in all the group members favoring the decision to an even greater extent. (See the discussion of consensus effects in Chapter 3.)

As with conflict, an understanding of the decision-making process can enable group members to influence decisions more effectively. Again, communication processes are crucial in decision making because it is through communication that we share and evaluate the information that is the basis of the decision, and through communication that we ultimately construct the decision and come to agree on it. Communication that encourages participative decision making and addresses both task and socioemotional needs contributes positively to both production and morale (Baird & Bradley, 1979).

Many explanations have been given to explain the decision-making process and its components. One three-stage model proposes that, in the first stage, groups eliminate weak or unacceptable alternatives. In the second stage, they compare the remaining alternatives. And finally, through continued talk and discussion, the group commits itself to a particular solution (Hoffman, 1977). According to Hoffman, in 80% of the cases, groups select as their final solution the first alternative that reaches a balance of having 14 more positive than negative responses to it from group members. However, this absolute threshold of " + 14" may be too high, and who makes the positive and negative remarks is ignored in this model, as it has been in others (McPhee, Poole, & Seibold, 1981). Although the particular details of this theory need to be worked out, it nevertheless provides a general overview of how decision making appears to work. Decisions, like leaders, appear to "emerge" from the group's interaction.

Although we could locate no studies specifically exploring sex differences in organizational decision making, some tentative speculations might be proposed. Decision making ultimately rests upon the exercise of power in the organization, and women are unlikely to occupy positions of power. Women are not likely to exercise power because of the sex segregation in occupations, the underrepresentation of women in upper-managerial levels, the gender-status inconsistency for women, and structural barriers to women's power such as lack of centrality of their positions, or any combination of these. When women do hold positions of power, those positions may be severely constrained in terms of authority and influence. Women's lack of power would suggest that they would have less influence than men in decision making. We would also bet, on the basis of research discussed in previous chapters, that decisions made by women are *perceived* to show less expertise, intelligence, "soundness," and effectiveness, and to be less accepted, than the *same* decisions made by men.

On the other hand, a number of studies show no differences between men and women in actual leadership behaviors, although the perception of male and female leadership styles may differ. This kind of evidence suggests that, if access to power were equal for women and men, sex may make no difference in the actual effectiveness or quality of decision making.

Finally, it is well known that groups tend to make higher quality decisions than the average of their individual members' private decisions. Women's superior performance at tasks requiring discussion and negotiation (Eagly, 1987) may enhance group decision making generally. Decision making appears to be a multifaceted process contingent on group members' characteristics and styles, task characteristics and requirements, and the situational context in which it occurs.

FEEDBACK

Feedback, the response listeners give to others concerning their behavior, plays an important role in organizations and small groups. Through feedback, we understand how others interpret our behavior so we can modify it to achieve desired results. Feedback enables us to assess our progress in reaching goals and in defining ourselves (Haslett & Ogilvie, 1988). In task groups, feedback monitors group activi ities and the group's progress in achieving its goals. Because women initiate and receive less communication than men, they generally receive less feedback. Less feedback is also available to women from informal organizational networks because they are often excluded from these networks. Remember from Chapter 1 that Kristin was kept so busy doing menial assignments and extra clerical work that she didn't have time to go out to lunch regularly with her male colleagues.

The effectiveness of feedback from other group members can be evaluated on several dimensions: its dynamism, trustworthiness, clarity, mood or general tone, and critical nature. When individuals evaluate feedback messages, they are concerned about whether the feedback is positive or negative, and about its clarity, accuracy, and relevance. The source of the feedback is important. A comment from a superior has different implications than the same comment from a peer or subordinate. The power and credibility of the feedback source will determine how individuals respond to the feedback and how satisfied they are with the feedback (Cusella, 1987). In addition, comments from sources judged to be trustworthy, responsive, and forceful have a different meaning and more impact than comments from sources lacking these characteristics.

Gender expectations may influence feedback in several ways. Women may be more effective in giving feedback because they have learned to be responsive and sensitive to others and adept at interpreting nonverbal communication. On the other hand, women's tendency to preserve harmony may lead them to avoid giving negative feedback. Their tendency to supervise subordinates closely may lead them to give feedback too frequently, but men's tendency to "leave subordinates alone" may mean they do not give sufficient feedback. Finally, subordinates' conscious and unconscious gender stereotypes and perceptions of their superiors will determine their acceptance of feedback from male and female supervisors, and their responses to it.

To be effective, feedback needs to focus on issues rather than personalities. Feedback should be as specific as possible and be given immediately. In addition, those giving feedback should support their comments with evidence and mitigate negative messages. To achieve maximum effectiveness, necessary negative comments should be combined with some genuine positive feedback as well (Haslett & Ogilvie, 1988).

Combine negative feedback with positive feedback.

Feedback is given by managers in performance appraisals. These appraisals can be both formal and informal. One leadership model links leaders' assessments of the causes of subordinates' performance with their responses to the subordinate. Supervisors may see subordinates' behaviors as stable, or as changeable and unstable, as being under the control of the subordinate, or as being controlled by external forces. For example, a supervisor will be less likely to punish subordinates if they fail because of lack of resources, an external influence, rather than laziness, controlled by the individual (Green & Mitchell, 1979).

Managers tend to attribute same-sex subordinates' failures to external causes rather than to causes controlled by the individual. In one study, female supervisors were influenced more by their subordinates' sex and likability than male supervisors were. However, the supervisor's belief about whether the poor performance was caused by internal or external factors influenced the corrective actions of both male and female supervisors. The men responded similarly to both female and male subordinates, whereas female supervisors responded more favorably toward female subordinates. Male supervisors appear to adopt corrective actions based on the principle of equity, making rewards and punishments proportional to contributions and deficiencies. In contrast, women based their corrective actions on both equity and equality principles. The equality principle equalizes outcomes for everyone and ignores minor differences in amounts of contribution or deficiency (Dobbins, 1985, 1986; Dobbins et al., 1983).

In a recent study, subordinates' sex exerted a subtle influence on managers' evaluations of their performance. The more internally controlled and stable the cause of the subordinate's inadequate performance was, the more negative the superior's evaluation of the subordinate. The subordinate's degree of control over his or her performance had the greatest influence on the supervisor's evaluation. However, when males failed, they were less liked and supported by their managers and less respected by their equals than were females suffering the same failures. Remember, from Chapter 2, that failure violates male gender-role expectations but is consistent with expectations for women. Both female and male managers viewed performance problems due to family demands as being within a person's control, yet a more stable condition for women than for men. "If family responsibilities are perceived as more likely to intrude into the work world for women, bosses may view women as less dependable and thus be less likely to push them up the corporate ladder" (Wiley & Eskilson, 1988, p. 461). Managers also indicated that, if problems created by family demands became chronic and if they appeared to be stable and continuing, their responses would become more punitive. Evidently, the playing field for men and women in organizations is not yet equal.

Feedback can also be directed toward an entire group by supervisors. Group feedback has been found to increase task motivation and involvement. Group performance can be improved through feedback that cues appropriate behaviors or increases motivation (Nadler, 1979). If a supervisor's feedback is positive, the group views itself as more cohesive, motivated, and open to change than if group feedback is negative (Staw, 1975). Finally, goal acceptance is important in feedback, and group participation appears to facilitate goal acceptance (Cusella, 1987).

SUMMARY

Group processes are vital to organizational functioning. Task groups in organizations are influenced by sex differences in communication. Both organizations and their work groups reflect and invoke the same status preference for males as does society in general. However, as individuals become better known, stereotypes are sometimes used less as a means of judging their performance and ability. Given the complexity of group processes, it should be apparent that the strengths both men and women contribute to group functioning are needed.

All small task-oriented groups have both a task and socioemotional dimension, and progress through definite developmental stages. The cohesiveness or "togetherness" of a group is an important factor in members' commitment to the group. The more cohesive the group, the greater the conflict a group can handle.

Within groups, women and men appear to behave in stereotypical ways—women being supportive and communal, and men being initiating or agentic. Men participate more, receive more comments, and are more influential than women in groups. Participation rates are influenced by the nature of the task: Women participate more in all-female groups than in mixed-sex groups, and when tasks are perceived as feminine.

Little is known about sex differences in conflict management. Available research suggests that women rely on reasoning as a strategy whereas men use a variety of conflict strategies. Generally, women appear to accommodate more in resolving conflict.

Although the deck seems stacked against women in terms of participation in small groups, they can enhance their performance through the following suggestions.

Participate. Effective group participation depends on participating. You must be heard as well as seen. If your remarks are ignored, repeat them or work them into the discussion at a later time.

Use the power and expertise you have. Even as a token or minority in the group, you may have valuable knowledge to contribute to the group. Create opportunities to share your expertise.

There is no single style of effective group participation. Different skills of problem solving, negotiation, conflict resolution, and the like may be needed for different group tasks and at different stages of group development.

Develop a range of communicative styles and conflict styles. Know when to apply certain styles and seek job experiences that help you develop a range of skills.

6
Leadership: Myth and Reality

Leaders play a critical role in organizations. They establish and transmit organizational standards, represent the organization both to their subordinates and to external publics, and make key policy and procedural decisions. It is for precisely these reasons that leadership is problematic for women.

Four themes, developed earlier in this book, recur repeatedly in this discussion of leadership: (a) Attitudes toward women in organizations, including women as leaders, are changing in some ways, but not as much as is popularly believed. Women are now more accepted as leaders, but the mythology of the old stereotypes still clouds how they are seen and treated. (b) When men and women behave in the same way, they are often seen and treated differently. Effective professional behavior, mistakenly defined as "masculine," is acceptable from a man, but not from a woman. This paradox creates the double-bind or damned if you do, damned if you don't dilemma. (c) Behavior on the job is shaped more by others' expectations and treatment and by the situational job conditions of real power and resources than by internal personality characteristics. (d) These conditions produce self-fulfilling prophecies. Stereotypical beliefs and expectations produce discriminatory treatment of women. This discriminatory treatment produces behavior by women and outcomes for them that then mistakenly seem to confirm the initially false beliefs and expectations.

LEADERSHIP IN ORGANIZATIONS

In organizations, leadership has two different but related meanings. Its broader, more inclusive meaning refers to planning, decision making, directing, supervising and evaluating the work of others, and bearing responsibility for the unit's performance. People who perform these roles are often called managers. The narrower meaning of leadership involves directing or being in charge of a group discussion meeting. Both meanings have much in common, and the same person often fulfills both functions, so we will treat them together except as specified.

Another important distinction is that between appointed and emergent leaders. An *appointed* leader is one who holds his or her position by virtue of appointment by some higher authority. Appointed leaders have legitimate, authority power. Most heads of units or departments are appointed leaders. An *emergent* leader is a member of an equal-status peer group who comes to act and be recognized as a leader without formal appointment by a higher authority. Emergent leaders have influence power. It is commonly believed that a leader emerges by making high-quality contributions to the group's task. In fact, however, recognition as an emergent leader depends on high *rates* of contribution, regardless of quality (Sorentino & Boutillier, 1975). In general, the group member who talks the most during the group meeting is recognized as the leader. Midway between appointed and emergent leaders are *elected* leaders, as in high levels of government, some university departments, and some boards of directors or trustees. Like appointed leaders, their positions are formally designated, but the "higher authority" in their case is the peer group.

Notice that, across all of its meanings and varieties, leadership exists only as a social relationship. You could not be a leader if you were stranded alone on a desert island. It takes at least two people in order for one of them to be a leader. Thus, leadership exists only in and through the process of communication. In order for one person to be a leader, that person must act like a leader, *and* the others must treat that person as a leader. They must acknowledge and accept the leader's authority and take the leader's ideas and suggestions seriously. A leader is one to whom authority and status are granted, formally or informally, by others (Calder, 1982). The biggest problem for women who are leaders or aspire to be leaders is being granted the necessary authority and status by others, both supervisors and subordinates, as well as clients, customers, or other associates with whom the woman must interact.

> The biggest problem for women leaders is being granted the necessary authority and status by others.

LEADERSHIP GENDER MYTHOLOGY

Although most educated people sincerely believe in equality of opportunity and in rewards based on performance, their perceptions, attitudes, and actions are still influenced, consciously or unconsciously, by the traditional gender stereotypes discussed in Chapters 2 and 3. The "masculine" stereotype, with its attributes of intelligence, dominance, rationality, and objectivity, implies competence, status, and authority. The "feminine" stereotype of emotionality, nurturance, accommodation, conformity, and deference, implies lesser competence, lower status, and no authority (Cohen et al., 1972; Linton, 1966; Powell, 1987; Sampson, 1969).

The "masculine" stereotype matches the "leader" or "manager" stereotype; the "feminine" stereotype does not (Heilman, 1983; Powell & Butterfield, 1986; Schein, 1973, 1975). Leadership is made easier for men because others "see" them as possessing the "masculine" attributes, whether they actually have them or not. Leadership is more difficult for women, because they are seen as possessing the "feminine" characteristics and as *not* possessing the "masculine" ones, again, regardless of their actual traits (Bellezza & Bower, 1981). As a result, men are automatically accorded higher status, power, prestige, and social value than women of equal position, ability, and personal characteristics (Deaux, 1976a; Dion, 1985). Because of these automatic assumptions, people unconsciously consider it either impossible or inappropriate for a low-status person like a woman to assume the high-status position or behavior of leadership. Or, in the case of a woman who has been appointed to a leadership position, others do not accept her authority, accord her ideas and suggestions as much importance, or take them as seriously as they would, automatically, for a male leader (Forgionne & Nwacukwu, 1977; Yerby, 1975).

Recently, when the authors were conducting a workshop for university administrators on recognizing women's achievements, all of the group members enthusiastically endorsed complete egalitarianism. But one woman blandly added to her denunciation of stereotyping that, of course, she preferred working for a male boss. When queried, she explained, "Well, you just have more *respect* for a man." Such is the power of our nonconscious mythology.

The old mythology is now mostly false. Mostly, but not entirely. The fact that it exists, in women's minds as well as men's, and that it dictates how women *should* behave as well as describing their alleged personalities, influences the behavior and attitudes of some women to some extent in some situations. However, even when the mythology is entirely false, it still has real effects on the way women are seen, treated, and evaluated as leaders, on the power they are accorded, and ultimately on how they behave.

"Good Leadership" is an Interpretation. There are two related reasons for the mythology's continuing influence. First, although the conceptual definition of leadership is clear, its representation in specific behaviors is fuzzy, even in familiar situations, so the extent to which a particular action represents "good leadership" is a matter of interpretation. The same action can be interpreted as "good" when it is approved or as "poor" when it is disapproved. Objectively, the behavior is the same, but its meaning to the perceiver is different (Calder, 1982; Deaux, 1976b; Lord et al., 1978; Pfeffer, 1977; Rush et al., 1977). Recall from Chapter 2 that the more interpretation an evaluation requires, the more unconscious stereotypes tend to influence it. Second, because of the definitional ambiguity, there is *no* objective measure of leadership quality. *Every* measure of leadership competence, expertise, value, or worth is similarly a construction of human inference (Calder, 1982; Rush et al., 1977).

"Leadership effectiveness" is usually measured by productivity, group cohesiveness (see Chapter 5), or group members' satisfaction with their leader (Hollander, 1985). In most work situations the measure of leaders' competence that counts is their supervisor's judgment. Judgments are interpretations. In many research studies, the measure of leaders' competence is the average of their subordinates' ratings of their effectiveness, or the subordinates' satisfaction with their leader. However, the subordinates' ratings are also interpretations. Because of the old stereotypes, subordinates may resent having a woman as an authority over them but *misinterpret* their genuine feelings of resentment as due to something about her behavior. Thus, they give her low performance or effectiveness ratings.

Subordinates may resent having a woman boss but misinterpret their resentment as due to her behavior.

Some researchers, and many supervisors, use what they consider to be objective measures of the leader's or the unit's productivity. Productivity records are, indeed, "hard evidence," but productivity depends upon the leader's power, authority, and resources, and the respect and cooperation of subordinates. Recall from Chapters 2 and 4 that women are accorded less of all these essentials than men with the same qualifications in the same positions. Thus, a female leader who actually does exactly the same things in the same ways as a male leader may actually accomplish less. However, her supervisor, unaware of her subordinates' and his or her own discriminatory treatment, attributes her lower productivity to her inadequacies. Notice the self-fulfilling prophecy. Because of the automatic stereotypes, supervisors accord the woman leader less resources and subordinates give her less wholehearted cooperation. As a result, the woman leader or her unit is less productive, thereby seemingly "confirming" the initial prejudice.

There is one almost-objective measure of the *amount* (but not quality) of group members' leadership in a discussion. This is the amount of time each group member spends speaking in the discussion, as clocked with a stopwatch. Even here, however, the stopwatches are operated by researchers whose biases can influence how quickly they press the button to start and stop the timing episodes, or cause them not to notice some episodes at all (see Chapter 3). The major result of the interpretation involved in leadership evaluations is that they usually reflect the old mythology, the old stereotypes about women's lesser competence and unsuitability for authority.

MYTHOLOGY EFFECTS: HOW WOMAN LEADERS ARE SEEN AND TREATED

Two major results of the old stereotypes are that women's actual leadership is often unrecognized, discredited, or undervalued, and that women leaders are treated in a discriminatory fashion (Gutek, 1985; Larwood & Lockheed, 1979; Nieva & Gutek, 1980; Porter & Geis, 1981; Rosen & Jerdee, 1978).

The Glass Ceiling: Hiring, Salary, and Promotion. Women are less likely to be hired for leadership and managerial positions than equally qualified men. When they are hired, they are paid less than men performing the same or comparable jobs. And they are slower and less likely to be promoted than men with the same performance records (Powell et al., 1984; Stewart & Gudykunst, 1982; Tsui & Gutek, 1984; also see Chapter 2). Remember from Chapter 1 that Kristin discovered she was paid less than a newly hired man in a similar position, and that neither Kristin nor Maria got the promotions they were seeking. One study found that Black women managers were promoted as fast as Black men managers, but the women were still receiving lower salaries (Nkomo & Cox, 1989). Sex seems to be a bigger factor than race in salary discrimination. Although Black men make less than comparable White men, women of both races make lower salaries than either Black or White men of comparable qualifications (Woody, 1989).

As a result of the discrimination in hiring and promotion, women are underrepresented in leadership, managerial, and executive positions, and the discriminatory bias increases the higher up one goes on

No matter what women do, how well they do it, or how many successes they achieve, there seems to be an invisible barrier, a "glass ceiling," that prevents them from advancing.

the organizational status ladder. This problem has been labeled *the glass ceiling.* No matter what women do, how well they do it, how many successes they achieve, there seems to be an invisible barrier, a glass ceiling, that prevents them from advancing beyond the middle levels of the corporate hierarchy (Blau & Ferber, 1985; Brown, 1981; McComas, 1986; Morrison et al., 1987; Olsen & Frieze, 1987). The glass ceiling, of course, is perceptual bias, the influence of gender stereotypes on perceptions and decisions (see Chapter 2).

The discriminatory bias is general. Although some studies find that women discriminate less than men against women leaders (Butler & Geis, 1990; Porter et al., 1985), others find that women discriminate against other women and against themselves as much as men do, and sometimes more (Rice et al., 1984; Watson, 1988); subordinates sometimes discriminate against their female managers as much as the managers' supervisors do. There are degrees of gender bias and discrimination. Some individuals are more biased and discriminatory than others. In general, those who are more traditional in their attitudes, less educated, and more authoritarian and personally insecure are more biased. Men who are insecure about their own masculinity may feel threatened by female leaders (Bormann et al., 1978; Powell, 1988).

Sex bias has decreased over the past 20 years, but it has not disappeared. As late as 1989, nearly 50% of the men and 20% of the women in a sample of young managers still believed that men are better managers than women. Business school students, both men and women, rated female managers as less competent or less knowledgeable, or as having poorer managerial skills, than male managers. When a male leader's group succeeded at its task, evaluators still attributed the success to the leader's ability, but they attributed the same success by a female leader's group to luck (Forsyth & Forsyth, 1984; Frank, 1988; McCallister & Gaymon, 1989).

Sex Bias in Treatment and Evaluation. The same prejudice exists in evaluations of group discussion leadership. In "leaderless" group discussions, leaders emerge by virtue of their higher rate of contributions to the group's task. However, women's contributions are often interrupted, overlooked, ignored, or "unheard" (Bunker & Seashore, 1975). In a study of mixed-sex "leaderless" group discussions, the women objectively contributed as much to the group task as the men. But after the discussion, both men and women group members rated the men higher than the women on "leadership" (Geis et al., 1985). Even when women are seen as leaders, they are rated as having less task leadership ability than men (Brown & Geis, 1984; Fallon & Hollander, 1976). And men's leadership is judged as superior in quality to identical leadership by women (Dobbins et al., 1985).

Gender stereotypes operate at such a deep level of human thinking that they produce emotional as well as cognitive reactions. In another study, both men and women group members smiled, nodded in agreement, and looked pleased in response to male leaders' contributions more often than to the identical contributions from female leaders. In addition, they frowned, scowled, and looked displeased more often in response to the female leaders (Butler & Geis, 1990). Obviously, the group members were not displeased at *what* the female leader said, the content of her contributions, because the same content from a male leader evoked approval. Rather, they were displeased that she overstepped the boundaries of the low-status role their unconscious assumptions prescribed for her.

These disapproving facial expressions can not only serve to discourage a woman leader, they can also have a devastating effect on how she is evaluated. Because people consciously (and sincerely) believe in equality, they do not recognize the true cause of the negative reactions. Instead, they assume that group members' disapproving expressions are evidence that they thought the contribution was poor in quality. This creates a consensus effect (see Chapter 3). Evaluators rated a leader's contributions as showing less leadership and poorer quality, and rated the leader as less desirable for hiring, as meriting a lower salary for a group discussion job, and having less capacity for authority and responsibility when the leader's contributions were followed by group members' disapproving facial expressions, than they rated the identical contributions by the same leader followed by approving facial expressions (Brown & Geis, 1984). This devaluation of negatively received contributions occurred for male as well as female leaders in this experimenter-structured laboratory situation. But in natural groups, when emotional expressions are spontaneous, the negative reactions occur primarily in response to female leaders, as just noted. As a result, their contributions are devalued.

Evaluators sincerely believe that they are judging the *content* of the leader's contributions, but in fact, the perceived "quality" of leadership is determined not only by what the leader actually contributes, but also by the evaluators' interpretation of others' reactions to it. The influence of others' reactions is entirely unconscious. Evaluators sincerely (but mistakenly) deny it. These studies explain, at least in part, why women are less likely to be promoted and are given lower salaries than men with the same qualifications and performance records.

The Subtle Status Assumption. The prejudice against women as leaders reflects two major components of the "feminine" stereotype. One is the *de*scriptive belief that women are less intellectually competent and rational. The other is the *pre*scriptive power and status assumption that a woman *should not* have more power or higher status than a man (see Chapter 2). A study (Ridgeway, 1982) illustrated this second, more subtle stereotype. In order to be accepted as a group leader, a woman not only had to prove her competence, she also had to convince the group that she was not in competition with other group members for personal status enhancement, but solely dedicated to the group's success. In contrast, a man had only to prove his competence. For men, competition for personal status enhancement is accepted.

A preference for male leaders, bosses, and managers illustrates the same power and status assumption. In the 1970s, most people still unabashedly asserted that they preferred a male boss (Ferber et al., 1979). Almost 10 years later, in another study, the participants chose traits they recognized as sex-neutral (like honesty and efficiency) as most important and valuable in a manager, but 80% of them still said they strongly preferred working for a male manager (Cann & Siegfried, 1987).

The old mythology of the gender stereotypes creates external barriers to women's leadership, the biased perceptions and treatment of them by others that we have just discussed, but it also creates internal barriers, forces within the woman herself (O'Leary, 1974).

MORE MYTHOLOGY EFFECTS: SEX DIFFERENCES IN LEADERSHIP

The question of whether men and women actually differ in their leadership performance, interest, ability, or style has no simple answer. Laboratory studies often find sex differences, but field studies of working leaders find fewer, smaller, or no differences. The important point to remember in considering sex differences is that behavior does not occur in a vacuum. Both men and women behave as they do partly because of their own individual characteristics and their perception of the situation, but also partly because of the way they have been treated in the past. As we noted earlier in this chapter, men and women with the same characteristics and qualifications are often treated differently. Thus, it is not surprising that they sometimes behave differently.

Laboratory Studies. The major sex difference in laboratory studies of emergent leadership is that women are less likely than men to become leaders of mixed-sex groups (Bunyi & Andrews, 1985; Eskilson & Wiley, 1976; Fallon & Hollander, 1976). For example, Megargee (1969) studied the effects of personal dominance on emerging as a leader. In pairs of two men or two women, the more dominant partner usually became the leader. However, when a dominant woman was paired with a nondominant man, the man was usually designated as the leader. Almost 20 years later, women were still less likely than men to become leaders, regardless of their previously measured personal dominance (Nyquist & Spence, 1986).

This underrepresentation of women in leadership roles could be caused by any, or a combination, of several factors. First, because of the stereotypic expectations, women's actual leadership may be unrecognized, discredited, or devalued. Second, female leaders may need to spend as much time and effort countering the negative stereotypes as they spend on their assigned tasks. As a result, they may have less time than comparable men to devote to the task, and thus actually perform less effectively. These two topics were discussed previously. Third, because of the stereotypic expectations and the social disapproval for violating them, fewer women may aspire to leadership or attempt to offer it. Fourth, some women who do aspire to leadership and attempt it may do so with less self-confidence than equally qualified men, and thus with less success. Finally, it is possible that there is some inherent difference between men and women that gives men a leadership advantage.

1. An Inherent Male Leadership Advantage? An inherent factor giving men a "natural" leadership advantage has not been identified. And you can be sure that researchers have looked for such a factor. On the contrary, men's overrepresentation in leadership roles is neither fixed nor immutable. Over the past 20 years, the percentages of women who have become leaders has increased—for example, from 15% of managers in 1964 to nearly 40% in 1984 (Powell & Butterfield, 1979; Blau & Ferber, 1985). Because male and female biology presumably did not change over those 20 years, but situational factors, like the acceptance of women as leaders, did change, the increase in female leadership suggests that situational factors, not biology, determine sex differences in leadership.

Research also shows that leadership is not a "natural male domain." When the assigned discussion topic is "feminine" (e.g., involving meal preparation or sewing), women are equally or more likely than men to become group leaders (Wentworth & Anderson, 1984). Similarly, women showed more leadership and higher rates of participation when they were (falsely) led to believe they had become leaders because they exhibited task-relevant skills (Eskilson & Wiley, 1976). Although most discussion topics in most organizations would be considered "masculine", the laboratory findings with "feminine" topics and manipulated skill beliefs suggest that the manifestation of leadership skill, initiative, and effectiveness are heavily influenced by socially shared stereotypes about participant's expertise. As women gain recognition of their expertise and knowledgeability in traditionally "masculine" areas, they should find increased opportunity—and recognition —for the basic leadership skills they already possess.

2. Participation Rates. The major behavioral sex difference contributing to the overrepresentation of men in leadership positions is that, in mixed-sex work groups of all kinds, women speak less and initiate fewer contributions than equally qualified men (Bernard, 1972a; Kimble et al., 1981; Zimmerman & West, 1975). As a result, women actually show less leadership (Nyquist & Spence, 1986). In addition, when a woman does speak, men are more likely to interrupt her, cutting off her contribution, than women are to interrupt a man who is speaking. Simply speaking more in a group seems to endow the speaker with a kind of psychological credit. Groups are more likely to accept an idea from a high participator than the *same* idea from a low participator (Hollander, 1964; Riecken, 1958). Not surprisingly, female leaders have less influence on decisions than males do (Adams & Landers, 1978; Porter et al., 1985). Speaking more frequently, for longer periods, and interrupting others all create and display dominance. Speaking less and allowing oneself to be interrupted create and communicate deference, acceptance of lower status. Remember that becoming an emergent leader depends on high *rates* of contribution. And, being recognized as an emergent leader is often the stepping stone to being appointed or promoted to a formal leadership position.

Again, the stereotypic expectations that women are less competent, less knowledgeable, and should defer to men may inhibit women from initiating or volunteering contributions. But even if a woman does not bow to social expectations, others' interruptions and disapproving facial expressions when she does contribute could effectively discourage her. The combination of disapproving expectations and situational signals may also cause women to offer suggestions in such a highly abbreviated form, anticipating that they will soon be interrupted, or with such a lack of self confidence, that other group members cannot appreciate their value or take them seriously. For example, even when a woman was given the correct answer to the group's problem, secretly, before the discussion, she could not get the group to accept it (Altmeyer & Jones, 1974).

3. Participation Content: Task Versus Socioemotional Contributions. As described in Chapter 5, men are more "task-oriented," women more "social-emotional" or "maintenance" oriented (Strodtbeck & Mann, 1956; Yamada et al., 1983). *Task-oriented contributions* directly address the item named on the group's agenda. They consist of information, opinions, or suggestions aimed directly at solving the problem or completing the task. *Maintenance contributions* are aimed at preserving the integrity, cohesiveness, and smooth running of the group. They consist of recognizing and supporting other group members, soothing hurt feelings, and reducing tension. Although researchers recognize the importance of socioemotional contributions, nonscientists equate "leadership" only with task contributions.

These contribution differences are reflected in self-perceptions. Men describe themselves in terms of power, skill, influence, and dominance; women describe themselves as open, social, attractive, and willing to get along with others (Forsyth et al., 1985). Female leaders are more self-disclosing (Hyman, 1980) and also give more information and positive support to their subordinates (Baird & Bradley, 1979). Men tend to be more directive, dominant, precise, and quick to challenge others' ideas.

This division of labor in the discussion group led people to assume that women do not know the task role, or are unable to perform it. Researchers, at least, always knew that men could perform the social-emotional role, because it was first identified in all-male discussion groups (Bales & Slater, 1955). However, men and women do not differ on personality tests of task versus socioemotional orientation (Chapman, 1975; Schneier, 1978). Not surprisingly, research on same sex groups reveals that both sexes know and do perform both task and maintenance scripts (Yamada et al., 1983). In fact, sometimes women are more task oriented than men. Winter and Green (1987) studied male and female leaders as they gave instructions to a male and female subordinate. Although all leaders used a task orientation with female subordinates, the female leaders were more task oriented overall than the males.

These findings suggest that women's usual focus on socioemotional contributions does not reflect a sex difference in personality, but rather the situational pressure of social expectations. Women may inhibit their task-oriented contributions in mixed-sex groups because such contributions are stereotypically "masculine" and women are disapproved and punished for violating the expected "feminine" role scripts (Butler & Geis, 1990; Petty & Lee, 1975). The dilemma for women leaders is that effective leadership behavior has been defined as "masculine" because only men were seen acting as leaders in the past. Thus, if a woman behaves as an effective leader, she is disapproved and punished for violating the stereotypic gender expectations. This is another example of the "double bind" or "damned if you do, damned if you don't" dilemma described in Chapters 2 and 5.

Effective leadership behavior has been defined as "masculine" because only men were seen acting as leaders in the past.

4. Self-Confidence. Although men and women score equally high on tests of general self-esteem and self-worth, women score lower than men on measures of self-confidence in succeeding at specific tasks, goals, or occupations (Lippa & Beauvais, 1983; Vollmer, 1984). Female managers evaluate their own ability and performance lower than male managers in similar positions evaluate theirs. In fact, the women are more accurate; men overestimate themselves (Deaux, 1979). Self-confidence affects both how a leader behaves and how he or she is seen by others. Leaders high in self confidence, both men and women, tend to use rewards, encouragements, and reasoning as their preferred methods of directing and influencing their subordinates. In contrast, both men and women who are low in self-confidence are more likely to use threats and bullying. In other words, they act like the stereotypical unpleasant woman boss—petty and tyrannical (Instone et al., 1983).

A lack of self-confidence also shows in women's nonverbal communication, such as body posture, gestures, facial expression, and tone of voice. Women, more than men, use such deference gestures as lowering the eyes, falling silent when interrupted or challenged, and hesitating or apologizing when offering an idea (Zimmerman & West, 1975). Women also use more uncertain speech forms such as tag questions ("The Zinger model seems to be the best, doesn't it?") which require another's active assent for confirmation. In contrast, the direct statement ("The Zinger model seems to be the best") gives the assertion the value of truth, providing no one actively *dis*agrees with it (McMillan et al., 1977). These nonverbal deference signals say to other group members, "This idea is not very important; this idea is probably wrong," and such nonverbal communications can have four times as much impact as the spoken content on listeners' interpretations of the message (Argyle et al., 1970). Here is another self-fulfilling prophecy. The old stereotype that women are less competent than men causes them to feel and be treated as less competent (Vollmer, 1986). This lowers their self-confidence, causing them to behave in ways that erroneously seem to confirm the initial prejudice.

5. Achievement Motivation. Finally, one clear *lack* of difference, even in laboratory studies, should be noted. Men and women do not differ in achievement motivation (Stewart & Chester, 1982). This absence of difference has also been found in Black men and women (Crew, 1982).

Field Studies of Working Leaders. Two laboratory findings also show up in field studies of working men and women leaders and managers. One is the prevalence of gender-stereotyped beliefs about men and women in general and male and female leaders in particular (Bass et al., 1971; Schein, 1973, 1975, 1978). The other is the lesser likelihood of women's becoming leaders or of advancing up through the status hierarchy of leadership in the organization. This "glass ceiling" effect was discussed previously.

However, looking for behavioral causes of women's lesser leadership opportunities and advancement presents a paradox: In contrast to the findings of leadership sex differences in laboratory studies, field research in natural work settings finds fewer, smaller, or no differences in how men and women leaders actually behave (Osborn & Vicars, 1976). These working men and women leaders, managers, and professionals appear to do the same things in the same ways with the same frequencies: They endorse the same management philosophies. They show the same levels of motivation for achievement and work success; they are equally effective and equally competitive. They use the same participative processes with their subordinates, in the same ways, with equal frequency; show the same competence and ability in communicating with their subordinates; and their subordinates are equally satisfied with their leadership. They use the same managerial styles, including the same balance of rewards versus punishments, and task versus socioemotional emphasis, and report similar self-perceptions of their styles and behavior. Most importantly, perhaps, women's self-confidence increases with increasing years of experience in leadership positions (Bartol & Wortman, 1976; Biles & Pryatel, 1978; Bunker & Bender, 1980; Day & Stogdill, 1972; Denmark, 1977; Dobbins & Platz,

1986; Instone et al., 1983; Offerman, 1984; Osborn & Vicars, 1976; Pyke & Kahil, 1983; Stitt et al., 1983; Szilagyi, 1980).

A few studies have found behavioral differences between male and female managers, mostly reflecting stereotypic expectations. Primarily, women show more concern for people and relationships. For example, male leaders have been found more assertive and aggressive in dealing with others, women more revealing of information about their feelings, beliefs, and concerns. Similarly, female managers are more accessible than males to their colleagues and subordinates. They are less likely to close their office door or use secretaries to screen out interruptions, and less likely to say no to requests. These findings suggest that women may undervalue themselves and the importance of their own time (Baird & Bradley, 1979; Chapman & Luthans, 1975; Denmark, 1977; Hyman, 1980; Josefowitz, 1980). A few studies have found sex differences contrary to the stereotypes. These will be discussed later. In brief, the field research suggests that excellent, average, and poor female leaders can be found in about the same proportions as excellent, average, and poor male leaders.

Laboratory Versus Field Studies. There are two possible reasons for the different results of the laboratory and field research. One is that the two types of research are studying two different populations. The participants in most laboratory research are random (unselected) samples of college students, representative of the more educated and middle-class half of the population. Field research studies a highly self-selected subpopulation—those particular men and women who have chosen business, management, or professional careers. It is possible that men and women in the broader population do in fact differ, on the average, but that those particular men and women who choose professional and management careers do not differ.

The other possible reason for the different results of the laboratory and field research is the point made in Chapter 2 that people's behavior is shaped less by their long-standing internal "personality" characteristics than by the demands, requirements, and opportunities of their role and status in the particular situation. This explanation says that men and women may indeed differ before beginning their careers (e.g., in college), but that, once on the job, they both develop the same repertoire of behavioral strategies and styles in response to the same forces and requirements of the job. Note that both explanations could be correct: Men and women who choose managerial careers could differ less from each other initially than men and women in the broader population, *and* once on the job, the forces of the job role could shape them to be even more similar.

There are three important points to remember in considering behavioral differences between male and female leaders, whether from laboratory or field studies. First, most of the behavioral sex differences in leadership could reflect the lesser resources accorded to women or women's lower self-confidence in leadership situations, or both (Powell, 1988). Second, behavior reflects the demands, expectations, and treatment by others, such as the leaders' supervisors, colleagues, and subordinates (see Chapter 3). Female leaders may behave as they do because that is the only behavior others will accept from them. Third, and perhaps most important, because leaders have traditionally been men, we tend to assume that men's behavior and leadership styles define "good leadership" (Powell & Butterfield, 1979, 1986). Thus, when women differ from men, we implicitly assume that the women's behavior is "deficient" or less effective (Hennig & Jardim, 1977). This assumption is unjustified. Women's styles may appear "less effective" *because*, and only because, they are less accepted, or because women as leaders are less accepted, no matter how they behave. Given equal acceptance, women's styles might be just as effective as men's, or even more effective.

> *Most of the behavioral sex differences in leadership could reflect less resources given to women or women's lower self-confidence in leadership situations.*

SUMMARY

Women as leaders are seen, treated, and evaluated differently from men. Traditional gender stereotypes, now mostly unconscious, decree that women are less competent than men and *should* be subordinate in status to men. As a result, women are less likely to be hired or promoted into leadership positions, and are paid less, than equally qualified men. This discrimination increases with increasing status level in the organization, producing the "glass ceiling" effect. However, it exists at all levels. Group members who greet a male leader's contributions with approval look displeased in response to the same contributions from a female leader. The displeased facial expressions could not only discourage a female leader, they also lead evaluators to view the contribution as poorer in quality. The combination of stereotypic expectations and differential treatment leads men and women to behave differently in some situations.

Laboratory studies find that although men have no "natural" leadership advantage, women make fewer contributions to task discussions and are thus less likely to emerge as leaders. Women tend to offer socioemotional rather than task contributions when they do participate, and show less self-confidence in their ability to succeed at particular leadership tasks. However, most of the field research on working leaders shows few, small, or no behavioral differences between men and women. If men and women differ little in behavior or effectiveness as working leaders, the continuing differences in hiring, evaluation, treatment, salary, and promotion would seem to reflect the influence of gender stereotypes, conscious or unconscious (see Chapters 2 and 3).

LEADERSHIP GENDER REALITY

Despite the negative effects of stereotypic expectations on women's leadership, it would appear that women have as much potential for successful leadership as men. Some studies directly contradict the old stereotypes and suggest that women might be *more* effective than men as leaders.

Stereotypes Bite the Dust. One finding should be of particular interest to women—and men. According to the stereotype, women are more emotional and therefore not to be trusted with important judgments or decisions, which are better left to men, who are more rational and objective. Contrary to the stereotype, however, the evidence shows that men and women do not differ on the rational-emotional dimension in decision

> In fact, women are less swayed by emotion than men are in their analyses and decisions.

making. And more recent evidence shows that women are *less* swayed than men by emotion and sentiment in their analyses, judgments, and decisions. Finally, women suffer no loss of intellectual or analytical ability, or control preceding or during their menstrual periods (Baron, 1987; Biles & Pryatel, 1978; Dipboye, 1975; Golub, 1976). Women may (or may *not*) express emotion more readily than men, but apparently they are less controlled by it.

Some studies of managerial motivation also favor women. Female managers have been found to have higher achievement motivation than male managers, equal motivation for personal power, power directed toward personal advancement, but higher motivation for socialized power, power directed toward task accomplishment and group success (see Chapter 5). Female managers have also reported more concern with opportunities for growth, autonomy, and challenge, less concern with work environment and pay, and more career commitment than men at the same occupational, educational, and salary levels. In brief, the women showed a more mature and higher achieving motivational profile than the male managers. Thus, they matched the ideal motivational profile originally developed for male managers better than the men did (Chusmir, 1985; Donnell & Hall, 1980; Powell et al., 1984).

Also contrary to stereotypes, no individual traits or personality characteristics have been found to identify leaders. Personal dominance and self-confidence appear to indicate who is likely to be selected as a leader, but do not indicate who might be an effective leader (Pavitt & Curtis, 1990). Generally, leaders seem to "emerge" as a function of task demands and group needs (Hersey & Blanchard, 1969). Finally, research suggests some solutions to problems discussed in the previous section. Perhaps most importantly, experience seems to reduce two of the major problems facing women as leaders: First, women's self-confidence as leaders increases with number of years of experience working as a leader (Instone et al., 1983). Second, the prejudice against working for a female supervisor is reduced by the actual experience of having a female supervisor (Ezell et al., 1981). Third, public acknowledgement of women's competence increases their leadership contributions and others' recognition of them (Bradley, 1980; Brown & Geis, 1984; Stake, 1981).

Task Versus Socioemotional Contributions. Research on actual working leaders and managers has identified two factors or components of successful leadership (Stogdill, 1963). One of these factors, called *initiating structure*, refers to the active, directive role of the leader. This role involves setting goals; planning strategies, procedures, work allocations, and sequencing to meet the goals; and directing and supervising the work of subordinates. This component of leadership represents the "task" orientation discussed above and in Chapter 5 that matches the "masculine" stereotype but not the "feminine" stereotype.

However, the other, equally important, component of successful leadership is called *consideration*. This factor refers to the leader's showing consideration for subordinates' needs, interests, wishes, welfare, and advancement. It may involve leaders' consulting with subordinates on goals, strategies, work allocations, and timing schedules, and it usually includes leaders' representing subordinates' needs to upper management and recommending their advancement. This consideration component of leadership matches the "feminine" stereotype but not the "masculine" one. It represents the "social-emotional" or group maintenance orientation more typical of women. This leadership component is more important than people realize. Major reasons for firing top executives are a lack of sensitivity and caring for employees, a bullying style, and cold, arrogant behavior (McCall, 1983). Thus, to the extent that the gender stereotypes are accurate, women have one advantage and one disadvantage as leaders, and so do men.

Remember (from Chapter 2), however, that the so-called "masculine" and "feminine" characteristics are created primarily by a long socialization experience of learning and practice, and are then maintained by the continuing pressure of role and status expectations. Thus, with conscious effort and practice, men can learn the consideration behaviors, and women can learn the initiating structure behaviors. Although when college students are assigned leadership roles, the men are more task-oriented and women more social-emotionally oriented, working male and female leaders do not differ in the relative emphasis they give to initiating structure and consideration (Dobbins & Platz, 1986). Indeed, in most studies, the most successful leaders were found to be high on *both* initiating structure and consideration (Stogdill, 1974). Most effective leaders are also high in verbal fluency, a complex communication skill involving both task competence and interpersonal relations skills (Mintzberg, 1973).

There is one important caution, however, in interpreting these findings on initiating structure and consideration. Most of the studies identifying these factors and testing their effects were done on *male* leaders and managers. We have already noted earlier in this chapter that women do not necessarily receive approval and high ratings for the same behaviors that bring approval and high ratings to male leaders (Wiley & Eskilson, 1982). There are other conceptualizations of effectiveness and success as a leader (see Hollander, 1985). However, we will not discuss them here, because their relevance for women is uncertain. Instead, we turn to three topics that provide some clues to *counteracting* the old mythology of gender stereotypes and their effects on women's leadership: power, female authority role models, and changing the stereotypes.

THE IMPORTANCE OF POWER

Power is the ability to exert a degree of control over persons, things (e.g., resources), and events. Leadership implies power (Hollander, 1985). As we noted at the beginning of the chapter, leadership involves being granted high status and authority (power) by others. Usually, of course, power is not used directly, but the knowledge that it exists serves the same purpose.

As explained in Chapter 4, power can come from a number of sources, but the two major categories are personal—such as dominance, charisma, relationships, or expertise—and situational—the structure of the job itself, the granting of power by the leader's supervisor and subordinates. Personal power can be developed and enhanced. Situational power is more problematic for women.

Power on the job determines much of a leader's style. Instone et al. (1983) studied strategies leaders use to influence their subordinates, such as giving praise or criticism; giving rewards or punishments such as bonuses, raises, salary cuts, promotion, demotion, or firing; promising rewards; threatening punishments; or appeals to friendship, reason, or group spirit. They found that men and women managers use the same strategies with equal frequency—*when* they have equal access to power *and* equal self-confidence. For men and women alike, a manager's style depends less on "personality" than on having real power in the work situation. This means having authority to make decisions and enforce them by rewards and punishments. It also means acceptance of that power by the manager's supervisor and subordinates and membership in the inner circle of influential people. Powerless leaders, men and women alike, often become punitive, petty tyrants. The problem for women is that they are often not accorded the same power and acceptance automatically granted to men with the same qualifications in the same position (Kanter, 1977). The Catch-22 for women is that effective leadership requires having power and using it: Because power is stereotypically masculine, it is acceptable for men but not for women (Johnson, 1976).

> *For men and women alike, a manager's style depends less on "personality" than on having real power in the work situation.*

Power, Status, and Nonverbal Communication. Power is also created and communicated nonverbally. It is situational power or status that controls nonverbal behavior signaling dominance and authority. When two people of unequal status discuss a topic, they use different patterns of looking each other in the eye (Dovidio & Ellyson, 1982: Exline et al., 1975). Low-status people gaze attentively at their high-status partner while the high-status person is speaking, but when the low-status people speak, they avert their gaze from the other's face. (Low-status partners have to formulate their contributions more carefully. The averted gaze permits greater mental concentration.) In contrast, high-status people do not gaze so attentively at their low-status partner while he or she is speaking, but they do look their partner in the eye more when they themselves are speaking.

In a study of these nonverbal dominance displays (Dovidio et al., 1988), pairs of men and women each held a series of three discussions on three different topics. For one of their topics, the man was given power, the high-status position. Either the pair was assigned a discussion topic on which he was an expert and she was not, or he was arbitrarily assigned high status by being put in charge of evaluating both of their contributions and allocating the reward between them. For another of the same pair's topics, the woman was given the high-status power position, either expertise or assigned status; and for their third topic, neither partner had a situational power advantage.

This study found a sex difference—but only for the neutral topic on which neither partner had a situational power source. The men used the dominant, high-status visual pattern, and the women used the deferent, low-status pattern. However, those very same women, talking with the same male partner, used the dominant, high-status visual pattern when they had situational role power—and the very same men used the low-status pattern when their situational role placed them in the low-power position. These results show that situational role power overrides internal personality factors in shaping this kind of dominance display.

Power Abuse and Exploitation. However, power is a coin that also has another side. If women are no worse than men at using and showing power when they have it, they are also no better. Women in all-female groups given power over another group exploited the disadvantaged group as quickly and heartlessly as men did in all-male advantaged groups. These women did not differ from other women in possessing the "feminine" traits of gentleness, nurturance, and sensitivity to others. Rather, their behavior was shaped by their situational role status, not by their "personalities." However, men and women in the disadvantaged groups did differ in their responses to the exploitation. The disadvantaged male groups resisted the exploitation and fought back more effectively than the disadvantaged female groups (Insko et al., 1983). Apparently, *both* women and men need "remedial training" in resisting the temptation to abuse power, but women more than men need "remedial training" in how to resist being exploited when their status superiors misuse power.

Here is an example: Lucinda is the manager of Accounts Receivable. Felipe, the Accounting Department manager and her supervisor, asks her to do some low-level clerical work. She first expresses understanding of his need to get the work done and concludes, "But you know, Felipe, that's not in my job description. I'm afraid if I did it for you it would make you look bad. People would think you were exploiting your female subordinates." This is an example of a win–win solution discussed in Chapter 1. Lucinda has avoided being exploited and she has helped Felipe, first by educating him as to what he is doing, and second by ensuring that he "looks good" to others. Felipe, of course, still has the problem of getting his work done. But, if he's smart, he'll take it to someone for whom it is appropriate.

THE IMPORTANCE OF FEMALE AUTHORITY ROLE MODELS

The visible presence of a number of female authority role models (one is *not* enough) can reduce or eliminate the effects of the gender stereotypes on how women leaders are seen and evaluated, and on their self-confidence and how they behave. When there were more female authority role models in the social environment, women leaders rated themselves, and both their supervisors and subordinates rated them, as equal to men in competence, effectiveness, liking, and respect. Also, as noted earlier, the experience of working for a female supervisor decreases the prejudice against women as bosses (Ezell et al., 1981; Tsui & Gutek, 1982). These results provide a clear contrast to the typical devaluation of women's leadership by supervisors and subordinates, and even by women leaders themselves, discussed earlier in this chapter.

The visible presence of multiple female authority role models increases college women's career interest and career achievement, their leadership skills of self-confidence and independence of judgment, their initiative and rates of participation in mixed-sex task discussions, even on "masculine" topics, and, perhaps most crucially, others' recognition of their leadership (Geis et al., 1984, 1985; Jennings et al., 1980; Tidball, 1973). These results show that the visible presence of female authority figures can reduce or eliminate the negative effects of gender stereotypes on women's performance as leaders and also reduce or eliminate their negative effects on evaluators' recognition and rating of the quality of women's leadership. Thus, increasing the visible presence of female authority figures in the work setting is a major solution to the problems women face as leaders.

Increasing the visible presence of female authority figures is a major solution to the problems women face as leaders.

The role models do not have to be persons with whom the women (or their supervisors or subordinates) have a personal relationship. They simply have to be visible. Neither do they have to hold exalted official positions. They do have to be seen acting like authorities and, most crucially, being treated as authorities by others. In some of the studies, the female authority models were women seen in domestic settings, with their husbands, in TV commercials rewritten to reverse the roles and status of the actors in the original network versions. In another study, male subordinates of dominant female leaders rated them as more effective when the group also included female subordinates than when it did not (Watson, 1988). Similarly, women were rated higher on task orientation when there were more of them in the group rather than just one (Frank & Katcher, 1977). In these cases, the visible presence of females (albeit subordinate) "doing the job" enhanced the men's estimation of the female leaders' effectiveness.

Finally, the role models also do not have to demonstrate the specific behaviors, skills, strategies, or responsibilities relevant to the woman's situation. The implications of "authority" seem to generalize from one kind of situation to another (Baumeister et al., 1988; Geis et al., 1985). The psychological dynamics behind the impact of visible female authority role models were explained in Chapter 2.

Having a female supervisor may be a significant advantage for competent women leaders. Evaluators rated a leader's performance higher when they saw the leader's supervisor personally endorse the leader than they rated the same performance by the same leader without the endorsement. This endorsement effect occurred for both male and female leaders, with either a male or female supervisor. However, the female supervisor's comments about the female leader carried more weight than the male supervisor's comments about her. The female supervisor's endorsement raised the female leader's perceived competence higher than the same endorsement by the male supervisor. But lack of endorsement by the female supervisor also lowered her ratings more than lack of endorsement by the male supervisor (Brown & Geis, 1984; Geis et al., 1990). The moral of this story seems to be: If a female leader is competent and can count on her supervisor's endorsement, she will get more recognition for the same performance working under a female supervisor than under a male. The female supervisor's authority and status seem to rub off onto the female leader, further enhancing her perceived competence and expertise.

The authority role model effect is not specific to women. The presence of more Black faculty, administrators, counselors, and advisors on a college campus yields higher Black student retention rates. Similarly, Black authority role models in organizations dispel the prejudice that Blacks are hired only to satisfy affirmative action demands

(Dickens & Dickens, 1982; McCombs, 1989). These findings emphasize that the female authority role models in a situation should include minority women.

It is possible that much of the devaluation of women's leadership, the discriminatory way they are treated, others' inability to accord them power, and their own alleged behavioral "deficits" may be a result of the scarcity of female authority role models in the work groups, organizations, and institutions of our society when the research was conducted. Notice that women's leadership has been devalued compared to identical or comparable leadership by men. Of course, there has always been an ample supply of visible *male* authority role models in groups, organizations, and institutions of all kinds. Men's mysterious ability to "succeed in business without really trying" has popularly been attributed to their "masculine" personality traits and skills. However, it may actually reflect the beneficial effects of the large supply of male authority role models throughout society—on men's performance, on their supervisors' ability to recognize their contributions, and on their subordinates' acceptance of their authority. The heartening news for women is that, when they have the same social conditions of same-sex authority role models that men have always enjoyed, they reap the same benefits in self-confidence, performance, initiative, recognition, and success.

When women have the same-sex authority models that men have always enjoyed, they reap the same benefits in self-confidence, performance, initiative, and success.

There is one problem with female authority role models as a solution to the difficulties faced by women leaders. Logically, it begs the question. It says, in effect, female leaders' problems will be solved when there are many other women who have already overcome the problems and are succeeding in leadership and authority positions to serve as role models. The question is, how do these other women overcome the barriers to begin with? In practice, the answer is "slowly, by expertise, extra effort, and some genuine egalitarianism in the work place." Although there have always been a few women in traditionally "masculine" occupations, the great influx of women into these areas did not begin until the 1970s. These early women pioneers met a wave of massive resistance and thus did not advance as fast or as far as their ability and

Every time any woman succeeds, her success increases opportunities for all women.

actual performances would have warranted. However, some of them did persist and survive, and even advance. The visible presence of such women weakens the stereotypes and creates more favorable attitudes toward women's leadership (Cheatham, 1984; Frank & Katcher, 1977). Increasing the number of female authority role models is a slow process, because of the barriers, but an incremental one. Every time any woman succeeds, her success diminishes the barriers and increases the opportunities for all women.

THE WINDS OF CHANGE

Despite discriminatory gender attitudes and treatment, despite their alleged personality and behavioral "deficits," increasing numbers of women are preparing for leadership and managerial roles in organizations, entering such roles, and succeeding in them (Blau & Ferber, 1985). "Society" has in fact become more accepting of women as leaders and less discriminatory against them since the 1960s. This change is probably the result of three related factors: The first is the genuine, sincere *conscious* ideology of egalitarianism endorsed by most educated men and women. A second factor is undoubtedly the national and state equal rights and affirmative action legislation that both called conscious attention to the discriminatory practices and made the more overt ones illegal. A third factor, and possibly the most important, is the still small but ever-increasing number of female authority role models in organizations throughout society, discussed above. These factors operate together. Each of them increases the impact of the other two.

There is evidence of change in both attitudes and behavior. For example, the percentage of male executives opposed to the idea of women as managers dropped from 41% in 1965 to only 5% in 1985 (Sutton & Moore, 1985). Women have also changed. Annual surveys of incoming college freshmen reveal that, from 1969 to 1984, freshmen women increased their commitment to "status attainment goals," such as having a high-level career, money and financial independence, and prestige (Fiorentine, 1988).

Similarly, McCallister and Gaymon (1989) surveyed 168 women and 172 men undergraduates and MBA candidates in business administration who were all currently employed in managerial positions in large organizations, and found more similarities than differences. When asked what they liked most about their jobs, both men and women mentioned the same three factors most frequently—the variety and diversity of the job, contact with people, and salary. The women mentioned people more than men did (the old stereotypes are diminishing but have not disappeared), and men mentioned salary more than women did, perhaps because the women had lower salaries. The same three factors were also mentioned most frequently by both men and women as things they *dis*liked most about their jobs—lack of variety and diversity, contact with unpleasant people, and inadequate salary. Again, there were minor sex differences, but the overall picture shows that these young men and women agreed on job values, what they liked when the job provided it, and what they disliked when it was lacking.

Other sex differences and similarities also indicated some real change but not total change. Few (about 14%) of the respondents mentioned organizational leadership as their primary goal. The women, perhaps responding to discriminatory treatment in their present positions, named entrepreneurial goals, owning their own business or corporation; the men listed fantasy goals such as being rich and famous, a movie star, or a professional athlete. When asked whether men or women make better managers, almost a third of the sample (29%) rejected both alternatives and wrote in that men and women are equal. And a sizeable minority (a third of the women but only 10% of the men) chose women as better managers. However, a full one-third of the sample still believed that men make better managers. When asked the reason for their belief, the women gave specific, behavioral examples as reasons, but the men tended to attack women's "personality" with abstract, stereotypic generalizations.

Analyzing these and other results, McCallister and Gaymon concluded that the women showed greater aptitude than the men as organizational leaders. The women showed higher task interest and better reasoning and communication skills. "Over half of the men in this research did not display these same skills and, in fact, were unable to support their assertions with any degree of verbal sophistication. Thus, if women are truly given equal opportunity, it is possible that they will outrank men in management positions by the year 2000" (p. 228).

Perhaps the most convincing evidence of change in attitudes toward women as leaders, and thus an increase in real opportunities for women, is an apparent increase in the number of research studies finding no evidence of sex bias in leadership evaluations or behavior. Different studies have found that male and female leaders were equally task-oriented; they also gave the same relative emphasis to initiating structure and consideration behaviors. Women spoke and interrupted men as often as men spoke and interrupted women. Women were as likely as men to become leaders, and the same behavior that brought leadership recognition to men also brought the same recognition to women. The female leaders' groups were as productive as the male leaders' groups. The female's followers were as satisfied with their leader as the male's followers were. And male and female leaders were rated equally high in leadership, dominance, intelligence, competence, effectiveness, industriousness, and supportiveness (Dobbins & Platz, 1986; Goktepe & Schneier, 1988; Kennedy & Camden, 1981; Offerman, 1984, 1986; Schneier & Bartol, 1980; Seifert & Miller, 1988; Stitt et al., 1983).

However, even in these studies, the stereotypes were not entirely dead. The Offerman study also found that all-female groups (female leader with all female followers) were seen as less likely to continue succeeding in the future. Recall from Chapter 2 that women's successes are stereotypically attributed to luck, which can change at any moment, whereas the same successes by men are attributed to their ability, a stable, internal factor that will continue into the future.

The major results of such studies provide encouragement for women as leaders and managers. However, the reader should keep two important cautions in mind. First, the studies showing egalitarian results are a *minority* of all the studies on women as leaders and managers published during the 1980s. The majority still show the devaluation and discriminatory treatment discussed earlier in this chapter. Second, most of the evaluators giving the egalitarian results were college students in the 1980s. This population will not provide the organizational evaluators and decision makers until approximately the year 2000 and thereafter. Although responses to women's leadership do seem to be becoming more egalitarian—slowly, sporadically, and unevenly—we are still far from the genuine "equal opportunity" we consciously and sincerely endorse. The winds of change may not be a gale, but at least they are breezes blowing in the right direction.

SUMMARY

Leadership is problematic for women. The traditional gender stereotypes, usually operating unconsciously, still shape supervisors' and subordinates' expectations, perceptions, treatment, and evaluations of women. Being recognized as a leader requires high rates of participation, being perceived as highly competent, and the granting of high status, power, and authority by those involved. Two major components of the traditional "feminine" stereotype, lesser competence and lower status, make leadership more difficult for women than for equally qualified men. The stereotypes are especially powerful in the area of leadership, because all leadership perceptions and measures are matters of interpretation.

As a result of the stereotypic mythology, women are less likely to be hired for leadership positions, are paid less when they are hired, and are slower and less likely to be promoted than equally qualified men. Female leaders are treated differently than male leaders in group discussions. They are interrupted more, their ideas and suggestions are less accepted, and others are more likely to greet their contributions with displeased facial expressions. All of these differential treatments serve to diminish the perceived quality of a leader's contributions. The discriminatory perception and treatment of women increases with increasing status level in the organization, creating the glass ceiling effect, the increasing underrepresentation of women at higher status levels.

The stereotypic expectations, combined with others' differential treatment, also influence some women's performance as leaders. Although no inherent factor giving men a natural leadership advantage has been found, in laboratory studies of mixed-sex task discussions, women participate less than men, and, when they do participate, their contributions are less task-oriented and more likely to address the social-emotional needs of other group members. In addition, women express less self-confidence in their leadership ability than men do. In contrast, field studies of working men and women leaders find fewer, smaller, or no sex differences in behavior or performance. It is possible that behavior on the job reflects situational demands of the job itself more than internal personality factors.

The reality is that women appear to have as much potential for leadership as men do. Their decisions are no more, or even less, swayed by emotion than men's are. Their motivation for power is more socially oriented toward the good of the group or organization, whereas men's power motivation is more directed toward personal advancement. Experience working as a leader increases women's self-confidence, and experience working for a female supervisor decreases subordinates' prejudice. Of the two components of successful leadership, initiating structure and consideration, one matches the masculine stereotype and the other matches the feminine stereotype, but both men and women can and do learn both types of behavior.

Power is the crux of the leadership problem for women. Leadership requires having power (being granted it by others) and using power. The stereotypic expectations that women are less competent and should have lower status than men makes people reluctant to grant women power or accept their using it. However, it is real situational power on the job, more than personality, that determines a leader's behavioral style, choice of influence strategies, and nonverbal definitions of his or her status and authority.

The crux of the solution to women's leadership problems is the visible presence of multiple female authority role models. When many women are seen being accepted and treated as authorities, women increase their career aspirations, their self-confidence, independence of judgment, and task-oriented contribution rates in group discussions. Perhaps most importantly, female authority role models break the stereotypes and allow evaluators to recognize women's leadership. Increasing the number of female authority role models is a slow process, because women who could become role models face the same barriers as all women.

Despite the continuing discriminatory perceptions, evaluations, and treatment, women's leadership is gradually becoming more accepted as a result of the sincere *conscious* ideology of egalitarianism, affirmative action legislation, and the slow but real increase in female authority role models throughout the organizations and institutions of society. Young men and women have become more alike in their expressed interest in status, money and prestige. Young managers of both sexes agree on scope of activities, social contacts and money as the most important job characteristics. Most importantly, although still in the minority, an increasing number of research studies show no evidence of sex discrimination in leadership recognition, acceptance, or evaluation. The stereotypes are not dead, but the future looks brighter than the past.

7

The Many Facets of Managerial Style

Although managerial work is varied and complex, its general qualities can be described. A manager's work reflects such factors as experience, hierarchical level in the organization, type of industry, type of organizational culture, and span of control (the number of subordinates supervised). Managerial work also varies with the characteristics of the industry and a given organization, job variables such as level in the hierarchy, personal variables such as personality and style, and situational variables such as timing factors. In this chapter, a discussion of the general characteristics of managerial work is followed by consideration of sex differences in managerial behavior.

CHARACTERISTICS OF MANAGERIAL WORK

MANAGERIAL ROLES AND FUNCTIONS

One of the most useful analyses of managerial work is that of Henry Mintzberg (1973). Mintzberg's study included observation and assessment of what managers do on a daily basis as well as a survey of the relevant research literature. Because his work is based on real organizational activities, it has a significant advantage over laboratory research or that based only on theoretical speculation.

Based on his data, Mintzberg concludes that:

1. Managers' jobs are very similar;
2. Managerial work is challenging and unprogrammed, as well as being routine;
3. Managerial power is based upon information, and information is vital in decision making;
4. Managerial work is varied; brief amounts of time are spent on fragmented activities;

5. Managers work primarily on the basis of verbal information and non-explicit assumptions;
6. Managerial work is very complex;
7. Managers are both generalists (processing information and handling disturbances) as well as specialists (managing specific tasks and skills); and
8. Managers spend about one-half of their communication time with outsiders, and about one-third to one-half with subordinates.

Managers perform 10 vital roles, all of which are interpersonal, informational, or decisional in nature. Managers serve as an "input-output system in which authority and status give rise to interpersonal relationships that lead to input (information) and these in turn lead to outputs (information and decisions)" (Mintzberg, 1973, p. 58). All of these roles are essential for managerial effectiveness; the loss of one role or function impedes managerial performance in the other areas. For example, if a manager does not function as a liaison to gain valuable information from external sources, then his or her ability to make decisions is limited by lack of information.

The roles and their functions can be diagrammed as follows:

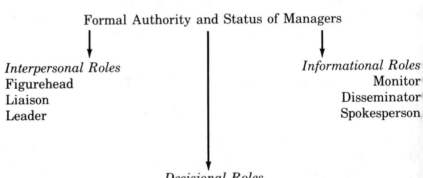

Formal Authority and Status of Managers

Interpersonal Roles
Figurehead
Liaison
Leader

Informational Roles
Monitor
Disseminator
Spokesperson

Decisional Roles
Entrepreneur
Disturbance Handler
Resource Allocator
Negotiator

The most basic and simple of the managerial roles is the interpersonal role of *figurehead*. Managers' formal authority requires that they act as organizational representatives. As a *liaison*, a manager deals with relationships with individuals from other departments and other organizations. Generally, the higher the managerial rank, the more extensive the manager's external contacts. Organizational power is most obvious in the manager's leadership role. These interpersonal roles are linked directly to the manager's status and primarily involve relationships with others, whether superiors, peers, or subordinates. As a *leader*, the manager defines how work is done, determines hiring and rewards, and maintains standards of performance.

Through their decisional roles, managers control how organizational decisions are made and influence what decisions are made. As *entrepreneurs*, managers initiate and design organizational change. As *disturbance handlers*, managers respond to unexpected circumstances or crises. Disturbances may vary from a subordinate's sudden resignation to the loss of a major client. As *resource allocators*, managers distribute organizational resources. Finally, as *negotiators*, managers may negotiate with other individuals or organizations for resources, opportunities, or to resolve conflict. Generally, these decisional roles reflect the manager's power in making and carrying out strategic decisions.

Another major managerial function is the collection and dissemination of information. As *monitors*, managers seek information in order to understand activities in the organization and its environment. As *disseminators*, they relay external and internal information to others in the organization. Such information may be factual or value-oriented. As a *spokesperson*, the manager sends information to other organizations, to the public, or to both. Both the public and key players in organizational environments must be kept informed by managers.

Managerial diversity can be seen in the way different roles are emphasized in a given situation. Mintzberg identified eight managerial job-types and the key roles associated with each of them. They range from being a political manager, in which spokesperson and negotiator roles are emphasized, to expert managers who emphasize the monitoring and spokesperson roles. Two general trends—more broad-based participation in organizational decision making and the increasing complexity of organizations—will force managers to place more emphasis on the figurehead, liaison, spokesperson, and negotiator roles.

This managerial model highlights the importance of communication in organizations. Two of the role categories, interpersonal and informational, depend heavily on communication skills. Interpersonal roles emphasize relationship skills such as team-building, while informational roles involve both interpersonal communication skills and also skills in mediated communication, such as command of new information technologies.

Another more recent study of managerial work focused on more specific tasks that managers perform (Luthans, Hodgetts & Rosenkrantz, 1988). Four major tasks and their subcomponents are listed below, including the percentage of time devoted to each.

TASKS

1. *Routine communication* (29%)
   a. exchanging information (15%)
   b. handling paperwork (14%)
2. *Traditional management tasks* (32%)
   a. planning (13%)
   b. decision making (11%)
   c. controlling (6%)
3. *Human Resource Management* (20%)
   a. motivating/reinforcing (5%)
   b. disciplining/punishing (not observed, done privately)
   c. managing conflict (4%)
   d. staffing (5%)
   e. training/developing (6%)
4. *Networking* (19%)
   a. interacting with outsiders (10%)
   b. socializing/politicking (9%)

Clearly, managers spend a majority of their time communicating with others. Routine communication and networking take up 48%, nearly half, of a manager's time. In addition, several of the tasks in human resource management, such as motivating and disciplining, directly involve communication skills. Communication skills, then, are essential tools for managers. The more effectively one communicates, the more likely one is to accomplish goals and interact effectively.

Effective management depends upon effective communication.

Managers interact with others for much of their daily activity, spending approximately 80% of their time communicating (55% in meetings, 15% writing or reading reports, 10% on the telephone). The majority of this communication is with subordinates. This downward communication with subordinates is done face-to-face roughly 75% of the time. Contacts with subordinates are fairly short, whereas interaction with superiors is longer, but less frequent (Luthans & Larsen, 1986).

Managers also rated the importance of their communication activities. Contacts with superiors and individuals outside the organization are regarded as most important and challenging, followed by peer and colleague contacts. Subordinate contacts were least important and challenging. Managers regard face-to-face interaction as more important and challenging than telephone contacts (Whitely, 1984). The most critical organizational decisions are handled by face-to-face interaction because most information is available in face-to-face settings (Short, Williams, & Christie, 1976).

Most managerial communication is face-to-face communication with superiors, outsiders, and subordinates. Thus, interpersonal, face-to-face communication skills are the most important. Written communication is relied on less frequently. However, as organizations become increasingly technologically advanced through telecommunication and computer systems, managers must also develop skills in utilizing these technologies to accomplish their goals and to communicate readily with others.

COMMUNICATING WITH NEW INFORMATION TECHNOLOGIES

As vast amounts of information became more accessible through new communication technologies, these technologies have transformed organizations. The organization's environment and its own internal activities are now capable of being more closely monitored. For example, managers' span of control can be expanded because of technology which enables them to monitor more subordinates, including those at distant locations.

These new technologies, such as fax machines, video conferencing, and data processing, have different degrees of "social presence" (Short et al., 1976). Social presence refers to the degree that various media or information technologies imitate the qualities of face-to-face communication. Face-to-face communication provides rich, diverse cues that indicate the speaker's meaning and intensity. For example, eye gaze, facial expression, vocal pitch, vocal emphasis and intensity, speech rate, body posture, and movement all provide cues that listeners use to interpret the speaker's message. The more cues available in a medium or technology, the more accurate listeners can be in their interpretations. From most social presence to least social presence, various technologies would be ordered as follows—television (video conferencing), audio communication (telephone or tapes), and written communication (mail or computer). For critical decisions, managers rely on face-to-face communication because it maximizes the likelihood of accurate interpretation.

Media richness is very similar to the concept of social presence. Media richness refers to an information technology's ability to *change* understanding, whereas social presence refers primarily to *clarity* of understanding. An information technology must be complex enough to handle the uncertainty, ambiguity, or equivocality of the information being transmitted. Put another way, the more ambiguous the information, the richer the medium transmitting that information has to be.

For maximum effectiveness, information should be transmitted in the organization on the basis of (a) its relevance to the work unit, (b) the degree to which the work unit depends on that information, (c) the sequencing of the work being done (who needs to know first, second, etc.) and its accessibility. Any medium selected for information must provide timely feedback; transmit multiple cues for meaning as required by the message's ambiguity; tailor messages specifically, and use varied language (Huber & Daft, 1985).

What factors influence a manager's choice among the various information technologies? Managers choose a particular communication medium because of situational factors such as time pressure and distance, symbolic reasons such as conveying concern or showing authority, and message ambiguity, for example, using face-to-face communication because of the greater number of interpretive cues given. Face-to-face communication was selected for content and symbolic reasons; the telephone and electronic mail (*E*-mail) were chosen because of situational constraints (Trevino, Lengel, & Daft, 1987). *E*-mail was used when colleagues were geographically widespread, and the telephone was preferred when there was time pressure (Steinfield & Fulk, 1986). The most effective managers are more accurate in matching the communication medium with message ambiguity (Daft, Lengel, & Trevino, in press). Organizational norms of use concerning various media, their characteristics, and a manager's own experience will also influence a manager's choice of medium (Fulk, Steinfield, Schmitz & Power, 1987).

Every medium also has a set of qualities associated with it. Face-to-face communication is associated with nonroutine messages; the need for many interpretive cues such as nonverbal cues; the need to discuss materials; to build trust and teamwork; to emphasize informality, and to express emotions. Written communication is used to process large amounts of information; for a detailed document, if a permanent record is required; if continued review is needed; or to emphasize authority or legitimacy. *E*-mail is used for routine, one-way messages and for efficient, speedy transmission (Trevino et al., 1987). In general, situational factors, like

Match the medium with the message.

time pressure or the need for discussion, are most important in determining media choice.

Organizations and managers considering use of media such as *E*-mail, voice messaging, and video teleconferencing need to have enough people using the medium to make it effective. Such media must be universally accessible and easy to use. People will not utilize a medium if only a few have it or if the system is difficult to use (Markus, 1987).

The new information technologies have important implications for managers. Quite simply, information is necessary for effective management. In order to perform effectively, managers must understand the complexities of the new information technologies and select appropriate technologies for monitoring the environment and disseminating information. Handling the new technologies will be more complicated for some female managers because of the sex segregation in mathematical and scientific fields. But knowledge of these technologies, and an understanding of their organizational implications, will be increasingly important for all managers.

As we have seen, a manager's work is very fragmented. Managers function in diverse ways, ranging from interpersonal to informational roles. These roles, of course, are modified by the type of industry, the manager's personality, and his or her particular work situation. Much of a manager's work involves communication, especially face-to-face communication with subordinates. However, managers view their communication with superiors and peers outside the organization as most important. Whatever particular roles managers play, they are organizational leaders.

MANAGERIAL LEADERSHIP

Different leaders may emerge to direct an organization at different developmental stages. In organizations with a long history and strong culture, managers may be "groomed" over a number of years to assume various leadership positions. As one procedes up the corporate ladder, leadership functions increasingly depend upon evaluating information and coordinating the activities of other organizational members. At virtually any leadership level, good interpersonal and communication skills are critical for success and fundamental in building teams, coordinating activities, and participating in decision making.

Traditional managers perform the conventional functions of planning, execution and evaluation. However, many managers also perform an important symbolic function. Symbolic managers focus on the values and corporate culture of an organization (Deal & Kennedy, 1982). They manage organizational values and shared meanings, not just tasks. They establish trust with others, build teams through shared values, prioritize activities in light of organizational goals, and uphold cultural values. As organizational cultures vary, so too do managers and managerial behaviors. However, many people still have difficulty imagining a woman as the symbol of their organization's identity and prowess.

Managers embody and transmit cultural values. They articulate a vision of the organization, both to external clients and publics, and internally to other organizational members. Specifically, they influence organizational activities through what they pay attention to, measure, and control; what they react to, such as critical incidents or crises; the role model they provide; what behaviors they reward, both materially and symbolically; and the power of recruitment, selection, and promotion. These behaviors, taken collectively, represent the valued activities and practices in the organization. Managers identify these values and reinforce them (Schein, 1985).

Specific managerial behaviors vary in different types of organizational cultures and at different developmental stages (see Chapter 4). In the early stages of an organization, a manager needs to articulate a vision of what the organization will be, and to enforce this vision. As the organization develops, managers absorb the anxiety and tension associated with growth. At organizational midlife, managers analyze the organization and intervene when necessary. Mature organizations may be maintained by managers or, if the organization stagnates, managers may have to change the corporate culture radically to revitalize it. Different managerial skills are thus required throughout an organization's lifespan (Deal & Kennedy, 1982; Schein, 1985).

Given competition among organizations and advances in science and technology, change in organizations is inevitable. Change may be entirely internal or involve external elements as well. It may be massive, affecting virtually the entire organization, or relatively minor, involving only a few departments. Change processes also differ depending on whether the organization is young, mature, or declining (see Chapter 4). It is the managers who identify what change is needed; program the change in stages, breaking it down into manageable tasks; handle the resulting conflicts; and ensure that organizational members are committed to the change (Schein, 1985).

New forms of organizations, built on new managerial assumptions, are required to deal effectively with continuous change and uncertainty. A new view of organizations and organizational leadership, focusing on a more integrated organization, has been advocated by Kanter (1983).

In order to cope with change, new assumptions are needed to guide organizations: (1) Organizations and their departments are interconnected, and their relationships to the business environment must be understood. (2) Multiple goals are present in organizations and emerge from bargaining across units and individuals. (3) Both individual factors and situational factors influence organizational decisions. (4) Specialization within units, and coordination among units, are increasingly important; thus communication skills are critical to both individual and organizational success. Increasingly, then, organizational members, and especially managers, will need skills in communicating, bargaining, and coordinating activities.

The basic managerial skills required in integrated organizations all depend upon the "power tools"—the gathering and use of information, control over needed resources, and the ability to generate support from others. Two of these skills—gathering information and generating support—depend directly on communication. In addition, the ability to persuade others, to manage problems through teamwork and employee participation, and to handle change processes are critical skills in organizations. Finally, scarce resources will foster more interdepartmental connections, and the role of persuasion and bargaining will thus become important in decision making.

MANAGERIAL STYLES

Managers handle change and tasks in different ways. Personal style differences among managers lead to different approaches to problems. Different managerial approaches will also be needed as a result of different organizational cultures. There is no single managerial style that is best; rather, different managerial types may be needed to cope with differing tasks, organizations, and personalities.

Managers must balance task demands and socioemotional needs (see Chapters 5 and 6). Several different managerial types reflect different balances between the two needs:

1. Bureaucrat—performs minimum work to maintain the organization (minimum attention to task, minimum to socioemotional needs);
2. Country-Club Manager—attends to group members' needs and thus facilitates a positive work environment (most attention to socioemotional dimensions);

3. Compromiser—performs necessary work with good morale (attention given equally to task and socioemotional needs);
4. Consultative—gains support for task by involving group members in decision making (emphasis on socioemotional dimensions to facilitate task achievement);
5. Taskmaster—emphasizes getting task done efficiently without interference from socioemotional needs (high task emphasis, no socioemotional emphasis);
6. Benevolent Autocrat—focuses on task, but without excessive, arbitrary control (high task focus, moderate socioemotional focus); and
7. Ideal Work-Accomplishment—accomplishes task using committed group members (strong focus on both task and socioemotional needs). (Blake & Mouton, 1964)

We can all recognize the tradeoffs in each managerial type. Depending upon the situation, different leadership styles might be required or most effective in a given set of circumstances.

As we have seen, managerial roles in organizations are becoming increasingly complex. The traditional model of authority being vested in one's position is being modified by the trends toward more integration, more coordination and more volatile business environments. Males still hold the majority of managerial positions in business, government, and academe, and thus the male model for leadership still dominates. The explicit and implicit male leadership expectations make it difficult for women to emerge as leaders, as discussed in Chapter 6. Women are not "seen" as leaders, and their leadership behaviors are negatively evaluated because they are counter to gender-role expectations.

Organizations are dominated by male values.

Perceptions of Sex Differences in Managerial Styles. Several studies have investigated female and male managers to learn if their managerial styles differ, and if so, how they may differ. Because most organizations are dominated by male cultural expectations, and men will frequently be of higher status in cross-sex conversations, it is likely that the male style will dominate and be reinforced. For women, then, organizational communication practices may tend to present them with yet another instance of conflicting role-expectations. Moreover, these conflicting expectations may be so sub-

Cross-sex interactions usually involve contrasting communication styles.

Women are viewed as supportive and expressive, whereas men are viewed as instrumental.

tle and pervasive that their effects are difficult to discern, and even more difficult to monitor, during actual encounters. Recall, from Chapter 6, that both communicative styles, being instrumental and initiating, and being nurturant and supportive, are appropriate and valuable styles in a variety of circumstances. A major problem is that the value of the considerate, supportive style is not recognized and valued, nor is it generally acknowledged that either sex can display either style.

Women show an accommodative managerial style: they are affiliative and attempt to minimize the distance between themselves and others. In contrast, men tend to keep a distance between themselves and others in order to maintain status (Wexley & Hunt, 1974). Women managers appear to pay attention to the socioemotional dimensions, whereas men appear to ignore that dimension. It may be valuable to assess your own style and consider the balance you achieve between socioemotional and task needs.

Remember from Chapter 2 that gender stereotypes operate as both facts and values. As facts, they consist of beliefs about sex differences on various personality, interest, and ability characteristics such as aggression or expressing emotion. As values, they consist of beliefs about how men and women *should* differ in personality, interests, and behavior. Both components influence behavior and how that behavior is evaluated (Terborg, 1977). For example, even people who believed women were capable judged them unacceptable as managers because of likely resistance to them by co-workers (Bowman, Worthy, & Geyser, 1965). Terborg suggests that the prescriptive rather than descriptive component of stereotypes may have influenced the results of that study.

The effects of stereotypes operating as values can be seen in a number of studies. Three different supervisory styles, portrayed by both male and female managers, were evaluated in a study by Haccoun et al. (1978). The styles were either direct and authoritarian; analytic and rational; or a friendly, emotional style. Female employees believed that the rational approach would be least effective when responding to a problem with a worker's low productivity. Male employees believed that a female manager using a direct, authoritarian style would be least effective. All subordinates perceived the male manager as more effective and were more satisfied with the male manager.

In an interesting departure from the laboratory or experimental simulation study, men and women managers and their secretaries evaluated managerial styles. Respondents were from a financial insti-

Women managers supervise closely and give support; men stress autonomy.

tution, a manufacturing firm, and a technical institute. Respondents reported that women managers were both task and people oriented, whereas male managers were viewed as focused on their image and autonomy. Female managers paid attention to detail and interacted frequently with their subordinates. In contrast, male managers focused more on themselves and managed their subordinates by "staying out of it" until they were dissatisfied with a subordinate's performance. Respondents expressed a strong preference for gender-appropriate behavior by managers; misunderstanding frequently occurred when cross-gender behaviors were exhibited. Women resented men who did not seem to contribute as much as others, and men resented women managers who supervised too closely and thus communicated an attitude of distrust (Stratham, 1987, p. 425).

Other studies have analyzed cross-sex managerial dyads in which sex of both managers and subordinates was varied. A dependent, friendly leadership style was rated more effective for managers of either sex when their subordinates were of the opposite sex (Rosen & Jerdee, 1973).

In general, several consistent sex differences have been found in managerial style. Men focus on the task, whereas women focus on both the task and social relationships. Women have an accommodating, informative, involved managerial style in contrast to the distant, autonomous style of men. As we shall see later in this chapter, these managerial styles mesh well with females' preferences for indirect communication and males' preferences for direct communication (Tannen, 1987). The male managerial style, however, is consistent with male-dominated organizational values. For women, their styles clash with masculine organizational values, and thus their styles are judged less effective as well as less acceptable.

Evaluations of and Satisfaction with Male and Female Managers. Men and women sometimes differ in how they respond to female managers. Women rated women managers more highly, rated women in general more positively, and viewed women as more competent communicators than did men. In addition, people who have worked with female managers rate them more highly than those who have no work experience with them (Berryman-Fink & Wheeless, 1985).

Although subordinates reacted favorably to a friendly style, supervisors were rated most favorably when their behaviors matched gender-role expectations. On the basis of paragraphs describing different types of leader behavior, men were rated as more effective than women in initiating structure, but women were rated more effective in consideration (Bartol & Butterfield, 1976). (See Chapter 6 for a discussion of initiating structure and consideration.) Subordinates were more satisfied with male managers who were high in initiating behavior and with female managers who were high in consideration behavior. The more women managers initiated structure, the less satisfied male subordinates were with them (Petty & Miles, 1976).

When group members knew only each other's sex and name, they perceived men as being more competent than women. Women displayed more positive socioemotional behaviors, such as being friendly, whereas men displayed more task-oriented behaviors, such as giving suggestions. However, when group members' competency status was given, no sex differences were found in competency judgments or group participation. Sex differences in competency judgments and interaction when status was unknown reflected the participants' assumption that the sexes differ in competency. Direct information about an individual's competence can sometimes block the stereotype that women are less competent (Wood & Karten, 1986).

Women managers were perceived as more attentive and concerned, gave out more information, and were more approving, friendly, and open. Male managers, in contrast, were perceived as domineering and challenging. The female managerial style was judged as being more effective by subordinates and resulted in higher morale (Baird & Bradley, 1979). Similarly, nursing employees reported greater morale and job satisfaction with female managers (nursing supervisors) who were perceived as managing in a stereotypically feminine style (open, receptive to ideas, friendly, showing concern, and giving information). Stereotypic male managerial communication was perceived as dominating, directing conversations, and quick to challenge. These results may reflect the sex-segregation in nursing (women dominate the nursing ranks) (Camden & Witt, 1983; Camden & Kennedy, 1986).

Women are rated as less desirable for managerial positions and receive fewer job offers and lower salaries (Terborg, 1977). However, gender stereotypes seem to influence evaluators more when little additional information about the woman is provided (Terborg & Ilgen, 1975). This finding seems similar to the situation of men's competence being assumed, whereas women's must be established.

Females have more favorable judgments about women managers and their communicative abilities than do males (Berryman-Fink, Heintz, Lowy, et al., 1986). Men and women also value communication with their superiors, and this communication is related to job satisfaction (Weider-Hatfield, n.d.). Supervisors' evaluations of female subordinates' leadership/management techniques and diagnosis of organizational problems were significant predictors of subordinates' promotions (Shockley-Zalabak, Staley, & Morley, 1988).

To summarize, managerial behaviors are rated most highly when they are consistent with gender-role stereotypes. In general, male managers are judged as more competent. Both sexes were less satisfied if their supervisor was a woman. In addition, some women managers reported having less job autonomy. Given the implicit assumption of males' competence and a preference for consistent gender-role behavior, female managers are caught in a dilemma: preferred management styles are inappropriate gender-role behaviors. Both men and women managers must be sensitive to this paradox, so that more flexible management styles are possible for both sexes.

> People are rewarded for gender-appropriate behavior.

There are three important points to remember in considering sex differences in managerial style. First, these results may be affected by whether or not the studies were laboratory or field studies (see Chapter 6). In laboratory studies, sex may be one of the most salient information cues present, whereas in field studies there may be many situational factors that influence findings (Koberg, 1985; Terborg, 1977). Second, the results represent subordinates' or associates' *perceptions* of male and female managers. Remember from Chapters 2 and 3 that perceptions are heavily influenced by the perceivers' beliefs, expectations and values. Sex differences reported by observers may reflect real behavioral differences between men and women managers, or they may reflect the observers' perceptual bias—or some of both. Third, people who have worked with female managers rate them more highly than those who have no work experience with them.

MANAGERIAL POWER AND COMMUNICATION

In a classic study, Pelz (1952) found that subordinates' satisfaction was contingent on the superior's access to power and resources for the unit. Because women are often found in limiting jobs, their access to power may be limited and thus their managerial effectiveness may be limited as well. In fact, some women managers report having less job autonomy than males in similar positions (Petty & Miles, 1976). Powerlessness often breeds powerlessness. However, perception of a manager's influence determined subordinates' satisfaction, rather than the manager's sex (Trempe, Rigny, & Haccoun, 1985). Similarly, in a field study of bank managers, female subordinates (84%) preferred male managers. Situational factors, such as male managers' greater experience and reported greater influence, were believed to explain female subordinates' preferences (Liden, 1985; Koberg, 1985).

Jablin (1980) found that subordinates' sex, superiors' access to strategic and work-related upward influence, and subordinate's job satisfaction were all interrelated. Both male and female subordinates were more satisfied with superiors perceived as having more power. Both male and female subordinates who perceived their superiors as supportive were significantly more open in their communication and more satisfied than colleagues who perceived their leaders as low in supportiveness. However, female subordinates were more satisfied and perceived more open communication with supportive supervisors than males did with supportive supervisors. Organizational values will also prescribe appropriate communicative behavior, and open communication between superior and subordinates may violate organizational norms (Reardon, 1981).

With superiors' preference for positive messages, and subordinates' desire to protect themselves, open and accurate communication between superiors and subordinates is unlikely to occur. In a study investigating the use of persuasive messages by subordinates, subordinates who judged themselves to be in highly centralized positions used significantly less open persuasion and less strategic persuasion (i.e., strategic persuasion is empathic and used open-ended means or open-ended outcomes). Male subordinates reported using significantly more strategic and manipulative persuasive messages than did females. Male subordinates also reported using more open persuasion in their messages to superiors than did female subordinates, but this difference was not significant. Interestingly, these sex differences remained even when other mediating variables were controlled (Krone, 1985). When attempting to persuade a subordinate to comply with an obligatory request, male managers used punishment-based tactics where female managers used altruism and rationale-based tactics (Harper & Hirokawa, 1988).

Subordinates also vary in how they respond to explanations of leadership failure. Men, but not women, found some explanations of failure (such as admitted poor judgment or blaming politics) reflected effective leadership. For managers with a past history of poor judgment, explanations emphasizing the unfairness of a decision or biased judgments by others helped the perceived leadership of males but did not influence females' perceived leadership (Giacalone, 1988).

Although studies disagree as to whether power of the manager or sex of the manager is most critical in influencing subordinate satisfaction and evaluation, the message for women managers is still strikingly clear. To be female is to be associated with powerlessness, and either actual or perceived powerlessness is a disadvantage. Thus, understanding and using power appears critical to a woman's success in organizations (Haslett, 1991).

SEX DIFFERENCES IN MANAGERIAL COMMUNICATION

Given the underrepresentation of women in managerial positions, peer interaction and communication with superiors is likely to involve cross-sex interaction for women. Sex and gender differences in style, interpretation, and judgments about acceptable behavior will influence cross-sex interactions and create misunderstandings. A politically savvy manager will understand these differences and develop strategies to deal appropriately with them. These differences can be used positively by managers to enhance their effectiveness. In what follows, cross-sex interactions and sex differences in communication will be discussed with special attention given to their managerial implications.

CROSS-SEX INTERACTIONS

In organizations, women encounter a model of appropriate managerial behavior that reflects male values and characteristics that have traditionally been considered "masculine," including preferences for male communication patterns. Women will likely participate in mixed-sex groups, or be the only woman or one of two or three women in a group. In cross-sex interaction, differences in male and female patterns of communication may lead to consistent misunderstandings.

Because much of women's interactions in organizations will occur with men, it is important to understand how cross-sex encounters may involve misinterpretations. In such situations, women ask more questions, do more of the "maintenance" work in keeping the interaction going (Fishman, 1983), use more positive minimal responses like *uhm-hm*, use silence as a response to interruptions, and use more pronouns (like *you* and *we*) that acknowledge the other person. In contrast, men interrupt more; challenge others' statements more; tend to ignore the comments of other speakers; control the topic, and make more direct declarations than do women (Maltz & Borker, 1982). Women tend to be more collaborative in their interactions, whereas men tend to be competitive. It should be noted that these are comparative differences, not absolute standards followed in any encounter. Within the context of cross-sex interaction, men and women interpret and evaluate communicative behaviors differently. First, women use questions to maintain interaction, whereas men view them as requests for information. Second, men tend to ignore preceding remarks, whereas women tend to refer back to them. Third, women tend to evaluate verbal aggressiveness as negative, disruptive, and personally directed, whereas men regard verbal aggressiveness as a strategy for organizing conversations. Fourth, women appear to develop topics slowly and collaboratively, whereas men tend to operate within narrowly defined topics and with abrupt topic shifts. Finally, when discussing problems and giving advice, men tend to give advice directly as experts, whereas women tend to share experiences and offer reassurance. These differences present a major potential opportunity for misunderstanding (Maltz & Borker, 1982).

In cross-sex interaction, men and women interpret and evaluate communicative behavior differently.

Because the male model is the preferred, familiar model for managerial interaction, women need to recognize communication differences in order to accurately interpret what is meant by a particular comment. Being able to accurately interpret various strategies enables one to react appropriately, rather than continuing to misunderstand the other's intentions. Obviously, communication would be facilitated, and organizations would function more effectively, if men learned to understand and adapt to women's communicative styles as well as women learning to understand and adapt to men's styles. However, the reality of the present situation, with women in the minority, is that the onus of adaptation falls primarily on the women. In order to maximize career mobility, managers—both men and women—need to be sensitive to these issues.

These interactional differences may also be confounded by differences in male and female managerial styles. Each sex is rewarded for consistent gender-role behavior, and negatively evaluated for inappropriate gender-role behavior.

SEX DIFFERENCES IN COMMUNICATIVE BEHAVIOR

Chapters 4, 5, and 6 discussed sex differences in organizational behavior, small group interaction, and leadership. The gist of these differences is that women tend to be more interpersonally oriented, cooperative, collaborative, and supportive of others, and less self-confident. Men tend to be more task oriented, direct, competitive, challenging, and self-confident. The other important point is that, even when men and women behave the same, they are perceived and evaluated differently, and it is usually women who get consistently underrated.

Men and women differ in some ways in their styles of communication. The Communicator Style Index measures 10 characteristics that define an individual's communicator style: impression leaving, contentiousness (argumentiveness), being relaxed, being friendly, attentiveness, openness, dominance, being dramatic, being precise, and being animated (Norton, 1983).

In a study measuring self-perceptions of communicative style, females viewed themselves as more animated than men, whereas men perceived themselves as more precise and more argumentative. For both sexes, dominance and impression leaving were the most important influences on overall communicator image (Bonagero & Pearsons, 1986; Montgomery & Norton, 1981). No sex differences were found in people's assessment of the differences between their own and ideal speaking behaviors (Kramerae, 1978b). When women and men rated their general social style, males viewed themselves as more assertive, but no sex differences were found in measures of responsiveness and versatility (Staley & Cohen, 1988).

When people assessed their own communicative style, few sex differences were found. However, those that were found did reflect gender-role stereotypes associated with men and women. These stereotypes appear to influence a person's judgment of his or her communicative style, even though they may be inaccurate and thus misleading.

It is also necessary to measure behavioral differences in communication to learn whether or not sex differences exist. In a review of sex differences in communication, a metaanalysis identified sex differences in the following communicative behaviors (Wilkins & Anderson, 1988). Men exceed women in all of these behaviors except numbers 4 and 6.

1. Emergent leadership behaviors;
2. Behaviors that facilitate communication, such as giving suggestions and explaining;
3. Autocratic leadership behavior, like dominating;
4. Democratic leadership behaviors, like attending to the socioemotional needs of the group;
5. Influence strategies reflecting persuasive messages;
6. Positive affect behaviors, like friendliness; and
7. Negative affect behavior, like displaying tension.

These behaviors reflect stereotypic expectations and evaluations of women and men, and their communicative behavior.

Considerable research has focused on differences between actual speech behaviors of women and men. Those speech characteristics commonly associated with women are regarded as less assertive and more polite. They include the use of *tag questions* ("It's a nice car, isn't it?" in which *isn't it* acts to weaken the initial comment); *qualifiers*, which indicate a reservation about a comment ("I kinda like that color," where *kinda* expresses uncertainty) and *compound requests* ("Won't you hand me that paper?" which dilutes the strength of the request, "Hand me the paper."). *Hedges*, such as statements like "Well, I don't know if this is correct, but . . ." also weaken the force of statements and are frequently used by women. Regardless of the speaker's sex, people judged tag questions as less assertive than a straightforward comment. Compound requests were judged as being more polite, and qualifiers were judged as warmer (Newcombe & Arnkoff, 1979). Men are more direct, talkative, and argumentative; women are more supportive, polite, and expressive (Haas, 1979).

Nonverbal Communication. There are important sex differences in nonverbal communication as well. Nonverbal communication is less consciously controlled and primarily conveys emotions (Burgoon, Buller, & Woodall, 1989; Pearson, 1985). Both verbal and nonverbal communication convey a message; listeners need to pay attention to both communicative dimensions in order to accurately interpret what is meant by a speaker (Haslett, 1987).

In general, women are more sensitive to nonverbal cues than men. Women also are more accurate at interpreting nonverbal cues than men (Bate, 1988). Some researchers suggest that women's nonverbal communication sensitivity makes them more expressive communicators. This also seems to fit the stereotype of men being taught not to express their emotions, and it being regarded as "feminine" to be expressive.

Eye gaze with others is used to regulate our interactions. Generally, speakers look away from listeners and listeners gaze at speakers. When speakers glance at listeners, it invites the listener to respond. The more dominant partner in an interaction gazes longest, whereas the submissive partner tends to look away from others. People with the highest status also control eye contact in an interaction (Eakins & Eakins, 1978). Women tend to look more and look longer than men. This is believed to account for, in part, women's greater sensitivity to nonverbal behavior (women are monitoring nonverbal cues more than men do).

Other sex differences in nonverbal communication have been found in facial expression, gesture, body orientation, and space. Women's facial expressions are more animated, and they smile more (Bate, 1988). Women's gestures are smaller, whereas men gesture more frequently and more expansively. Both men and women gesture more and use more diverse gestures when interacting with members of the opposite sex. Women are also touched more and approached more closely than men. Finally, men have less direct body orientation when interacting than do women, and use more space. In general, nonverbal behaviors of women are similar to those of lower status and less dominance in an interaction.

Great care should be taken in interpreting nonverbal communication. Nonverbal behaviors vary as a function of sex, ethnicity, and culture. Using your own cultural patterns of nonverbal behavior to judge the nonverbal behaviors of other cultural or ethnic groups will result in serious misinterpretation. Effective interaction requires us to be aware of these differences so that we can accurately interpret another's messages.

In general, men's communication behavior, both verbally and nonverbally, conveys authority, status, and dominance. These masculine communicative behaviors are also valued in managers, whereas the feminine communicative behaviors, such as expressiveness and politeness, are not valued. Because we positively evaluate appropriate gender-role behavior, women who "switch" to a more masculine, assertive style may still be negatively judged. As pointed out in Chapter 6, however, women can switch styles and be positively evaluated but only if those changes are limited (i.e., change limited to a few behaviors, rather than a more comprehensive shift).

Powerful versus Powerless Speech. Powerful speech has also been compared to powerless speech styles. People evaluating different messages judged powerful, polite messages as being both powerful and effective. Direct statements without modifiers; intensifiers like *very*); deictic messages ("That man over by the chair . . ."); hedges and tags; and hesitations were ranked, in order, from most to least powerful and effective.

Speakers using powerful speech were judged as significantly more dominant, but not as competent as speakers using powerless forms of speech (e.g., tag questions, qualifiers, etc.). Qualifiers may make the speaker appear more open-minded and thoughtful, and thus more competent (Warfel, 1984). Those respondents who had strong sex-typed identities associated powerful speech with dominance. Powerful speech styles are also judged as more credible, persuasive, and attractive (Erickson, Lind, Johnson et al., 1978).

Although the power of one's speech style is important, some situations may be handled most appropriately by a powerless form of speech. People using powerless speech are more accepted when they are also judged as trying to be sociable. Messages are judged in terms of the speaker's intention (Bradac & Mulac, 1984). Bradac and Mulac's study found no differences between male and female interviewees in their use of powerful or powerless forms of speech. Perhaps the context of interviewing obscured sex differences, or perhaps, low-power people (interviewees) found powerless speech an appropriate response in this situation. Recall from Chapter 6 that situational power status overrides internal personality characteristics.

However, women's speech has been associated with powerless speech forms. Two interpretations have been put forth to explain this association. The deficit view suggests that women lack power because their actions (speech behaviors) lack power. The discrimination viewpoint suggests that powerless forms of speaking are associated with women because women are stereotypically viewed as less competent (Berryman & Wilcox, 1980; Bradley, 1981; Erickson et al., 1978; Johnson, 1983; O'Barr & Atkins, 1980; Warfel, 1984). As discussed in Chapters 2 and 6, both explanations could be true, and together they create a self-fulfilling prophecy. Because women are stereotypically viewed as less competent, they use less powerful speech and others accept only less powerful speech from them. Then, because women use less powerful speech, they lack power and therefore effectiveness—thereby seeming to confirm the initially mistaken perception of lesser competence.

Women's speech is regarded as powerless speech.

In brief, very striking stereotypes differentiate between female and male speech patterns. Men's power is expressed in their greater level of participation, more directive remarks, more interruptions, and greater control over conversational topics. In general, women's speech is perceived as more polite, less assertive and less powerful than men's speech. However, the empirical research supporting this general finding is mixed. Many factors—such as the context, the relationship between interactants, cultural expectations, social roles, and the speaker's intent—may be more important than the speaker's sex in determining the most effective communication style (Aries, 1988). Women, however, need to be aware of prevalent stereotypes and adjust their messages accordingly. Speech styles may vary as a function of the situation, personal goals and the task. No one style fits all circum-

Communicate according to the situation and your relationship with others.

stances. Knowing your own personal communication style will help you develop communicative strategies appropriate to your style, and indicate areas of your strength and weakness. Generally women rely on fewer types of strategies than do men, and thus limit their effectiveness. Understanding your communication strengths and weaknesses will ultimately enhance your organizational as well as personal effectiveness.

TOWARD A NEW MANAGERIAL STYLE

One of the themes running through this book has been that sex differences exist and that these differences should be *appreciated*, not *punished*. There is no single most effective style of management, of leadership, or of group participation—rather different styles are appropriate for different contexts. Given the advantages of diversity in style, managers must become even more flexible than before because they must adapt to increasingly complex organizations and organizational environments.

Different managerial strategies are needed in different situations.

What should this new managerial style be like? We suggest that it should capitalize on human resources in a more meaningful way than has been the case in the past. Managers should be able to accept people for what they are, treat all courteously, and trust others (Bennis & Nanus, 1985). Women's communication and managerial styles of consideration and supportiveness should fit this new management focus and result in increased subordinate participation and satisfaction.

What strategies might women pursue to maximize their access to power, and create opportunities for advancement? On the individual level, a number of different tactics can be pursued. First, women should participate actively in meetings, task forces, and daily interactions with colleagues. Effective participation requires that one be prepared and, on the basis of that preparation, make comments when appropriate. Being heard may also require persistence because women are often not "heard." Give your suggestions and claim credit for them.

Second, demonstrate your knowledge and competence. Seize opportunities to learn new skills and extend your expertise, especially if it involves interdepartmental meetings and projects. Be visible through your participation and, again, claim credit for your ideas and contributions.

Third, become part of an active network, both inside and outside the organization. Such contacts expand your understanding and knowledge about your own organization as well as providing information about job opportunities. It is particularly important for women to

Develop strong cross-sex networks across the organization.

participate in mixed-sex networks since all-female networks tend to work with more limited information.

Fourth, find and invest in the power tools of information, resources, and support (Kanter, 1983). Information is power: Gain access to information, but share it selectively and reciprocally. Build support through networking.

Information is power: Share it selectively and reciprocally.

Fifth, competence multiplies. That is, if you are perceived as competent, you have increasing opportunities to demonstrate and use your skills (Kanter, 1983). Put another way, power leads to more power. Be ready to take risks. For career and personal growth, some risks are necessary. However, as you consider risks, calculate the probable outcomes of an action, both in terms of the best scenario and the worst. Then decide if the probable gains are worth the risk.

Finally, in so far as it is possible, expand your job opportunities by participating in a variety of projects, particularly those that will develop your own professional skills or enhance your visibility. Increasingly, corporations will be led by those who have varied job experiences, not just specialized knowledge in a single area. The complexities of organizations and environments require multifaceted managers who can cope with the turbulence and change in the business environment.

These individual strategies may enhance career advancement, but systemic bias can occur and impede career development. These biases must be attacked on a systemwide basis. In order to take action, you need to analyze the company and its corporate structure and to mobilize support for change. The systemic bases of bias may be identified by investigating the following areas. First, one needs to understand the organization's culture. Know what the core mission and goals of the organization are, the means taken to obtain those goals, and how they are measured. Are these goals and measures equitable for all? Second, understand the value and reward system in the company and identify any sources of bias, implicit or explicit. Third, assess the sources of information and power within the organization. Are these sources accessible and fairly administered? Fourth, identify important leaders in your organization and analyze their ability to help support change in the organization.

Once sources of systemic bias have been identified, specific data concerning bias should be collected and documented. On the basis of such information, collected by colleagues as well as yourself, a plan of action to correct the problem can be developed. Action plans will vary across companies, situations and personnel. However, it is always a good strategy and more effective if you can to work within the existing structure of the organization. If you are unsuccessful, then other steps may need to be taken, but you have at least worked through appropriate organizational channels. Broad-based group support is required to effectively counter systemic bias, so forming coalitions and building networks are important and will support efforts to remove bias. If the bias is deeply ingrained in the system, it may be better to change jobs to where the working environment is less biased.

Effective managers need a business environment which permits diversity and recognizes the value of different styles. As Bennis and Nanus point out, trust is an important part of the new managerial style: Trust is developed through recognizing and appreciating different talents and abilities, and providing a corporate climate which responds to an increasingly diverse workforce.

While this chapter has focused on managerial skills and suggested some strategies for further developing communication skills, subsequent chapters will deal with specific situations women may encounter in the workplace. Suggestions will be offered as to how one might analyze and react to such situations.

Section IV
The Bottom Line:
Combining Research and
Experience in the Real World

Research can provide valuable information about "what usually happens" and why it happens. Experience is also a valuable source of knowledge, but individual experiences are limited to specific situations and personalities. The powerful combination of both research and experience produces a sum greater than its parts. This combination can be a very powerful tool in combatting sex discrimination.

The two chapters in this section combine both research findings and the experience of many years in resolving problems that women experience during their careers. Some of the issues are relatively clear. Savvy women can resolve them on their own. Others are more subtle and elusive, difficult to identify as sex discrimination, and even more difficult to handle.

Chapter 8 presents case studies involving sex discrimination. Each study is followed by an analysis of the problem, some possible options for response, and suggested solutions. One study focuses on getting the right start in a new job. A second stresses communication and the technique of successfully presenting a proposal. Others illustrate the issues involved when a young woman is promoted over older men, job elaboration and power space, and dealing with various forms of sexual harassment. Of course, in any given situation, there are many specific factors that influence the nature of the problem and which particular solutions would be viable or even possible. In some areas, there are no short term solutions because the problems have been part of our culture for many years.

Chapter 9 summarizes and integrates the problems and solutions discussed throughout the book. It focuses first on the effect of sexism on women, including how women discriminate against themselves. A second section presents a series of questions designed to identify invisible sex discrimination and focus on specific situations in organizations. Knowing the right questions to ask can be crucial to acquiring the knowledge to identify a problem and determine whether sex discrimination is "alive and well" but invisible to everyone, including those who perpetuate it.

The third section presents suggestions for enhancing your career success, for counteracting sexism in organizations, and for dealing with existing sexism effectively. The need to empower yourself is emphasized and followed by suggestions of how to start gaining some power. There are important strategies that are not used as much as they might be, because men do not know them and many women revert back to, or never escape from, the stereotypical supportive role of helping colleagues and ignoring their own needs. Still other men and women would like to have more control over their working lives but do not know where to start. A third, more sophisticated group have a good start on their careers but have been stalled for unknown reasons. The suggestions in this section are designed to address these problems.

A central theme of this book is that knowledge is empowering. The goal of this section is to apply that knowledge to create win–win solutions that benefit everyone.

8
A Matter of Choice: Some Frequent Problems and Possible Strategies

This chapter offers case studies illustrating some specific problems that women in the workforce have encountered. They are typical, prevalent, current, and well documented. The suggestions and options that are described in these situations are some that are available to women and have proved effective in dealing with those situations. There are always additional options available to a creative thinker. However, every strategy has its costs, including the strategy of taking no action at all.

The choice of an option should be made after reviewing the alternatives available and assessing the risks. The gain must be worth the potential pain. In most situations, there is seldom a clear or correct single solution, or only one correct solution. However, every woman has a choice of options she can use, at least one of which should be appropriate for her.

> The gain must be worth the potential pain.

There are some aspects of each case that represent issues that women must face, sometimes on a daily basis. Women who understand the dynamics of sex discrimination are in a much better position to develop effective strategies to counter it. To begin with, they are less likely to blame themselves and have a higher self-confidence.

The first case study, *A New Beginning: Starting in an Organization*, deals with a woman changing to a new job. It includes suggestions to counteract the poor judgment that she inadvertently used in her previous position due to her lack of knowledge of perceptual bias and the dynamics of the workplace.

The Art of Presenting a Proposal, the second case study, emphasizes the extensive early preparation needed to establish the climate for acceptance and adoption of a new proposal. Many of the steps suggested will become automatic once a woman becomes skilled at establishing such a climate for her proposal.

One of the subtle ways to discredit a woman competing for a job is discussed in the case study, *Sexual Harassment: Discrediting the More Competent Woman*. Sometimes when no legitimate way can be found to compete successfully against a woman, very subtle sexual harassment is used. One of the difficulties for a woman is that neither she nor others may recognize such subtle harassment for what it is until it is too late to repair the damage.

A Collision Course: Power Space vs. Job Elaboration, describes what happens when a very competent and underemployed woman inadvertently invades her manager's power space through job elaboration that her manager encouraged.

The Perils of Rapid Advancement is concerned with the difficult problems that a very hard-working and competent young woman faces when she is promoted over men with more seniority. It includes handling of sexist jokes, interruptions at meetings, and dealing with the old boy network.

An important study, *Sexual Harassment: The Unwanted Attention*, offers suggestions to deal with this growing issue of sexual harassment. Before the federal law was enacted, there was little hope of combatting sexual harassment because the victim usually was perceived as guilty for "enticing" the man. It is now recognized that sexual harassment is based on power and control rather than sexual attraction. It does not stop when it is ignored; some action must be taken.

These case studies illustrate how women can take some control over their situations on the job. Research and experience have been the basis for the proposed solutions. When a working woman is faced with a difficult situation, two of the most important things to remember are: (1) knowledge is empowering, and (2) a win–win strategy is the most effective way to solve a problem.

CASE STUDY 1
STARTING IN AN ORGANIZATION:
THE FIRST STEPS

Each organization has its own culture. Identifying and understanding the culture of an organization is basic to success within it. It is a complex environment that takes time to unravel and understand. From the first day on any job, there are certain factors of which to be aware.

A woman must work to establish her own credibility and integrity within the new environment.

Vivien, an enthusiastic but cautious young woman in her late twenties, has just changed jobs and is starting to work as an accountant for a different company. She knows only a few employees whom she had met at professional conferences. She left her former job, where she had worked for 4 years because it appeared to be a dead end for her. She is very excited about the possibilities in her new position. In her previous job she had been sure that her work was as good or better than the work of Alan and Bill, both of whom had been promoted over her. As she had been taught, she had been modest and had assumed her work would speak for itself. However, she did not advance.

David, her former boss, did not seem to take Vivien or her professional goals seriously. Instead of answering her questions about work problems, he always interrupted her. He would tell her how attractive she looked in her new dress or about the problems he and his wife were having with their twins. Vivien also wondered if company politics were involved. She had ignored the constant rumors on the "grapevine" and the office politics because she thought it was the safest thing to do. How can she get off to a good start on her new job? What can she do differently in her new position?

PERCEPTUAL BIAS: GAINING RECOGNITION FOR YOUR WORK

Research has shown that work done by women is perceived by both men and women to be of less value and less importance, even though the work is identical to or better than that done by men. If Vivien was aware of this research and its implications on the job, she would have realized that she needed to do more than just "let her work speak for itself." She needed to "sell" herself and highlight the quality and quantity of her work in appropriate ways. Providing objective comparative data is one of the best measures, if the data are available and can be used. Subjective evaluations of work seldom help women, even though they may help men. Objective evaluation by others, especially a blind evaluation, is another effective method. For example, when one professional journal used blind evaluations, there was a surprisingly large increase in the acceptance of articles written by women. One option Vivien has is to continue "letting her work

Subjective evaluations of work seldom help women even though they may help men.

180 THE ORGANIZATIONAL WOMAN

speak for itself." However the result would be a similar lack of advancement. A more effective option is to be less modest and highlight her contributions to the work of the department

INTERACTING WITH MALE COLLEAGUES

Men are comfortable with women in traditional roles—mother, sister, wife, or girlfriend. It is very difficult for them to change their "normal" behavior toward women to behavior appropriate with a professional colleague. Most men are not aware that they even have a problem dealing with women in the workplace.

Working women need to find the right balance between maintaining their femininity and being taken seriously as a professional colleague. The solution is to maintain a delicate balance between the stereotypical female behavior and professional behavior considered appropriate to your job level. For example, be professional when it counts and more feminine in less critical situations. A woman needs to establish that balance to avoid the usual sex-role stereotyping, and educate her male colleagues in order to maintain it.

Vivien has the option to be friendly to Orvill, her new boss, only in a professional way rather than a personal way. That option was not a realistic one with David, her former boss, who seemed unable to have a professional, rather than the stereotypical, relationship with women who worked for him.

One way men limit competition from women on the job is by treating them according to the stereotypical social role and ignoring them as serious professional colleagues. Vivien's former manager had treated her that way. It was inappropriate for him to discuss personal matters and not answer her questions. Vivien needed to direct the meeting back to professional matters. Often, men are not even conscious of such behavior. If women behave or encourage others to behave stereotypically on the job, of course, they do not have to be taken seriously. There are many subtle ways to "keep women in their place."

PROJECTING A PROFESSIONAL IMAGE

Vivien should ask herself why she might not have been taken seriously in her former job. Did she take herself seriously and project a professional image, or did her social role, as a woman, cloud her self-perception and confuse the perception of others? There are many ways to give messages about the perceived commitment an employee makes to a job. If Vivien's image on the job was primarily that of a socially oriented female, it may have been projected through her clothing (tight sweaters, frilly low-necked blouses, high-slit skirts) and her body language as well as by what she said and did. In this case, she may say she is professional, but the nonverbal messages may contradict her; the result is a confusing mixed message. Again, the solution is a sensitive balance between the two extremes in dress and behavior. A question Vivien might ask herself is, "Do I look and act serious enough to request and receive $100,000 to initiate and implement a new program?"

THE GRAPEVINE AND OFFICE POLITICS: AN IMPORTANT SOURCE OF INFORMATION

Vivien must realize that, in an organization, no work can be done effectively in isolation. She cannot afford to repeat her earlier decision and ignore the "grapevine" and office politics, because they directly affect her ability to do her job. This informal communication network often interprets the meaning of a more formal communication and can anticipate change. Often, the rumors are based on fact and are true. Vivien does not have to get personally involved in office politics, but she must know what is going on, as it directly or indirectly influences her own work options and opportunities. She is missing vital information, often related to timing, that is available to others. Knowledge is empowering, especially when it involves appropriate timing and can be used constructively. She needs to remain relatively neutral regarding office politics and listen carefully to rumors circulating on the "grapevine."

ESTABLISHING CREDIBILITY: KNOWLEDGE, RELIABILITY, AND ACCURACY COUNT

In establishing credibility on the job, use only accurate data and facts to back up your work. Vivien must be able to support her statements by knowing the relevant laws, statistics, and research. She must *not guess if she does not know the answer.* If she guesses incorrectly, someone else will be happy to correct her. She would not only have been identified as someone who does not do her "homework," but she would have to work twice as hard in the future to prove her statements because of the earlier mistake. The message that she gave

Important information is power and can be exchanged, not given away.

was that she could not be trusted to be accurate. Others could not act on the basis of her information. Thus, few would request or exchange information with her in the future.

When Vivien is in the powerful position of having accurate information others want or need to know, she has the option of trading it rather than giving it away. If she can establish herself as one who provides accurate and reliable information, she will have greatly empowered herself.

LEARNING FORMAL AND INFORMAL POLICIES AND PROCEDURES: A NECESSITY FOR SUCCESS

If Vivien was not given a company handbook of policies and procedures, she should request one. The formal policies are usually found in the company handbook. However, she must learn both the formal and the *informal* company policies. It is equally important to know whether or not the policies are followed and how they are enforced. Informal procedures and policy enforcement may be difficult to identify; however, Vivien must be aware that they exist, and she should consciously work to identify this valuable information. Even better, if she has identified someone as a trustworthy colleague, she can learn "the ropes" from him or her. Policies may remain the same, but their interpretation and implementation may vary with the person in charge.

SUMMARY

Starting a new job is an exciting opportunity. There is an entirely new environment to be understood. Some good advice is to "make haste slowly" until you find out whom you can trust, who is out to exploit you, who is the office gossip, and who is reliable. Many of the issues that women face, and some of the options they have, especially in a new organization, have been discussed. Some sensitive issues that women sometimes ignore to their peril include: gaining recognition for work performed, interacting professionally with male colleagues, projecting a professional image, office politics, establishing credibility, and knowing the formal and informal company policies and procedures and how they are enforced and interpreted. Not all are of equal importance. However, appropriate attention to these issues can significantly influence a woman's success on the job.

CASE STUDY 2
THE ART OF PRESENTING
A PROPOSAL SUCCESSFULLY

Strategies can be developed to assist women in overcoming some of the sex discrimination in treatment and communication resulting from perceptual bias. Many of these strategies are good techniques for anyone. However, for most women, additional preparation is usually necessary because their work is frequently judged more critically than the same work done by men. To establish a climate for success, the problems need to be clearly defined and preparation done carefully.

A serious, attractive, tall woman in middle management, Ramona has worked hard for over a year to learn her job. She thinks she has identified a problem in the sales and billing area that could be measurably improved. It would require some reorganization and cost the company a great deal of money to implement her idea; but it would pay out in 3 years or less. She has noticed that new ideas from junior women, especially those costing money, are not always welcome in her department. She wants to make a proposal for the change but is concerned that she might not get any support from Joe, her manager, a conservative, short man. Joe has been on the job for 10 years and does not like to "rock the boat" with a new idea if he can avoid it.

FIRST STEPS: HOW TO START

Ramona needs to know if her proposal is as good as she thinks it is, and whether it has been considered and rejected before. She can check back files to find out if a similar project has ever been considered. If one has been turned down or postponed, she should review the concerns and objections to it, possibly modifying her proposal to resolve any problems that may still exist. She could ask senior colleagues if anyone had developed her ideas before. If so, she could find out whom she should talk to and where to find a record of the earlier proposal.

Back-up data must be impeccable and well-organized. A short overview can be very helpful as few people will read through 10–20 pages of detail.

Timing is very important. If there has just been a budget cut, this may not be the right time to present a high-cost change. Ramona should find out when advance budget planning is done and present her proposal in ample time to have it adopted and built into the budget before the deadline. It may be possible to "sell" only the first step in one fiscal year, but it will be a start.

A CLIMATE FOR SUCCESS: CAN IT BE DEVELOPED?

Proper presentation of a proposal is an art. Although women are very adept at persuasion, especially in their private lives, they seldom transfer this valuable skill to the workplace. Ramona is aware that Joe himself will be taking a relatively high risk if he advocates her ideas because she is a relatively new employee and female. Ramona must develop a win–win strategy and present her proposal so that it is clear that her boss, her department, and the company will benefit, especially Joe, her manager. She must address her manager's concern for the most controversial issues and his objections, such as how soon it would pay out, and any necessary changes in personnel, both in the number of people and any change in job functions. However, the *big* question for Joe is, how will it make him and his department look, better or worse? How much additional work will it be for him? These issues must be addressed, so that Joe will view the change as "worth the risk."

> The big question for Joe is, how will it make him and his department look, better or worse?

Ramona must not just "drop" the proposal on Joe, her manager, "out of a clear blue sky." In that case, his first response would probably be negative, as it usually is with a new idea. He would know all the reasons it would not work.

Most administrators do not react well to "surprises." Ramona needs to ask Joe informally if he thinks the billing system is as efficient as it might be. She might also add that improving the system would be a major credit to their department's image. The question will assist Joe in recognizing the problem and, perhaps, cause him to think about it. After a week or two, Ramona can tell him, again informally, that she has been thinking a lot about it and has some ideas she would like to explore. At this time, Ramona may also wish to do some similar preparation with senior members of the department.

After several weeks, Ramona can tell Joe that she has informally outlined a procedure that might work, and ask him if he will think about her ideas. When she meets with him, seated at a table as she does not want to tower over him, she outlines her ideas to him verbally, carefully noting his response, verbal and nonverbal. It is very probable that he may start out being negative. It will be necessary to talk through his concerns, stressing how Joe, the department, and the organization will benefit.

Joe might identify an area that Ramona had overlooked or have additional data otherwise unavailable to her. If that happens, Ramona should leave to modify the proposal, thanking Joe for his interest and time. Becoming defensive or emotional would defeat the entire project.

Joe might have other agenda items with his manager and ask Ramona to wait a month or two. Ramona will have to accept his request to wait in order to gain his necessary support.

If the proposal is now refined enough to put on paper, Ramona can make another appointment with Joe and request that he review the draft. If he is strongly against it, however, and Ramona is convinced she is correct, it would be better not to push much farther at this time. It is important to remember that, "If at first you don't succeed, try again another way." However, she always has the option of dropping the whole idea.

If everything does go well, and the proposal is now refined, Joe may suggest that Ramona present it at their next staff meeting for review and possible changes. Now, Ramona may want to share her proposal informally with her colleagues in advance of the meeting. Just as with Joe, it is better for Ramona to know their objections or proposed revisions in advance so that she can evaluate and incorporate them or be prepared to answer them with data. At this time, she should also work for support of her plan by building some alliances with her colleagues.

PRESENTING THE ACTUAL PROPOSAL: DOES IT STILL NEED ADDITIONAL PREPARATION?

Ramona already has a good start for presenting her proposal. She has refined the idea with her manager and has interacted with colleagues, requesting their suggestions. Her idea has already been through several preliminary drafts, each draft incorporating more of her colleagues' suggestions. The result is a better proposal which has gained some support from her colleagues because she has incorporated some of their suggestions. Because many people know about her proposal, it is securely identified with her and no one else can adopt it as their own, as has sometimes happened to her other ideas.

Ramona is on the agenda of the staff meeting, and she cannot be ignored by her colleagues. She has requested and been given 30 minutes for her presentation. She must keep within the allotted time and have a well-organized presentation. She must make every minute count. Her concise written summary must be well-organized and distributed with the agenda. She should take her more detailed backup information to the meeting. Ramona wants several areas brought out in the discussion, and she has decided not to leave anything to chance. She has lined up several supportive colleagues to ask the important questions and to start the discussion following her presentation.

INTERRUPTIONS: CAN THEY BE CONTROLLED?

Ramona has had some bad experiences at previous staff meetings. At her first meeting, she had an idea to reduce wasteful duplication of effort that she planned to present. No sooner had she started to explain her idea, however, than a senior man interrupted with a negative comment disguised as a joke. When Ramona tried to resume her presentation, another man interrupted, changing the subject. After a few more meetings, Ramona realized that her comments were almost always interrupted. She was determined to prevent that from happening this time.

Ramona knew that, by preparing a written proposal to distribute at the meeting, at least everyone would have a complete picture of her project. Also, through her earlier individual contacts, colleagues would be familiar with the idea. When she alerted her friends to ask the "right" questions, she also requested that, if the usual interruptions occurred, they should state that they wanted to hear the rest of her proposal. This is a good technique to use at any meeting. Ramona had already done the same for them. This support needs to be reciprocal within her special network, which includes both women and men.

Ramona decided that, at the meeting, she would request that questions be held until she had completed her presentation, explaining that she had a limited amount of time and that the last 10 minutes would be for questions and discussion.

POWER OF THE CHAIR: CAN IT BE USED?

Because interruptions have been an ongoing problem, Ramona decided to discuss this issue with Joe, her manager. She explained that she needed the full allotted time for the presentation and asked his help as chair of the meeting to see that she received it.

The chair of the meeting has the power to control interruptions. Often that person does not seem aware of what is happening when only women are interrupted. Unconsciously, he or she may believe that what women say is less important than what men might say. However, if the chair does understand what is going on and permits interruptions to continue, there is a message in it. In other words, the chair does not want you to say or complete what you started. Without some support from the chair, it is more difficult to deal with interruptions.

The easiest way to respond to an interruption is to ignore it. Interrupt the interrupter, if possible, and continue with your presentation. This option may or may not work, but Ramona decided it was worth one try if she had the support of the chair, who would be alert to her problem.

HANDLING CRITICISM: EXPECT THE WORST AND HOPE FOR THE BEST

It is always better to expect the worst and hope for the best. You will seldom be disappointed. It is important to listen to any criticism carefully as you can always learn something. A serious problem for career women is not receiving honest and frank criticism from their superiors. Without knowing what is wrong, women cannot make the appropriate corrections.

The best option in handling criticism at a meeting is to turn it to your own advantage, if possible. When someone brings up something that was omitted, it is a good idea to thank them and proceed to elaborate on it from your own perspective.

A defensive and emotional response is usually the first impulse which should be quelled. That kind of response is unproductive and will not win in the long run. In the future, people will not take you seriously. You will be denied their valuable evaluation of your work, as they will not take the time and energy to critique it. Of course, criticism often involves something we would rather not know. Naturally, none of us likes to be criticized, but it is one of the most important ways to learn. It is very easy to "not see the forest for the trees." However, be alert for criticisms that are "covers" for some hidden agenda such as a power play. An idea is usually improved when there is a diversity of perspectives incorporated into it.

Be alert for criticism that is a "cover" for some hidden agenda.

Never confront colleagues directly in a meeting or in front of others unless it is part of a specific strategy. It is even more dangerous to confront your manager in such a situation. Managers cannot afford to let a member of their staff defeat them in public. If it was permitted, others would try that technique to meet their own needs, and the manager would lose control. Respect your manager's power space.

It is only natural to receive some negative comments, and it is necessary to be prepared for them. Ramona already knows the weakest part of the project, and needs to give it special attention. She can be certain others will find it.

Being too emotionally involved with an idea may result in overlooking valid criticism. An attack on the proposal must not be viewed as a personal attack or allowed to cause her to lose her temper. Even if it is a personal attack, Ramona must not permit herself to respond emotionally in public. If she did, she would be "fair game" for everyone there. It is dangerous for her not to have her brain in control of her actions. Under such circumstances, people say things they do not mean and regret it later. However, those comments may be the only things that other people remember.

When someone poses an objection, the response can be, "On what basis do you say that?" It is legitimate to seek the basis of the remark or the source of new information. It may be more current information or information with limited distribution that was not available to Ramona earlier.

If Ramona thinks that she has the answer to the question but needs to present it in a way that will not embarrass anyone, she could say "I had the same problem in the beginning, but upon further examination of the data, I found this . . . ."

THE VALUE OF A WIN–WIN PERSPECTIVE: IS IT WORTH THE EFFORT?

Whenever a change in organizational structure is suggested, everyone becomes very nervous. People like the security of the current structure, because they know where they stand and how it works. They are very concerned personally about whether they will "win or lose" when any change occurs.

Ramona must remember that her proposal will probably require some reorganization. All the people at the meeting will be wondering how it will affect their individual jobs:

1. Will it mean more or less work for them?
2. Will it enhance their status or decrease it?
3. Will their budget be cut or increased?
4. Will their staff be reduced or increased?

Ramona will need to answer their unspoken questions and allay their fears, pointing out the advantages that will result from this proposed change. These are emotional issues as well as substantive ones. When a person is threatened with the loss of power or status, or has a personal grudge, the response will be emotional rather than rational. If a person does not want to do something due to personal or emotional reasons, you can have all the reasons and the data in the world to justify the action; however, nothing will happen until their personal needs are met. If the emotional needs are not recognized and dealt with, she will not have a successful presentation. It is much easier for a win–win proposal to succeed when it has something for as many people as possible.

SUMMARY

It is not just luck that accounts for success in presenting a proposal. Ramona's extensive early preparation planned to gain support of her colleagues and manager is very important to a proposal's acceptance. Ramona recognized that it was crucial to gain the backing of her manager through a win–win plan. Her ability to handle criticism, especially legitimate criticism, increased the chances for the proposals adoption. Some women may become discouraged when they recognize how much work can be involved in the successful presentation of a new proposal. Not every proposal requires such extensive preparation. However, when it involves a large budget and changes related to personnel, people have to become comfortable with the idea and make it their own. If Ramona is well prepared, there may be no problems. If she does not prepare carefully, it probably will not go very smoothly or produce the desired result.

CASE STUDY 3
SUBTLE HARASSMENT: DISCREDITING
THE MORE COMPETENT WOMAN

When men become professionally threatened by a competent woman, they may treat her in a way that casts her into the stereotypical role of girlfriend, wife, mother, daughter, or outcast. This diminishes women as professionals and as being serious about their work; it also allows others not to take them seriously.

Shelly, an attractive and sophisticated single parent in her 40s, has a solid record of professional achievement. She is well-respected by her colleagues and in her profession. It is rumored that she is one of six candidates for the job of a regional vice-president in her company. One secret of her success is that she can accomplish her goals without alienating others and, as a result, has few enemies. Suddenly, she has found Dan, one of the other possible candidates, starting to ask her extensive detailed questions about her two children. How was their health? Were they doing well in school? Did she worry about them when she traveled on business? Did she find it hard to work late and leave them home alone?

She became very suspicious of this sudden solicitude when a few of her colleagues started voicing the same concerns about whether she was neglecting her children. She realized that Dan's goal was to have her perceived as a mother who worked when her "real" job was at home rather than as a professional who was also a mother. A popular topic of discussion among her staff became whether it would be fair to her children if she took the vice-president's job.

TAKING CARE OF YOURSELF: ARE OTHERS TRYING TO TAKE CARE OF YOU?

Shelly identified the problem as Dan's way to "put her in her place" and discredit her for the promotion. She could not be faulted on her job performance and ability, so he started focusing on her personal life and her role as a mother. However, it was very difficult for her not to feel increasingly guilty about her children, although she had very good supportive household help. Of course, this was part of Dan's strategy. Although this harassment was personal and could only be used against a woman, it is not usually identified as sexual harassment, as underhanded and difficult to counter as it is. This kind of harassment can be viewed as a sign of the harasser's weakness because he cannot find another way to discredit the woman.

A solution is not easily found when personal issues are involved. Over the years, Shelly had demonstrated that she was able to handle her responsibilities to her children and that they did not interfere with her job performance. If she had been vulnerable to the subtle accusation of neglecting her children in the past and they had serious problems, she would have a hard time countering Dan's subtle undermining. Shelly can choose the option of ignoring Dan's attack. However, it would be better to call attention to her record and state that she is tired of the ploy that Dan is using. She must not spend too much time denying the rumors, as that could focus attention on an inappropriate and damaging issue. She needs to touch base informally about what is happening to her with her boss. Although important if not clarified, the harassment should not be a major issue unless it starts to escalate abruptly. Shelly can challenge Dan and ask him why he is suddenly focusing on her children. She can explain that she is aware of what he is trying to do and that it will not work. As she could anticipate, Dan's reply would probably be, "I am only thinking of you and your children."

SUMMARY

Such subtle harassment must be recognized for what it is: an attempt to disqualify women who meet or exceed the qualifications of others who are competing for the same position. It is necessary to alert your boss about the false and inappropriate remarks. You need to call attention to your record and state that you resent the underhanded attack. Do it once, firmly, clearly, and briefly. It is best not to draw additional attention to the issue by spending an excessive amount of time defending yourself once you have countered the attack, as that would appear to give the accusation credibility.

CASE STUDY 4
A COLLISION COURSE: POWER SPACE
VS. JOB ELABORATION

Many women have a wide range of talents and are underemployed. In cooperating with others, women may inadvertently assume broader job responsibilities. However, this can be dangerous for both the woman and her manager, depending on the extent of the job elaboration or expansion of her work responsibilities above and beyond her job description. It can be fatal if she enters her manager's power space.

Jean, a well-organized, middle-aged administrative assistant, was happily married and loved her job in the advertising world. She had returned to work after her second child left for college. She had a flair for detail and could also quickly identify the implications of any proposed policy changes. When people had a question, they often discussed it with her rather than bother Al, her boss, a friendly but not too competent young man. Jean had tried to lighten his work load by attending to some of the problems herself without "bothering" him. When Jean started the job, she found Al very supportive and helpful. He seemed pleased that she learned so quickly and encouraged her to handle more and more of "the details" on her own. Of late, however, Al seemed to have changed. He was becoming more abrupt and not sharing as much information with her. This behavior seemed to have started when she corrected him about the needs of one of their more important clients at a staff meeting. Jean knew he was "mixed up" on the issue and thought she was helping him out, because his mistake could have had major financial implications for that account and the organization. Jean thought everything was going well until this puzzling change in Al's behavior occurred.

POWER SPACE: IS IT SACRED?

The problem is that Jean, unwittingly, had entered into Al's power space. The final blow occurred when she corrected him in front of the entire staff. Al began to recognize that Jean was making financial decisions for him that were far beyond her job responsibilities. In fact, she had done an excessive amount of job elaboration, often encouraged by Al to take on additional responsibilities. Now, he felt threatened by her competence and the power he had given her. At that point, Al had no choice except to limit her and reassert his power.

However, Al also liked the heavy work load she handled. He gave her the job assignments that he did not want to do, and then usually took credit for them in the cover letter. He always rewarded her with a very good evaluation, but when it came time for any significant salary increases or a promotion, they were not forthcoming. For a long time, the praise was enough, but as the work environment became more hostile, Jean realized that she was not getting the recognition she deserved or any tangible rewards for her hard work. The message given by the evaluations directly conflicted with the lack of tangible rewards for her work.

High performance evaluations for a woman do not mean that she will be tangibly rewarded.

JOB ELABORATION: IS THERE A PRICE FOR DOING MORE?

Jean is in a difficult position as an officially unrecognized, yet very competent, woman who has expanded her job responsibilities and now wants to get recognition and pay for her work. The complication is that Al cannot permit her to continue in the same status as much as he might like her to do so. Not only has she entered his power space, she has done so in front of the whole staff. She publicly embarrassed him, an unforgivable action, even though she was right and thought she was helping him.

Managers will defend their mistakes to the end if they are "corrected" in a public meeting, especially by a woman and one of their subordinates. That subordinate usually will continue to pay a high price for his or her mistake.

As unfortunate as it may be for both of them, Jean's best option may be to transfer to another area. She could ask Al for a discussion of the problems, which must include either trying to convince Al that she should have a promotion and increased responsibilities written into her job description or reducing the scope of her work if she maintains her present job, an option Jean would find difficult. Neither of these options would be completely satisfactory for either of them. Jean deserves a good recommendation from Al as she seeks a transfer, and, preferably, a promotion to another area, but Al might not give it to her. He has become too dependent on her and wants her to continue doing all the work she did before *and* to respect his power space. However, Jean has outgrown the job. She has also gained some of the political savvy necessary in the working world.

When a very skilled and competent woman is underemployed, job elaboration or an expansion of her work beyond the designated level of her job and her job description often occurs. The issue is not whether she can do the work and do it well, but whether she has a defined responsibility to do it, and can she get the recognition and pay for her work? It is very easy for a manager to encourage a willing, interested and competent employee to pick up an additional work load without fully realizing that it can cause serious problems. The more work Jean did, the more she was assigned.

> *A manager would rather be wrong than be corrected by a female subordinate.*

Al will have to increase his own work load considerably by picking up the more routine jobs he previously encouraged Jean to do. He will have to reassert his role as manager with his colleagues and staff. He is realizing that he practically gave his job to Jean.

Jean was disillusioned that her job turned out the way it did. Al had encouraged her to take on additional work but had done nothing to increase her salary or upgrade her classification in exchange. Jean mistakenly assumed he would be fair to her and that her work would "speak for itself."

When she corrected him at the meeting, she was surprised that he was so upset. She knew what he said was wrong. It slowly occurred to her that she should have spoken to him privately after the meeting, which would have allowed him to make his own correction. He would rather be wrong than be corrected by her in public.

SUMMARY

Many women are surprised to find that they are not necessarily rewarded for doing additional work. If you voluntarily assume additional job responsibilities, try to negotiate a change in your job description and a salary increase. If you are assigned excessive additional work on a regular basis, read your job description carefully. It may be necessary to change it to reflect the additional or changed responsibilities that you have been given, and delete others that are less desirable. Do not assume that you will automatically be rewarded for the extra work.

It is important to respect the power space of your manager. Whether they want to or not, managers cannot permit anyone into it beyond a certain point, or they lose their own power to manage and possibly their job.

CASE STUDY 5
THE PERILS OF RAPID ADVANCEMENT

When a young woman is promoted over older employees, especially older men, there are many built-in challenges that are not easily met. Her age and sex will be perceived negatively by her new staff and make it more difficult for her to gain their cooperation. In this situation a woman must be very sensitive to the working environment and search for ways to make it less hostile. However, there are some strategies that can be used to ease the situation.

Elizabeth, an intelligent and ambitious young woman in her late thirties, through hard work, ability, and a strong mentor, moved up the managerial ladder very quickly. After 5 years in the company, she became a director of a large department employing around 100 people, 75 men and 25 women. Jim, recently promoted to vice-president and her former director, is an older, conservative "company man." He has worked 30 years in the organization and is 6 years from retirement. He is a believer in the informal "old boy network" as a way to get things accomplished. He says that he does more work during a Saturday golf game than in a week at the office.

Elizabeth does not think that she was his first choice for the job. She recognizes that her sex, comparative youth and inexperience may be viewed by the men and women in her department as very negative, and knows that they will "test" her. She was not encouraged when she looked around the table at the first regional manager's meeting and found only White males looking back at her. She knows that she is expected to make several unpopular organizational and personnel changes as soon as possible for the health of her department. She hopes to accomplish them quickly in order to get the department moving again.

When Elizabeth sought the job, she recognized that it was a high-risk situation, especially for a young woman. However, she also recognized that it was a visible challenge and that important recognition would be given to anyone who could do the job successfully.

A HOSTILE ENVIRONMENT: CAN IT BE TURNED AROUND?

Elizabeth must be alert to the many opportunities as well as challenges in her new position. The problems of being a female manager in a male-dominated work environment pop up, usually when you least expect them and are least prepared to deal with them. Some will hold both Elizabeth's age and sex against her. Her speed of promotion, no matter how much she has earned it through competence and hard work, is another negative for her. She may be viewed stereotypically by most men, and many women as well, as being "too smart for a woman" and "not knowing her place." She will be perceived as "not having paid her dues." Her promotion, especially over older men who were bypassed, leads to a scenario full of problems. She will be resented, and her staff may find it emotionally difficult, if not impossible, to accept her as their manager. It is possible that certain employees will try, consciously or unconsciously, to sabotage her.

There are several creative approaches to the problems. The research on perceptual bias and communication will give her the basic information she needs to know: what is happening and what to expect. It will assist her in understanding that people do not recognize their own biases. Elizabeth might hope for more cooperation from the women, but she may not receive it. She will need to evaluate negative reactions thoughtfully and look for the cause. They could be based on:

1. Unconscious perceptual bias against a female manager
2. Purely emotional responses
3. Differences in male and female communication styles
4. Additional knowledge and data unknown to Elizabeth

Elizabeth can do little about her age and sex. She can dress conservatively. She will need to listen carefully and "make haste slowly." Her department will need time to become accustomed to the idea of a young woman stepping into the top position. She will have to prove herself to be tough enough to assert her power, handle difficult situations, establish her credibility—and at the same time, attend to the socioemotional needs of her group and, to some degree, conform to some female stereotypes.

A PRODUCTIVE WORK CLIMATE: HOW CAN IT BE DEVELOPED?

As Elizabeth starts her new position, she needs to have personal contact with as many of her staff as possible. One option is to have a series of small informal breakfasts and/or luncheons, with no more than eight carefully selected people attending. With a limit of eight people, no one can avoid direct eye contact with her. The small numbers also will generate more information and discussion. It may be time-consuming, but the time and effort should be worthwhile.

These small groups would provide an opportunity for her to introduce herself and to listen to any staff concerns. Also, she could seek information and suggestions for solving some of the current work problems, as well as presenting her goals and objectives for the department. The small group meetings would allow Elizabeth to integrate both task and socioemotional objectives. She should not establish an advisory committee because she may not wish to take its advice, which could create a serious problem, especially in the first year.

> Do not establish an advisory committee unless you are prepared to take their advice.

COMMUNICATION: WHAT ARE THEY REALLY SAYING?

Elizabeth needs to be aware of the messages that her colleagues send her, both verbally and nonverbally. She should seek the underlying message when she is told that something cannot be done. There may be more than one reason. Is it that:

1. They do not want to?
2. They do not know how to?
3. They do not see the purpose or value in doing it?
4. They do not accept her as manager?
5. They do not think she really knows what is going on?
6. They do not trust her judgment?

Elizabeth must remember that there may well be valid reasons. She will need to ask for the facts, evaluate them, and then make a decision. She may need to acknowledge that she may not have communicated the reason for the change as carefully as she needed to. She will need to watch for passive aggression. When people are in a subordinate position and unable to act out their anger, they can place many obstacles in the way to sabotage what their boss is attempting to do.

MAKING CHANGES: WHY ARE THEY ALWAYS DIFFICULT?

The staff had become very comfortable in a relaxed environment and did not want any "change in pace" made, especially by a young, hardworking woman. They will strongly resist any change unless it is to their advantage to accept it. If Elizabeth can develop a win–win strategy to get the department moving, half of the job will be done. Of course, she may need to use both a carrot and a stick to accomplish her goal.

Elizabeth has a reputation of cutting through to the heart of the problem and moving quickly ahead. Although she will find it difficult to slow down enough to bring her colleagues along with her, their support is necessary to accomplish any job. She will have to understand that few people can "see" things as quickly as she can. If she moves too quickly ahead in making changes, even if they were necessary, the changes will probably not be successful because her staff may not work to make them succeed.

It may be difficult to develop support for much change, but the most successful and lasting long-term changes endure because they were based on understanding the need for the change. The best ideas incorporate diverse viewpoints. Many options need to be considered, and the proposal refined to meet most, if not all, objections. Also, Elizabeth will need to build coalitions within and without her department to make some of the desired and necessary changes.

THE OLD BOY NETWORK: CAN A WOMAN WORK WITH IT?

With the encouragement and support of the former manager, now their new vice-president, the old boy network was operating in high gear. The problem for Elizabeth is that it was operating without her and around her. Knowing it would be almost impossible to penetrate, Elizabeth realized that she had to counter it. She consciously started to develop new written procedures in her area related to decision making and policy. She decided that any decision in her department needed to be confirmed in writing before it was reworded or reinterpreted on the golf course. The golf game provided an opportunity for some of her senior men to go directly to the vice-president without her knowledge, much less her approval. Her staff knew information before she did that directly related to her area. Knowing it had to be stopped, she did two things.

She met with Joe, her vice-president, and requested that a weekly meeting be set every Friday afternoon to exchange any relevant information, especially that which she needed to know. The meeting provided an important opportunity for her to communicate with him directly to give him an up-to-date picture of her area without that information being filtered through a subordinate's perception on the golf course. She could then identify what decisions were made during the golf game. If decisions continued to be made on the golf course, she would have to ask Joe on what basis they were made. She would need to make it clear that she must be included in the discussion before a decision was made or a policy reinterpreted that affected her area.

In addition, Elizabeth made it very clear to those working for her that they worked directly for her. They were to inform her first of any information or proposed decision. Also, any information to the vice-president must flow directly through her, not around her. She realized that this was a sensitive issue that might be easily circumvented.

Of course, one way to deal with the old boy network is to try to penetrate it, but that is often almost impossible for a woman to do, even if she learned to play golf. A second option is to establish a collaborative relationship with a member of the network, one who could be trusted to keep her fully and accurately informed, and to represent her thinking and interests at the golf game. A third option is for Elizabeth to discuss with Joe the unnecessary work problems caused by poor communication (the old boy network). She would need to have some suggestions available and emphasize their necessity in order for her to do her job properly (getting the work done and making Joe look good). If she could devise a win–win strategy that would make a positive and discernable difference for Joe, she might be successful.

Such a strategy might be an informal Friday or Monday breakfast or luncheon including all managers and featuring Joe. Another might be a 1-day retreat to discuss policy and procedures. If Elizabeth could demonstrate that her presence resulted in better decisions and that she did not threaten the "old boys" by her approach, she would have a better chance of being included.

MEETINGS AND SEXIST JOKES: WHEN THE JOKE IS ON YOU!

As Elizabeth looked around the regional manager's staff meeting and saw that only males were in the senior positions looking back at her, she knew there would be additional problems. From experience and knowing the research on women, she was not surprised when she heard the usual sexist and off-color jokes. She also knew that they expressed the men's anxiety, anger, and resentment. However, such jokes were still a socially acceptable way, in that organization, for men who felt threatened by a competent woman to "put her down" or control her. As the only woman there, she knew that they were testing her and that everyone would be watching her reaction.

When Elizabeth heard the first "dirty" joke, she decided not to laugh with the "boys" or even smile. When the second joke was told and they waited for her reaction, she said, "I must not have heard you clearly. Would you please repeat it?" Somehow, it does not sound quite as funny the second time. After the third joke, she said, "I didn't understand the joke. Would you please explain it?" It can be very uncomfortable to explain a sexist joke to a woman, especially if it is an offensive one. Sexist jokes can be a difficult situation to handle when there is no other woman to support you, but many times a man will become supportive and fewer jokes are told. Eventually, as they come to know you as a person, and the level of anxiety, anger, and resentment is reduced, sexist jokes are seldom told. However, if a man is really out to get you, that is a weapon he might use. Recognize it for what it is!

> As your male colleagues come to know you as a person, and their level of anxiety, anger and resentment is reduced, hostile humor is seldom used.

MEETINGS AND INTERRUPTIONS: WHAT IS A SAVVY APPROACH?

At the regional managers' meetings, the interruptions started occurring as Elizabeth anticipated. She was aware that her colleagues were seldom conscious that she was usually interrupted before she could finish expressing her idea. However, she tried not to take the interruptions personally. Elizabeth remembered that she needed three other managers at the meeting to form the critical mass for a mutual support system in order to stop the constant interruptions.

SUMMARY

When a young woman receives a fast promotion to a high level position over men and women, it presents a very challenging work situation. Her age, sex, and the resulting work environment present significant challenges. Although there are problems that can be anticipated and strategies developed in advance to deal with them, not all of them are easily identified. It is very difficult to survive in a hostile work climate. It is even more difficult to make the necessary changes to turn it around. Elizabeth has an especially difficult situation with her vice-president and his use of the old boy network. It is crucial that Elizabeth develop some sort of a support network, including external contacts. This work environment requires a woman to have a lot of savvy, time, patience, and understanding to be successful. After all the options have been tried and have failed, and when there is no improvement in such a hostile environment, the only solution may be to change jobs.

CASE STUDY 6
SEXUAL HARASSMENT,
THE UNWANTED ATTENTION

Sexual harassment is an increasingly common problem for working women. It is against the law, and women do not have to endure it. Because men hold most of the power positions, there are many more opportunities for them to sexually harass their subordinates, who are usually women. There are many reasons why women do not report sexual harassment. However, women need to tell someone who can help them. Sexual harassment does not stop of its own accord.

> Sexual harassment does not stop by itself.

Barbara, a short, stocky, single woman of indeterminate age, who habitually wore polyester pantsuits, started work in the laboratory of Tom, a bald, middle-aged, married researcher. She proved to be very good at her job until there was a subtle change in the working climate. Tom replaced the picture of his sailboat in his office with a large photograph of a nude woman. Barbara had short daily meetings with him in his office and found the picture very disturbing, making it hard for her to concentrate. As Tom got to know her better, he started telling sexual jokes, which she did not wish to hear. One day he asked her to work late to finish a project. When they were alone in the building, he put his arms around her, drawing her close, and tried to kiss her. She became frightened. It became even worse when he suggested that they adjourn to his apartment to complete the finishing touches on their project. Barbara knew that his wife and children had left for their summer home at the shore. She found an excuse and left the laboratory immediately, but she was seriously worried about what might happen in the future.

Barbara was very upset and unable to do much work. She had liked working for Tom but was now afraid of him. She felt guilty and wondered what she had done to encourage him to make such sexual advances. As the sole support of herself and her aged mother, she desperately needed the job and she was afraid to tell Tom to stop sexually harassing her. She dreaded going to work each day and her health began to deteriorate. She kept hoping that the sexual harassment would stop, but it not only continued, it became worse. Although she knew it was illegal, she did not report it to her director because she thought no one would believe her and nothing would be done about it.

VICTIMS OF SEXUAL HARASSMENT: CAN THEY STOP IT?

Different people experience sexual harassment differently. People need a variety of options, both formal and informal, to resolve complaints, and in fact varied channels appear needed to even bring forth the complaint (Rowe, in press). Many people may not pursue a complaint because they believe they have insufficient evidence, or they may be unwilling to accept the additional stress involved. Given the increasing diversity in the workforce, flexibility is needed in resolving such concerns (Rowe, 1990).

Tom's behavior has created a major problem for Barbara. He created a poor working climate with the nude photograph and dirty jokes that disturbed her. These are common forms of sexual harassment. His unwanted physical advances to his subordinate are also sexual harassment. All are illegal. Tom was using his power position to illegally intimidate a woman employee.

There was no reason for Barbara to feel guilty. It was a power play for Tom, not a romantic interlude. The solution starts with Barbara taking some control and refusing to continue playing the "victim." She will need to keep a detailed chronologue, documenting dates, times, how his sexual advances made her feel, and a description of his sexually harassing activities. She needs to stop laughing nervously at his dirty jokes and to tell him clearly that she does not appreciate them. As soon as he starts, she must request that he stop. She must also request that he remove the photograph of the nude woman, as she finds it offensive. Barbara has a legal right to a working environment free from such harassment. If Tom refuses to take the picture down, she can insist that their meetings be conducted in the laboratory instead of his office and report his refusal to the director. She must take a photograph of the nude picture in Tom's office for future documentation.

Barbara needs to tell other people what is happening. A check with Tom's former technician to see if the same thing happened to her might prove productive. Barbara had read that women often leave a good job rather than confront or report sexual harassment. If a pattern of sexual harassment by Tom was established, Barbara's story would have greater credibility. Barbara knew Tom's behavior was illegal, but she did not know how to handle it. Her self-esteem was diminishing each day.

This classic case of sexual harassment toward a vulnerable, unattractive woman who needs the job is typical. Barbara was afraid to report it because she thought:

1. She would suffer retaliation from her boss.
2. People would think she asked for it.
3. People might think that she misread the intentions of her boss.
4. She would be blamed for the behavior of her boss.
5. No one would believe her.
6. Nothing would be done.
7. She might lose her job.

Although telling someone might be uncomfortable for Barbara, the risks involved are frequently smaller than most people imagine, especially when compared to the prospect of silently accepting and dealing with demeaning harassment alone. It is important to discuss the situation with a person who can help you.

Sexual harassment includes any unwanted sexual attention or conduct such as:

1. Staring, leering, and ogling
2. Sexual teasing, jokes, and gestures
3. Continuing to ask for dates after being told they are unwanted
4. Sexually demeaning comments or pictures
5. Inappropriate touching, pinching, and assault
6. Attempts to kiss or fondle
7. Pressure for sex
8. Suggestions that sex can be exchanged for raises and promotions.

Does a woman have any options about what she can do? Barbara could:

1. Say no. She should have told Tom that his advances were unwanted and that she wanted them stopped.
2. Do something about it immediately. She needed to pay attention to the cues or comments that indicated harassment. If Tom's earlier behavior made her uncomfortable, she should have said so.
3. Know her rights. Sexual harassment is a violation of federal law. She needs to know her organization's sexual harassment policies and procedures.
4. Keep a diary. If the harassment continues, she should keep track of dates, times, and places as well as statements about how she felt, possible witnesses, and any relevant documentation, including the photograph of the nude picture in his office. Such information can support a complaint.
5. Talk to others. She should discuss the situation with co-workers and ask them whether they also have been harassed, because incidents of harassment are often not isolated; sexual harassers are likely to exhibit a pattern of such behavior. A co-worker can watch for any sexual harassment and serve as a possible witness.
6. Write a letter to Tom expressing how she felt and tell him to stop it. The letter should be dated, and a carbon copy kept. This letter could serve as documentation, if needed.
7. Report Tom's behavior to his director or to the person in the organization who is designated to deal with sexual harassment. If that is not effective, she should go to the local or state human rights commission.
8. Request a transfer to another laboratory or department.

SUMMARY

Sexual harassment remains a serious problem for many women in the workplace. It can be a devastating experience and one that does not go away. The price of not taking any action and remaining a "victim" is very high. It is important for a woman to know the legal definition of sexual harassment, her legal rights, the organization's policy, and how it needs to be reported and documented. There is no win–win solution in this issue. What is necessary is to stop the harassment. Although retaliation by Barbara's employer is illegal and needs to be reported, she should expect that she may need to change jobs with the help of her employer. Barbara may want to request a transfer to another laboratory.

CONCLUSION

This chapter presented a realistic, pragmatic approach to the invisible problems that women working in organizations experience. These case studies represent the application of research findings and experience to some of the very real issues confronting working women. One goal of the case studies is to show that women can take some control of their lives. Second, they demonstrate that there are a variety of options from which to choose in resolving a problem.

However, there is a risk that accompanies every option, including the decision to do nothing. The risk must be assessed and the rewards must be worth the effort and possible pain. Before a choice is made from the range of options, it is important to collect all the relevant information available in order to have the best basis for your decision. Knowing the research on sex discrimination that explains what is happening and why it is happening is essential to developing effective strategies to resolve the problem. Such knowledge can make a significant difference in solving a problem.

The belief, conscious or unconscious, in society's stereotypical perspectives of what is appropriate behavior for men and for women must be anticipated in others. It can be difficult to see aggressive and task-oriented behavior rewarded when it is done by a man and penalized when done by a woman. Even though the situation might call for such stereotypical "male" behavior, usually both men and women perceive such behavior as inappropriate for a woman. The long-term solution is to educate everyone about the continuing influence of gender stereotypes and their effects. Meanwhile, however, it is very helpful to understand the basis of what is happening. The win–win strategy is one of the best tools for accomplishing a goal and overcoming the limitations of perceptual bias.

9

Overcoming the Barriers to Career Success: Summary and Conclusion

This chapter presents a pragmatic, positive approach to some of the basic issues faced by women who work in organizations. This constructive approach is based on both research and experience and summarizes the main themes of the book. It first reviews the influence and power of sexism over all women and men and then presents a series of questions to help identify possible sex discrimination in your job situation. Their purpose is to alert you to discrimination that may be unrecognized. The questions may also help explain puzzling situations at work. Finally, the chapter describes how men and women can enhance their career success and what they can do about discrimination, including a number of ways to empower themselves. The three sections together summarize the problems and solutions presented throughout the book.

SEXISM: WHAT DOES IT MEAN TO YOU?

Although sexism still exists, it is not necessarily deliberate. Most people are not even conscious of it. Sexism influences the thinking and behavior of *both men and women*, and results in discrimination against women. Women discriminate against other women, and women discriminate against themselves. *Everyone* discriminates against women.

> Everyone *discriminates against women.*

Sexism creates *perceptual bias*, the automatic distortion of perception to match unconscious stereotyped beliefs and expectations, and perceptual bias causes discrimination. The stereotypes that women are less competent and *should be* subordinate and deferential to men are powerful because they operate as expectations—as both facts and values—and because they are consensual in society. The research discussed throughout this book documents discrimination against women in organizations. Women are less likely to be hired than equally qualified men. When women are hired, they are given lower-level jobs, more routine work, fewer opportunities, lesser resources, less power—and lower salaries. When, despite these disadvantages, they perform as well as men, their work is seen and evaluated as lower in quality or importance, and they advance more slowly, if at all. In everyday encounters and small groups, women are treated as unimportant. Their ideas are interrupted, unheard, or discounted, and their speech and communication styles are devalued. Their abilities and potential as leaders and managers are not recognized.

Do Women Discriminate Against Themselves? Subconsciously, women discriminate against themselves, not recognizing that they are doing so. For example, many women may say that they could not possibly succeed in some particular academic course, for any number of reasons. Yet their academic record clearly indicates that they are fully capable of succeeding in that course. In fact, they are discounting their own abilities. It is important to distinguish between self-discrimination and accurate assessment, especially in the work environment. A woman may not always have the education, background, skills or experience required for a particular position, but that would not stop many men, who often overestimate their abilities. Before a woman limits herself in any way, she should carefully review all aspects of the situation and ask if she is discriminating against herself by inflating her limitations and failing to recognize and acknowledge her abilities. It is important to review the objective information, both positive and negative, about other candidates very carefully. Women need to keep in mind that they may "lose" by being "too accurate and objective," which may result in underestimating their qualifications and abilities.

WHICH KIND OF SEXISM: INDIVIDUAL OR ORGANIZATIONAL?

Two kinds of sexism exist. It can be found on an individual level as well as being systemic in the organization. Individual sexism is discrimination, exploitation, or domination of women by an individual or group of individuals, conscious or unconscious, intentional or unintentional. In an organization, sexism often masquerades as "professional judgment," which cannot be

Sexism often masquerades as "professional judgment."

countered, disproved, or even identified as sexism. Organizational or systemic sexism involves policies and procedures resulting in discrimination against women. Such discrimination is often not recognized. For example, organizations may have many more male than female managers, even though many women have the necessary skills. Systemic discrimination is also reflected in entire professions that are predominately female, such as teaching, or male, such as medicine.

It is important to identify which type of sexism is present in a specific instance, and it may be both individual and systemic. Because sexist attitudes and practices were woven into the fabric of our culture, they are naturally built into organizational structures. It is an unusual organization that does not discriminate against women in some way. Systemic discrimination is difficult to recognize, because we have lived with it all our lives. Politically astute women often discover instances of systemic discrimination even after years on the job. It is very difficult to identify specifically and even more difficult to change. Upfront personal discrimination is the easiest to recognize. However, most personal discrimination is invisible, to the perpetrator as well as the victim, and that is when it is most destructive, especially to a woman's self-esteem. Understanding the research on sexism and sex discrimination is the first step to identifying basic problems. Empowering yourself, and dealing with sexism constructively, is the first step to any solution.

QUESTIONS THAT NEED TO BE ASKED

Savvy men and women who want to ensure maximum utilization of their own and other employees' abilities, as well as fairness, will continually monitor their work situations for indicators of sex discrimination. This is especially necessary when events keep happening that do not appear to be based on facts or reason. Depending on the situation, your sex, and your role, you can ask yourself one or more of the following questions:

Managers' perceptions of women shape how they will be treated and how they will perform.

1. **What is the central theme or schema of your impressions and thoughts about women colleagues?** When you first see a new woman in your area, is your first thought of her sexual attractiveness? Do you see her as the solution to getting all the routine jobs done? Or do you wonder what ideas and expertise she might contribute to the group's major tasks and problems? The central theme or schema of your private impressions and thoughts influences how you will see her,

how you will treat her, your expectations for her, and how you will evaluate her contributions. In turn, your expectations and how you treat her will shape how she will behave and how she will perform. Notice that the first two themes above represent schemas that are irrelevant to her professional assignment, and detrimental to her performance and to your ability to interact with her professionally. Women should be viewed as professional colleagues.

2. **Do you expect the women you encounter at work to behave professionally, but then find yourself feeling annoyed or affronted, feeling that the woman has been domineering, arrogant, or "uppity," when she fails to act in a "feminine" manner?** Nearly everyone who has dealt with women in organizations has had this experience. It is hard to recognize that we all, men and women alike, have expectations for women that are directly contradictory. Consciously, we expect women to behave professionally, but because professional behavior has traditionally—and erroneously—been defined as "masculine," when women do behave professionally we feel it is inappropriate for them. On the other hand, when women conform to "feminine" expectations, we see them as "unprofessional" and either ignore or discount them.

3. **Do you sometimes find yourself searching for legitimate facts to justify a hiring, promotion, or evaluation decision?** If the decision benefits a man and disadvantages a women, the fact that you then have to search for legitimate reasons to justify it may indicate that unconscious gender stereotypes actually determined the decision. Go back and list *all* the objective facts about both candidates. It might be interesting to weigh the facts that support the opposite decision, and then compare them to those that support your original decision.

4. **Are the rules and policies strictly enforced for women but not for men?** For example, if a woman takes time off to transact some personal business, is she required to take a vacation day, or can she take compensatory time for the overtime she works? Did her colleague Ron have to take a vacation day when he had a similar need? Is a woman reprimanded when her report is completed a day late, when Joe's work is 4 days late and accepted without comment or penalty? (He must have had "other important things to do.")

5. **Are women continually assigned the routine, unrewarded stereotypical work "appropriate for women?"** Are women the only ones in their area expected to do some of their own typing or answer telephones during the lunch hour, when male colleagues are excused from the low-profile jobs and go out to lunch together? When colleagues need help to finish a job, do they always automatically expect a woman to assist them and then give her no credit for the

work? The unconscious assumption that only women need to do "women's work" is still prevalent in many organizations. It keeps women "in their place" and prevents them from competing professionally with men.

6. **Do women have salary equity with male colleagues?** This is often difficult to discover. However, if men receive the higher profile challenging work, it can be expected that they would be appropriately rewarded. But even if women and men do the *same* work, men may still be paid more.

7. **Are women promoted as fast and as far up the ranks as men?** If women hold 40% of the entry level positions, then, if there is no sex discrimination, 4 out of every 10 managers should also be women at all of the higher levels, all the way to the top. The underrepresentation of women at high ranks is the glass ceiling effect. It is partly a result of perceptual bias— "seeing" the abilities and performance of women as inferior to identical abilities and performance by men—and partly the result of past patterns of employment, conscious sex discrimination, and other factors.

8. **Are women frequently interrupted by male colleagues at meetings before they complete their question, comments, or presentation? Are women's ideas ignored?** Has a male colleague made the same suggestion 20 minutes later, and has everyone thought it an important new concept? These things happen, not because women might have soft voices, but because their colleagues consider what a woman thinks or says less important than what a man thinks or says.

9. **When a woman does manage to speak in a group, do other participants frown, scowl, or look displeased, compared to looking pleased when a man speaks?** These subtle, fleeting facial expressions may not indicate that they dislike her idea, but that, unconsciously, they do not expect a woman to offer substantive contributions. However, other participants who also see the disapproving facial expressions will interpret them as indicating that her contribution was poor in quality. As a result, the woman will be discredited and discouraged, and the group will lose a valuable idea. Are you aware of other subtle differences in how men and women are treated? Men sometimes distance themselves from a female co-worker by turning their face or body away from her. This deprives the woman of the feedback signals that all co-workers need for cooperation and maximum effectiveness. In addition, women are often addressed or given assignments in ways that imply lesser competence or lower status. This treatment leads them to confirm the implicit expectations, with a resulting decrease in their own and their unit's productivity.

10. **Are you aware of subtle verbal and nonverbal communi-**

cation differences between men and women? For example, women smile more than men, and this is viewed as a sign of deference. Men frequently speak louder, and this is recognized as part of an aggressive communicative style. Perceptions of the same nonverbal communicative behavior may be interpreted differently. When men's vocal quality is throaty, they are perceived as more mature and well-adjusted, whereas women are viewed as naive, neurotic and less intelligent. Do you use tag questions at the end of statements? It's hard not to do, isn't it?

11. **Does the manager introduce male visitors, job candidates, or new hires with praise and a personal endorsement, but introduce female visitors, job candidates, or new hires with only perfunctory facts?** An authority figure's praise or personal endorsement raises the perceived value of identical ideas or performances.

12. **Are sexist jokes told at staff meetings?** Although all the men laugh, the purpose of such jokes is to "put women down" or "keep them in their place." They can be very successful in doing so if they are permitted to continue. Jokes, hostile humor, and laughter are often used when men feel insecure or threatened by a competent woman. The best way to deal with hostile humor involves a series of actions. In response to the first hostile joke, say nothing but do not laugh. In response to the second, ask the person who told it to repeat it because you are not sure you heard it correctly. In response to the third, ask the joke teller to explain the joke. This makes the teller very uncomfortable and conveys the offensiveness of such jokes to everyone present.

13. **Does a male colleague continually bump into a woman or drape his arm around her shoulders when she does not want him to?** This behavior is not based on sexual desire but is a personal power play to control or intimidate the woman. It is best for the woman to tell him tactfully the first time to stop immediately. If a second time is required, it is necessary to tell him less tactfully and very clearly to stop it before it progresses to a more dangerous level. Such behavior does not stop by itself, as much as we wish or hope it would.

14. **How is evidence or data interpreted? For approximately equally good reports, is a woman's work criticized for minor mistakes and the substance ignored and a man's work praised for the substance and minor mistakes ignored? Is a woman's work always found wanting no matter how good it is?** This issue of perceptual bias is difficult for both men and women to handle. Women begin to doubt their own competence. It is difficult to fight the power of consensus alone on such an issue. For a fairer evaluation of the work, a blind evaluation by a third person could be helpful.

15. **Are women's travel or training requests rejected because their work is "so important" that the organization could not**

spare them? Are they rejected because the departmental budget is tight? Or do women not even request funding support for professional conferences because they think there is no travel money? Were you surprised when Phillip decided he wanted to go, and, even though he was not on the program, the manager found the funds? In some organizations, the travel money is equally divided. In others, it is allocated at the discretion of the manager. Under the latter arrangement, women usually receive less than their male colleagues. However, unless a request is made, travel or training support is seldom received.

16. **Were you surprised that a male colleague was not reprimanded for greatly overspending his budget for his latest project and was complimented for the fine results, when a female colleague kept within her budget and still produced an equally good result but received no commendation?** Again, unconscious perceptual bias by both men and women is the source of this unequal treatment. It is important to recognize the basis of the problem before you begin to believe that Ellen's work really is not as good as Ethan's, even though you know it is as good or better.

17. **Have women been receiving consistently high job evaluations and praise for their work from their manager, but no corresponding salary increases?** Often women are rewarded with praise and high employee evaluations. Men are rewarded with salary increases.

18. **Have you wondered why some people are evaluated so much higher than others? Is the evaluation instrument full of subjective personal opinions disguised as seemingly objective appraisals?** Women almost always benefit when evaluations are based on as much objective data (specific concrete facts) as possible, with the objective questions the same for everyone. When evaluations require interpretation (*"How* important was the project?" "Are three major successes worth an 'Excellent'—or just a 'Very Good'?"), perceptual bias takes over.

19. **Is there really a risk for a woman in being the only woman in an area? Or working in an organization with few if any women in high-level positions?** For women who plan to progress in their careers, these are serious drawbacks. When organizational colleagues are not used to seeing or working with women in high-level positions who have power in their own right, the stereotypes concerning women are still firmly embedded. Everything a woman does or does not do will be noticed, commented upon, often resented, and usually devalued, consciously or unconsciously. Meetings will be sprinkled with sexist jokes, and she will be constantly interrupted. Men will seek and use subtle ways to "put her in her place." Some women feel that "it is

better to be on the bus than to miss it altogether," even if it means a token job. The opportunity may be valuable for their careers, if there is something important to learn in that job and they do not plan to stay very long. The chances that they will be allowed to move toward the top in such an organization are small.

COUNTERACTING SEX DISCRIMINATION: STEPS TOWARD SOLUTIONS

An early step in dealing with discrimination is to empower yourself in appropriate ways. It is important for women to have a proactive or assertive approach and not be a "victim." For both men and women, it is necessary to take some control over your professional life. Of course, no one working in an organization is free of all external control. However, you can control your perception and your attitude toward your work. A problem can be viewed as an opportunity. More importantly, taking some control over your life influences how you feel about yourself and how you act. A positive attitude does not suggest failure, but a consistently negative one is usually a self-fulfilling prophecy. It is vital to anticipate problems and to look for answers and solutions in advance rather than only react to the actions of others. The proactive strategy communicates to others that you are seeking solutions, not just complaining or being difficult.

A problem can be viewed as an opportunity.

The only way to empower yourself permanently is to do it yourself. Others, such as a mentor, can assist you, but no matter how much you may wish it, no one else can do it for you. If someone else empowers you, that same individual can take that power away. Another danger is that, when you are empowered by others, they may have ulterior motives and may try to manipulate you in the future. You will be in debt to them and they will expect to "collect" on that debt. A person who has empowered himself or herself is more likely to be granted the situational power required for successful job performance.

We emphasize that no one approach will "cure" the problems caused by sexism. Rather, as many approaches as possible should be used simultaneously. We also emphasize that the process of reducing sex discrimination is slow—to be evaluated over years, not over weeks or months. Sexist attitudes, perceptions, and behavior have been learned and practiced over everyone's entire lifetime. They can be unlearned, but it takes time, effort, and practice. The following suggestions offer

(a) strategies to counteract and reduce sexism in an organization, (b) strategies to cope with existing sexism, and (c) general strategies to enhance the career success of any organizational member. Many of the suggestions fall into two or all three categories. Together, they summarize and integrate the solutions suggested throughout the book.

1. Understand the Process of Sexism and Sex Discrimination
2. Increase the Number of Female Authority Role Models
3. Educate Your Colleagues
4. Support Women At All Levels
5. Collaborate With Others
6. Understand the Organizational Culture
7. Understand the Organizational Structure and Goals
8. Establish Credibility
9. Participate Actively
10. Deal With the Double Bind of the "Damned If She Does, Damned If She Doesn't" Dilemma
11. Handle Criticism
12. Avoid the Emotional Label
13. Know When and How to Negotiate
14. Develop a Range of Communication and Power Styles
15. Analyze Before Acting
16. Assume Power
17. Develop Networks
18. Take Calculated Risks
19. Develop Self-Confidence
20. Persist
21. Recognize the Bottom Line

UNDERSTAND THE PROCESS OF SEXISM AND SEX DISCRIMINATION

"Knowledge is empowering." This version of a familiar saying relates directly to knowing the research on sex discrimination and perceptual bias. When you understand the causes of sexism, how it works, and how it influences all aspects of your professional and personal life, you will be better equipped to develop constructive strategies to deal with it. First, such knowledge helps to identify and clarify the problem. If women do not understand why men often have larger expense accounts, go to more professional meetings (while they have to "mind the store"), or are usually advanced over women even when the women are equally or more qualified and experienced, it is only natural for women to internalize failure and blame themselves. It is much harder to identify the true culprit as subtle sex discrimination. After a discussion of these issues, working women have often said to us, "So that is what has been happening. I feel much better knowing it is not just me."

Knowledge of the research can free women from blaming themselves when things go wrong and from not taking credit for their successes. If you watch carefully, men do just the opposite. Men blame luck or the situation when things go wrong, and take personal credit when things turn out well. It can be very interesting to keep a tally by sex to see how different the factors are to which men and women attribute their successes and failures.

Also, knowing that the problems that result from sex discrimination and perceptual bias happen to many women can make an enormous difference in a woman's own self-image and self-esteem. Understanding that the problem may not be just herself or her behavior is important. The impact of sexism is felt by all women. It is not always identified or expressed in the same way, but the result is always the same.

INCREASE THE NUMBER OF FEMALE AUTHORITY ROLE MODELS

The most effective way to counteract sexism is to increase the number of visible female authority role models in the work situation—from the board of directors on down through the ranks. First, female authority role models break the stereotypes. Authority positions require behavior that is competent, assertive, rational, objective, independent, decisive, ambitious, and leaderlike. In fulfilling their responsibilities, female authorities disconfirm the subordinate-status characteristics that have traditionally been labeled as "feminine." Second, the presence of multiple female authorities makes them familiar and dispels the anxiety of dealing with the unknown and unpredictable. Third, female authorities reduce or eliminate perceptual bias. Evaluators of both sexes suddenly recognize and acknowledge the actual quality of women's performances and achievements. Fourth, by breaking the stereotypes, female authorities enhance other women's behavioral effectiveness. Women increase their career ambition, their self-confidence and independence of judgment, and their participation rates in group discussions. The female authorities do not have to be known personally, nor do they have to demonstrate the particular skills or behavior relevant to particular women's jobs. They simply have to be visible and be visibly treated as authorities by others.

The multiple female authority role model strategy is the most effective solution to sexism because it works automatically, without visible pressure or implications of blame, but it is probably the most difficult to achieve. The same unconscious stereotypes that hold all women back also make it difficult to get and keep women in authority positions. Women who would serve as role models must first be hired or promoted, and then they must be supported: They must be given real power, resources, authority, respect, and wholehearted cooperation; they must be listened to and their ideas taken seriously. Achieving these conditions requires constant awareness, alertness, and monitoring.

The multiple female role model strategy is the most effective solution to sexism because it works automatically, without visible pressure or implications of blame.

Individual Action. Individuals, both men and women, who themselves hold positions of authority can recruit and support competent women for authority positions over which they themselves hold power or influence. For example, a department director can recruit and support competent women as managers of his or her various operating units.

Group Action. Individuals who do not hold authority positions can form alliances, preferably including some people with influence, and present a group recommendation for more female authorities to those who have the power to implement it. The recommendation will be more effective if it is backed up with facts—the inequity and loss of productivity caused by the failure to recognize and advance competent women. The recommendation may have to be presented to a number of power figures in the organization, and it may have to be presented a number of times, formally and informally and in different ways. A key factor in the success of this strategy is the number of people included in the alliance and representation of as many different areas in the unit or organization as possible. This strategy represents a positive use of the power of consensus.

EDUCATE YOUR COLLEAGUES

Educating the people with whom you work is the next best way to change "what has been" to "what should be." Rarely are men and most women even aware of what is happening until the data are compiled and interpreted from a broader perspective, one that includes and identifies women.

How can managers and colleagues be educated, especially if they are not interested? There is no denying that education is a long-term project. Many factors enter into such a situation, and no one way always works. It usually takes many different strategies. Factors that must be considered include your age, seniority, established credibility, status, and rank in the organization, your positive or negative interpersonal interaction with others, the quality and quantity of your data, your personal persuasiveness, and the number and influence of your allies.

Formal Strategies. One type of formal strategy involves persuading the management to authorize or mandate collecting comparative data and presenting the results of the comparison to the top management. For example, one organization with highly educated and aware top leadership established a standing salary equity review committee. Every 2 years, salaries of women below those of men comparable in status, experience, and productivity were raised to maintain equity. Individuals can also collect different types of data. In another organization, a senior woman who sat on the committee to evaluate junior executives suspected that perceptual bias was influencing the committee's interpretation of the objective data. She kept a record listing individuals' specific accomplishments and the ratings they received. Then when a woman came up for evaluation and the committee members expressed doubts about her effectiveness, the senior woman could point out to them that, last year, Albert had been rated an enthusiastic "excellent" for the same objective evidence, and that the year before, Steve had been encouraged with a "very good" on even poorer evidence.

A second type of formal educational strategy is to hold workshops for key organizational members, preferably from the top down, to discuss the issues of perceptual bias and sex discrimination. This strategy requires the authorization and support of top management to ensure attendance at the workshops and serious attention to their content. The workshop discussions can be led by two or three organizational members or by invited outside experts. The higher the leaders' status, established credibility, topic expertise, articulateness, and tactful assertiveness, the more effective the workshops will be. About a week before the meeting, it is helpful to send each workshop participant some brief educational materials such as the pamphlet *Seeing and Evaluating People* (Geis, Carter, & Butler, 1986) as background and to serve as a discussion guide. Each workshop session should include no more than six to eight participants. Small groups encourage everyone to participate. People are more likely to remember what they themselves have said than what they have only read. (But they need to do the brief reading first, to learn what the problem is and what to say about it at the meeting.)

Informal Strategies. Effective education can also occur informally. A female university professor who habitually wore pantsuits to work was asked by a male colleague, in front of others, "Jessica, why don't you wear skirts sometimes, so we can see your legs?" (This is a blatant example of attempting to enforce the value or "should" component of stereotypes.) Jessica immediately replied, as if good naturedly, "Tell y' what, Maury, you wear a skirt tomorrow, so I can see your legs, and I'll wear one the next day so you can see mine." Everyone in the group got educated.

In a research laboratory, a male guest speaker, presenting his research on male rats' mating behavior to the assembled researchers, used mildly crude sexual language. Then he apologized to the "ladies" present, thereby isolating them and treating them as females, not as professional colleagues. A senior woman interrupted him: "Stanley, I think you can assume that people with similar professional background and training have similar standards and tolerances." Again, everyone got educated. Note that interrupting a formal presentation in this way requires a certain amount of age, seniority, established acceptance among colleagues, and personal assertiveness.

In a university, a woman faculty member was discussing sexism in the department with a sexist male colleague when he confided that he could not help noticing female undergraduates' attractiveness and having sexual fantasies about them. The woman replied, "That's okay, Harry, as long as you follow each one with a second fantasy that the woman is our department chair evaluating your work and setting your next year's salary." Note that sexual fantasies are not "okay." They create a sexual schema in the fantasizer's mind rather than the appropriate task-focused schema. However, sometimes small gains are better than no gains.

These informal educational efforts need to be repeated, often over and over, with the same people in different situations, as long as they are needed. The best strategy, when you have time to think in advance, is to devise a win–win solution where both of you gain something that you want, and which also includes an educational component. For example, at yet another university, high-level administrators were requested to judge papers for a contest on research on women for a prestigious award. They received prestige and favorable notice. And, by reading the research papers concerning women or women's issues, they broadened their thinking about women and related issues.

SUPPORT WOMEN AT ALL LEVELS

In an organization, all women benefit when any woman is successful, whether in accomplishing an important project or in achieving a high-status position. She provides a role model for other women and men in the organization, and, by her performance and interactions, she educates others about women's competence. It is important to support women at all status levels by granting them the same authority, resources, power, and "benefit of the doubt" as men at the same level, and to encourage colleagues to do so. It is particularly important for authority figures to give the same enthusiasm, praise, and personal endorsement to women as they accord, automatically, to men in the same positions. The authority figure's commendation and visible readiness to back up the junior person increases the perceived value of that person's ideas and performance. Authority support is especially important in hiring and promotion deliberations.

Nonverbal support is also important. When a woman offers a substantive contribution in a group meeting, other group members frequently show fleeting facial expressions of displeasure, but when a man offers the same contribution, they look pleased. The displeased expressions not only discourage the woman, they also lower the perceived value of her contribution. It takes awareness and practice to monitor one's own facial expressions. Meanwhile, when you see others look displeased in response to a woman's contribution, remember that they do not think her ideas are poor; rather they are discomfited because she has violated their unconscious expectation that women should remain subordinate and deferent.

Avoid disparaging women in public either verbally or nonverbally. Particularly if you are a woman, as you disparage other women, you disparage yourself. To counteract the stereotypes, a positive consensus effect can be created by listening to women's ideas and suggestions, objecting to others' interrupting them, recognizing their authority, and insisting that others do, too. Also, publically recognizing women's contributions and accomplishments will eventually improve the image of all women in the

> Avoid disparaging women in public either verbally or nonverbally to avoid disparaging yourself.

organization. Admittedly, supporting women is a slow process, but it will be effective over the long run.

A problem arises when there is a genuinely incompetent woman in your work setting. Remember that women, like men, come in all degrees of competence. One problem is that authorities, seeking to avoid a woman they perceive as "threatening," sometimes hire a less competent woman over a more competent woman candidate. The second problem is that a given level of incompetence will be noticed more quickly and more widely in a woman than in a man. When you disparage an incompetent woman you only support and increase this bias.

We do not advocate going out of your way to praise or make false excuses for incompetent colleagues, male or female. Remember to protect your credibility. However, while they remain on the job, they are due the respect, attention, and cooperation appropriate to their positions. Note also that a few incompetent men remain in authority positions, with high salaries, for years. Everyone pretends not to notice their incompetence. Sexism is not dead when a female Einstein advances faster than a male Twiddle de Dum, but when the Ms. Mediocres advance as far and as fast as the Mr. Mediocres.

COLLABORATE WITH OTHERS

An important way to empower yourself is collaboration with others. What one person cannot accomplish alone can often be done with a group. The process involves the following:

1. Identifying a group with a common issue. Participants do not have to agree on other issues or have anything else in common.
2. Establishing a group consensus concerning the desired goal.
3. Generating the will to act together.
4. Negotiating the final plan or document.
5. Reaffirming the commitment to support the document's implementation.

This process requires time, effort, and skill. There is often a considerable amount of negotiation required. The final outcome may not be exactly as you had planned. It is crucial that you remain flexible and willing to settle for what you can negotiate at that time. However, if a win–win strategy is the basis for the effort, and the collaboration makes everyone look good, the effort will probably succeed with minor adjustments. The identity, type, and number of collaborators varies with the task and goal. Collaboration can be an important path to power and an effective means of gaining acceptance for strategies to counteract sexism.

UNDERSTAND THE ORGANIZATIONAL CULTURE

Do not underestimate the importance of the culture of the organization. Learn as much as possible about it. The first step is to become a member of the organizational team. People who do not fit in or accept the organizational norms of behavior are seldom successful. Being part of the team also enables you to get the information and cooperation necessary to do your job well. For instance, if getting to work on time has a high value for the organization, it must have a high value for you, too. If a certain standard of dress is required, you must conform or pay a penalty, as your colleagues will not "see" you as a member of the team. If the organizational culture is unacceptable to you, it may be time to move to a different department or area in the organization, or to find another job. It is seldom productive to spend time and energy fighting or trying to change the organization without the support of a "critical mass" among your colleagues.

Do not underestimate the importance of the culture of the organization.

UNDERSTAND THE ORGANIZATIONAL STRUCTURE AND GOALS

Not only do you want to be perceived as loyal to the organization, but knowing the organizational structure and goals will also allow you to focus on what the organization considers important. Know what the core mission and goals of the organization are, the means taken to obtain those goals, and how they are measured. Understand the value and reward system and your own position relative to those values and rewards. Assess the sources of information and power within the organization. Evaluate your own position relative to those power centers and develop strategies for tapping into those power bases. An additional advantage is that this knowledge will enable you to place your personal goals in the context of the organization. If you cannot accept the goals of the organization, it is time to change organizations.

ESTABLISH CREDIBILITY

One of the first things any person must do in an organization is to establish credibility, not only in an area of expertise but also as a colleague. It is especially important for a woman not to make mistakes through carelessness or lack of thoroughness, as colleagues will be watching and checking her work for mistakes much more carefully than that of a male colleague under similar circumstances. It is risky to guess and fatal to lie. If you feel that you know your own area well, explore some related areas that would help your future advancement. Also, you must be a person who can be trusted to keep information confidential when necessary and provide accurate feedback to others when required.

It is risky to guess and fatal to lie.

PARTICIPATE ACTIVELY

High visibility results from active participation in appropriate activities such as meetings, task forces, and daily interaction with colleagues. Not only does participation give you and your abilities broad exposure and provide increased professional contacts, it also can be a learning experience. Appropriate participation can be a way to leadership and power in an organization. Becoming an emergent leader depends on high rates of participation, and recognition as an emergent leader is often the stepping stone to promotion to formal leadership positions. Your participation needs to be timely, relevant, and well documented. Take credit for your work and competence. Create opportunities to talk positively about your work and your department. Participating in activities in which you meet decision makers provides valuable access and visibility for you and your department. But appointing a woman to chair the social committee may only reinforce limiting sex role stereotypes of "women's work."

DEAL WITH THE DOUBLE BIND OF THE "DAMNED IF SHE DOES, DAMNED IF SHE DOESN'T" DILEMMA

The problem is that much effective professional behavior, such as participating actively in group discussions, is erroneously perceived as "masculine" because only men were seen performing in professional and authority roles in the past. At the same time, unconscious gender stereotypes lead people to expect and demand "feminine" behavior from women, and, unfortunately, some of the "feminine" characteristics are associated with less competence and lower status because, again, virtually all women were seen in domestic and subordinate status positions in the past. The effective solution to this problem requires the long-term strategies of understanding sexism, increasing the number of female authority role models, and educating your colleagues discussed above. However, while you are waiting for these strategies to work, you still have to deal with the dilemma on a daily basis.

Strategies for men and women differ on this issue, primarily because men do not face the same contradictory expectations personally. However, both men and women who want to encourage their unit's maximum productivity and morale can learn to be aware of the unconscious gender-role expectations in themselves and others and encourage, support, and reward women for behavior that is professionally appropriate, even if it is not stereotypically "feminine."

For women on the receiving end of the contradictory expectations, the effective strategies are more precarious, especially when colleagues are unaware of the problem. One approach might be called the "This But Not That" or the "One Step At A Time" strategy. Adopt one professional behavior or activity that is most important to your career success but remain conformingly "feminine" in other behaviors, activities, or situations. For example, realizing that active participation is professionally valued, a personally dominant woman might decide to speak out and contribute assertively in group meetings and other interactions, but dress conservatively, refrain from excessive bragging about her successes, from "one-upping" male colleagues, and from displaying knowledge, ability, or interest in sports. Then, after establishing her credibility, value and acceptance in this role for a few years, she can adopt another professionally valued behavior or style, for example, treating her own needs as important. If she stays with the same group or company long enough, by mid-career she may have worked herself out of the dilemma.

Adopt one professional behavior or activity most important to your career but remain conformingly "feminine" in other behaviors, activities or situations.

This strategy may be particularly effective when a number of women in the same unit collaborate, each of them choosing a *different* nontraditional behavior or activity. For example, one woman could participate actively in group meetings, another assertively demand pay equity, another refuse to type or answer phones during her lunch hour unless everyone takes a turn, another base her requests or ideas on her own expertise instead of on rewards or friendship, and another treat her own time and needs as important. Each needs to support the others. Stereotypes are most effectively disconfirmed when the disconfirmations are dispersed over many members of a group. With this collaborative strategy to break the stereotypes instead of just coping individually with their effects, each of the women will be accepted sooner using all of the effective behaviors. Colleagues who have learned to accept a particular nontraditional behavior from one woman then learn more quickly and easily to accept it from other women.

A second strategy is the "Little Bit of Everything" or "Easy Does It" approach. The woman moves her behavior and style *slightly* away from the stereotypic "feminine" patterns toward the professionally valued "masculine" patterns on all fronts at once. The key word here is the *little bit*. Again, over the years, with acceptance, she can keep increasing the little bits. With either of these strategies, moving to a new organization or a distant department in a large organization usually means starting over at the beginning.

> Move your behavior slightly away from the stereotypic "feminine" patterns on all fronts.

The double-bind situation is a no-win situation, for it rigidly limits behaviors and strategies and thus results in unproductive and ineffective management. Both men and women need to be aware of creating double-bind dilemmas or participating in them. Being aware of "double-binds" requires that we understand our basic beliefs about men and women. Only then can we, as a society and within organizations, move toward effective flexible behaviors and multiple strategies which are required by an increasingly diverse workplace and society.

Masculinity and Femininity. The personality characteristics and behavioral styles traditionally labeled as "masculine" and "feminine" are not a result of biological sex but of the traditional division of labor, roles, and status between the sexes. The traits erroneously labeled as "masculine" are actually those required by employment outside the home, high status, and authority. Those labeled as "feminine" are the traits required by domestic roles, subordinate status, and lack of authority. In fact, both sets of characteristics are neither masculine nor feminine, but human. Women vary among themselves in their natural predispositions to both types of traits, and so do men. But both men and women can and do learn and perform both types of behavior. Both men's and women's behavior is shaped partly by their own predispositions and heavily by their role, status, and real power in the situation.

Some of the so-called "masculine" traits are desirable and effective—for both sexes—at work, for example, intelligence, objectivity, assertiveness and leadership, and expertise. Some of the so-called "feminine" traits are also desirable and effective for both sexes—for example, sensitivity, consideration and caring for others, friendliness, warmth, and sharing. In an ideal world, women would be feminine by definition—because they are female—and men would be masculine because they are male, regardless of personality characteristics. Then individuals of both sexes could develop and practice whichever traits were comfortable for them and effective in the roles they occupied. Individuals of both sexes would be freer and more effective, and organizations would be more productive.

HANDLE CRITICISM

Because many women have low self-confidence and blame themselves excessively for their failures, they tend to take criticism of their work personally and feel devastated by it. First, neither men nor women should take criticism personally. Second, even a serious mistake or failure does not mean the end of one's career. Third, when you receive criticism, *think*. Evaluate the comments objectively and learn from them *if* they are valid. For example, Kay's boss, Don, told her at the last staff meeting, when she was making a progress report on her project, that she did not know what she was talking about and that she had made a poor decision that could affect the budget of the entire department.

Instead of feeling helpless and guilty that she had made a bad mistake, Kay should consider and explore what might have caused his behavior before she internalizes "a failure" in herself. When Don makes that kind of a comment, Kay needs to decide why he did it in order to plan her own response. First, Kay needs to ask Don for the basis of his statement. She might make this request at the meeting, but often it is more effective, and more informative, to follow it up, later, privately, for more detail. With this information, Kay has several options under her control as she assesses the incident.

1. Don might be right; she should carefully review her report.
2. Don made his judgment either on wrong information, lack of information, or incomplete information. Kay can offer supporting data as a basis for her decision.

3. Don did it deliberately to embarrass her or keep her in her place. Kay will never win when the issue is emotional or personal. It is best to drop it for now.

4. Don is making a political maneuver to impress or influence someone else. The alleged problem in her report is not a real problem.

5. Don is covering the fact that the budget had already been cut for an entirely different reason, possibly his mistake. Kay might recognize an emotional outburst and just let it go at the meeting, then follow it up with a later meeting for clarification.

The basis for Kay's judgment includes her knowledge of Don, information from others, including "the grapevine," and her own intuition.

AVOID THE EMOTIONAL LABEL

It is essential for women not to be stereotyped as "too emotional" and thus unable to do "important" work. Women are often perceived as being "emotional" when they are not. If this happens, the woman, or someone else of either sex, can ask on what basis that conclusion was reached. Be aware that such labeling may be used to discredit a woman when no other way can be found, if she is perceived as too threatening to her boss or colleagues. Such unfair accusations are very difficult to handle without becoming emotional. This is especially true when an emotional male in the group is not perceived by the others as being emotional. Although a man's emotional response may be to swear, it is seldom perceived as such, especially by other men.

> Women are often perceived as being "emotional" when they are not.

For women, as well as men, appropriate professional attitudes mean no crying or temper tantrums in public. People who lose their emotional control will be discounted in the future and be judged as "not objective" about their work by colleagues. When people respond emotionally, their minds are seldom in control and they will lose the argument. It is dangerous enough to verbalize an emotional response, but it is even worse to write it in a memo—and send it. If you are a woman, your opponent will have evidence that you are "only an emotional woman" and that you can be discounted. Provocation can also be a preplanned tactic by others to make you angry so that your opponent can exploit you in the conflict.

However, an angry response can also be a conscious strategy to attain your goal. But even when it is appropriate to "get mad," it can be very empowering to contain your emotions and use your mind to "win." In the earlier example, Kay could have responded to the criticism emotionally either by crying or getting angry and yelling at her boss that he was unfair and did not know as much as she did about the issue. Neither response would have been effective. The wisest response would be to talk to him privately at a later time when Kay had gathered and rechecked her data. It is possible she was wrong. However, if that was true, Don did not use an effective way to communicate that information to her.

KNOW WHEN AND HOW TO NEGOTIATE

The art of negotiation can be immensely helpful in dealing with every day situations in addition to more critical issues. It is prudent to marshal the resources needed to win as often as possible. Remember however, the best solution is the win–win solution—one where all participants gain. It is not always easy to find such a solution to a problem, but you may be surprised at what creative thinking can devise, and the rewards are well worth the effort. When everyone gains, seldom can anyone resist the proposed solution.

Going back to our earlier incident, a possibility for Kay to turn a bad situation around is for her to ask Don privately to clearly define the problem on which he based his remarks. Once she understands what it is, she can suggest a compromise that benefits Don, the organization, and herself. It may be:

1. Additional or less data included in her reports
2. More detailed explanation
3. Broader interpretation or reinterpretation of the data
4. Developing a cost-saving strategy
5. Streamlining the entire process
6. Different or more accurate accounting procedures or both.

The possibilities are many. The result of her proposed solution must accomplish Don's goal, be acceptable to her, and related to the goals of the organization.

In preparing to negotiate, gather all the information that may be relevant. Knowledge is empowering, especially in negotiation. Anticipate all possible compromises, and decide on your "bottom line" in advance. If things do not go as you anticipated, it is better to withdraw temporarily from the negotiation than to lose. That will enable you to return with additional information to support or back your position, or to present a new or modified proposal based on what you learned during the first session.

In selling a new idea, it also helps to be quietly persistent in working toward a specific goal, but only to the appropriate point. It does not pay to "beat a dead horse." In fact, it alienates people when you go too far. "If at first you don't succeed, try again another way."

When you enter into negotiation, it is important to identify the emotional involvement of the participants. When people are operating on the basis of an emotional need such as "putting you in your place" or increasing their power, it is almost impossible to negotiate with them, even with a win–win proposal. They will find a hundred reasons to justify their position if they do not want to do something. On the other hand, if they want you to do something, they can also find a hundred reasons to justify that it needs to be done. No rational arguments can change their minds. It is best to cut off negotiations, as there is no way to move forward.

In the earlier example, when Kay's manager told her that she had made a serious mistake and put the department's budget in jeopardy, Kay needed to gather and organize her back-up data. She cannot ignore such an outburst but must deal with it on a one-to-one basis in an objective manner. She can request the data he used for his judgment. There might be something she did not know. If that is true, she will need to leave, regroup, and return with a modified proposal. However, if the outburst is based on an emotional or personal need, there may be little Kay can do to turn the situation around.

DEVELOP A RANGE OF COMMUNICATIVE AND POWER STYLES

Communication is the medium through which power is developed and used. Be aware that women and men who are perceived as using strategies consistent with gender-role expectations are usually also perceived as more effective. Remember also, however, that perception is not an accurate mirror of reality. Women who are perceived as effective may be described as "feminine" because they are liked or appreciated, and for the same reason, effective men may be described as "masculine." Nevertheless, although men are liked and approved for using the "feminine" strategies of friendliness and consideration, women who are perceived as using the "masculine" strategies of initiating structure or being directive are disliked and disapproved. Women are perceived as more effective when using reward power. Men are more effective using expert power. A woman may say and do exactly the same things that a successful male colleague does, but her actions will be viewed differently, especially if her behavior is not compatible with "feminine" expectations.

However, these discriminatory perceptions and evaluations become more egalitarian when there are more female authority role models in the work setting, or when the evaluators have more experience working with or for female supervisors. In fact, working men and women leaders and managers are often perceived as using the same balance of consideration versus task-structuring behaviors, and they are equally liked and rated as equally competent and effective. The most effective managers are described as using high levels of both consideration and task structuring. Thus, it would appear advantageous for both men and women to develop a wide range of communication and power styles. Different styles provide both men and women with additional options to initiate contacts or respond to others. Flexibility to respond appropriately to different situations is an important negotiation tool.

ANALYZE BEFORE ACTING

The maxim "look before you leap" holds true in organizations. It is important to examine all aspects of any issue or problem at work from all participants' viewpoints and anticipate the results of different actions. Your analysis can involve timing, who will benefit and who will suffer, whether the risk is worth the gain, financial cost and payout, relevancy, and whether the proposed solution advances the organization's goals.

Impetuous action can be very dangerous, because the results of such action have not been carefully thought through. Such action is often based on personal or emotional needs rather than on a rational analysis. A woman may pay a high price for such a mistake, especially when it fits a limiting gender role stereotype that women are "too emotional" for high level positions. She may lose her credibility and be viewed as "flawed."

ASSUME POWER

Initially, assume power until you are explicitly told that an action, responsibility or task is outside your job responsibility. Women are usually given less power than men in the same position. For men and women alike, an important strategy for getting and being given power is to act as if you already had it. One problem for women is that having and using power too obviously violates stereotypic expectations for women's behavior. Women should be prepared for some negative reactions, but persist unless the costs outweigh the gains.

Both men and women should be selective in their choice of additional tasks or responsibilities. It is important to be conscious of the dangers of job elaboration, such as intruding into your manager's power space. A second power strategy is to form networks or coalitions to extend your power through the exchange of information. Accurate information is power that too many women unthinkingly give away. Such information can be traded for other information. It can also assist in providing access to some important networks from which you would normally be excluded.

DEVELOP NETWORKS

A network of women and men colleagues is very important as a source of support, valuable information, future contacts, referral, and power. A network is an informal mutually supportive group and implies a certain amount of trust by members in each other. Note that it is mutually supportive. A member has certain responsibilities that include being discrete, reliable, and a contributor to the group network. The group can provide a forum to test new ideas as well as to check out rumors. One may have several networks that relate to different purposes or areas. Some of the most effective networks include both men and women, because men often have better access to information. The value of networks in providing information necessary for you to perform your job responsibilities effectively should not be underestimated.

TAKE CALCULATED RISKS

Risk taking is an area of many options. The trick is to decide which risks are worth the possible gain with the least possible pain. The decision should be influenced by the degree to which taking the risk will advance you toward your desired goal. The greater the risk, the greater the reward should be. Playing it safe 100% of the time will not get you very far. You may be uncomfortable taking risks, at first, but practice reduces the anxiety. (You take a calculated risk with your life every time you ride in a car.)

The preparation for deciding whether to take a risk is similar to preparing for negotiation. The first step is to gather as much information as possible concerning the issue. The second step is evaluating the risk, how important the possible gain is to you personally, how the required action relates to your value system and personal integrity, and whether the action will advance you toward your desired goal. As we have emphasized, it is important to make an informed and deliberate decision rather than an emotional one.

An easy way to start is by trying a small risk. Once you find that you are rewarded, or that the penalty was not as bad as you expected, it is easier to move on to bigger and better opportunities. However, before deciding to take a risk, it is valuable to visualize a worst case scenario. After careful evaluation, you may find that the consequences may not be as dire as you first anticipated, and that the risk is worth trying, even if it does not work out as you had hoped.

DEVELOP SELF-CONFIDENCE

Having more self-confidence makes work less stressful, more fun, and actually increases the quality of your performance. Self-confidence has two components, an internal component of what you feel, and an external component of what you reveal and express. No one, including scientists, can tell how much internal self-confidence another person has. We only know what others express and reveal. Women claim less self-confidence than men in their ability to succeed at specific tasks and occupations traditionally labeled as "masculine." One way to increase your self-confidence, for men and women alike, is to learn to act as if you already had self-confidence. "Whistling in the dark" really does work! As you practice acting self-confident, you actually begin to feel more confident. Although excessive false bravado would be obvious and self-defeating, moderate degrees of "faking it" are practiced on occasion by most successful professionals. A second way for women to increase their self-confidence is persistence. Women's self-confidence increases with increasing years of experience at work.

PERSIST

Despite high ability, effort, commitment, and using all of the knowledge and approaches suggested in this book, a woman still might not advance as fast in her career as a comparable man. The forces of sexism are powerful and pervasive. However, persistence is often rewarded. Women should not be discouraged and think that their good efforts are fruitless. It may be that their results just need more time to accumulate and be recognized. On the other hand, there are situations in which sexism is so entrenched that they are in fact dead ends for women, and a woman's wisest strategy is to cut her losses and move. Whether the situation requires persistence or exit is a judgment call, and outcomes cannot be predicted with certainty. However, with more women moving into organizations and moving upward in organizations, persistence should pay more often than not.

RECOGNIZE THE BOTTOM LINE

There is a point where any discussion of issues become irrelevant. That point is known as the bottom line. It is only concerned with the final result. From management's point of view, what counts is whether an employee either "comes through" or does not "come through." Extenuating circumstances are no longer of interest. It is important to recognize when management has reached the "bottom line" where intent, data, negotiation, and persistence no longer apply. It can be a hard deadline, or a controversial issue where a stand can be related to loyalty to the organization or to an individual. Either you do it or you do not do it. If you do not do what is asked of you or told you, there can be serious ramifications.

It is *crucial* not to let an issue get as far as the bottom line. The best way to prevent it is to find a win–win solution to any prospective problem issue before it gets to that point, even though you may not come out very far ahead. When the issue is translated into one of a superior's power to enforce and your power to refuse, you will not win. A manager's power space should not be challenged directly. If the issue is so important to you that you decide you must challenge your boss, your only option may be to resign from your position.

CONCLUSION

Sexism exists in the minds and actions of both men and women. Reducing sexism means that men must change, as well as women. Empowering yourself is something that you can do. For both men and women, empowering yourself means enhancing your own effectiveness, counteracting sexism in the organization, and dealing with existing sexism. There are numerous ways that you can start these processes. They are ongoing projects and usually do not produce dramatic results immediately. Rather, the incremental and sometimes invisible results accumulate and gradually yield a sum greater than their parts. The choice of action, including no action, is up to you.

After reviewing the situation and your own strengths, you can examine many options and their possible risks. Usually more than one way is used to start on the road to increased power. If you never make

The best solution is the win–win solution—one that benefits all participants.

the decision and the commitment to start taking some proactive control over your life, the situation will remain the same or deteriorate. The frustrating problems will not go away on their own accord, no matter how much we may wish it. No action is also a decision. Guard against exploiting others, especially women, and also against being perceived as one who can be exploited. The list of questions to be asked will help to identify such situations. The list of solutions will help cope with them and gradually counteract them.

The choice of option is both personal and situational. What is right for one person one time with one set of circumstances may not be appropriate for another person at another time, or in another situation. However, if you can develop and suggest a win–win solution to resolve the problem, you have made an important first step.

References

Adams, K., & Landers, A. (1978). Sex differences in dominance behavior. *Sex Roles, 4*, 215–223.

Allen, V.L., & Wilder, D.A. (1980). Impact of group consensus and social support on stimulus meaning: Mediation of conformity by cognitive restructuring. *Journal of Personality and Social Psychology, 38*, 1116–1124.

Alperson, B.L., & Friedman, W.J. (1983). Some aspects of the interpersonal phenomenology of heterosexual dyads with respect to sex role stereotypes. *Sex Roles, 9*, 453–474.

Altemeyer, R.A., & Jones, K. (1974). Sexual identity, physical attractiveness and seating position as determinants of influence in discussion groups. *Canadian Journal of Behavioural Science, 6*, 357–375.

Argyle, M., Salter, V., Nicholson, H., Williams, M., & Burgess, P. (1970). The communication of inferior and superior attitudes by verbal and nonverbal signals. *British Journal of Social and Clinical Psychology, 9*, 222–231.

Aries, E. (1977). Male–female interpersonal styles in all male, all female and mixed groups. In A. Sargent (Ed.), *Beyond sex roles*. New York: Free Press.

Aries, E. (1988). Gender and communication. In G. Powell (Ed.), *Women and men in management*. Newbury Park, CA: Sage.

Arvey, R.D. (1979). Unfair discrimination in the employment interview: Legal and psychological aspects. *Psychological Bulletin, 86*, 736–765.

Asch, S.E. (1956). Studies of independence and conformity. A minority of one against a unanimous majority. *Psychological Monographs, 70*(9) (Whole No. 416).

Bacharach, P., & Baratz, M. (1962). Two faces of power. *American Political Science Review, 56*, 947–952.

Bacharach, S., & Lawler, E. (1980). *Power and politics in organizations*. San Francisco, & CA: Jossey-Bass.

Baird, J.E. (1976). Sex differences in group communication: A review of relevant research. *Quarterly Journal of Speech, 62*, 179–192.

Baird, J.E., Jr., & Bradley, P.H. (1979). Styles of management and communication: A comparative study of men and women. *Communication Monographs, 46*, 101–111.

Bales, R.F. (1950). *Interaction process analysis: A method for the study of small groups.* Cambridge, MA: Addison-Wesley.

Bales, R.F. (1953). The equilibrium problem in small groups. In T. Parsons, R. F. Bales, & E. A. Shils (Eds.), *Working papers in the theory of action* (pp. 111–161). New York: Free Press.

Bales, R.F., & Slater, P.E. (1955). Role differentiation in small decision-making groups. In T. Parsons, R.F. Bales, & J. Olds (Eds.), *Family, socialization and interaction process.* Glencoe, IL: Free Press.

Bandura, A., & Walters, R.H. (1963). *Social learning and personality development.* New York: Holt, Rinehart & Winston.

Bar Tal, D., & Frieze, I. H. (1977). Achievement motivation for males and females as a determinant of attributions for success and failure. *Sex Roles, 3*, 301–314.

Bargh, J.A. (1984). Automatic and conscious processing of social information. In R.S. Wyer, Jr., & T.K. Srull (Eds.), *Handbook of social cognition* (Vol. 3, pp. 1–43). Hillsdale, NJ: Erlbaum.

Baron, R.A. (1987). Interviewer's moods and reactions to job applicants: The influence of affective status on applied social judgments. *Journal of Applied Social Psychology, 17*, 911–926.

Bartol, K.M., & Butterfield, D.A. (1976). Sex effects in evaluating leaders. *Journal of Applied Psychology, 61*, 446–454.

Bartol, K.M., & Wortman, M.S. (1976). Sex effects in leader behavior self descriptions and job satisfaction. *Journal of Psychology, 94*, 177–183.

Basow, S. (1986). *Gender stereotypes: Traditions and alternatives.* Belmont, CA: Brooks/Cole.

Bass, B.M., Krusell, J., & Alexander, R. A. (1971). Male managers' attitudes toward working women. *American Behavioral Scientist, 15*, 221–236.

Bate, B. (1988). *Communication and the sexes.* New York: Harper & Row.

Baumeister, R.F., Chesner, S.P., Senders, P.S., & Tice, D.M. (1988). Who's in charge here? Group leaders do lend help in emergencies. *Personality and Social Psychology Bulletin, 14*, 17–22.

Bellezza, F.S., & Bower, G.H. (1981). Person stereotypes and memory for people. *Journal of Personality and Social Psychology, 41*, 856–865.

Bem, S.L. (1974). The measurement of psychological androgyny. *Journal of Consulting and Clinical Psychology, 42*, 155–162.

Bem, S.L. (1981). Gender schema theory: A cognitive account of sex typing. *Psychological Review, 88*, 354–364.

Bem, S.L. (1985). Androgyny and gender schema theory: A conceptual and empirical integration. In T.B. Sonderegger (Ed.), *Nebraska Symposium on Motivation 1984: Psychology and Gender.* Lincoln, NE: University of Nebraska Press.

Bennis, W., & Nanus, B. (1985). *Leaders, the strategies for taking charge.* New York: Harper & Row.

Benokraitis, N., & Feagin, J. (1986). *Modern sexism.* New York: Harper & Row Publishers Inc.

Benson, P., Winther, D., & Sauser, W. (1984). *Behavioral characteristics of heterogeneous groups: The case for gender.* Paper presented at the International Congress of Cross-Cultural Psychology, Acapulco, Mexico.

Berger, J., & Zelditch, M., Jr. (1985). *Status, rewards, and influence: How expectations organize behavior.* San Francisco: Jossey-Bass Inc., Publishers.

Bernard, J. (1972a). *The sex game.* New York: Atheneum.

Bernard, J. (1972b). *The future of marriage.* New York: World Publishing.

Berryman, C.L., & Wilcox, J.R. (1980, Winter). Attitudes toward male and female speech: Experiments on the effects of sex-typical language. *The Western Journal of Speech Communication, 44,* 50–59.

Berryman-Fink, C., Heintz, M.A., Lowy, M.S., Seebohm, M.L., & Wheeless, V.E. (1986, November). *Perceptions of women as managers: Implications for organizational success.* Paper presented at the Speech Communication Association Convention, Chicago.

Berryman-Fink, C., & Wheeless, V.E. (1985). Perceptions of women managers and their communicator competencies. *Communication Quarterly, 33,* 137–148.

Bies, R. (1988). Managing conflict before it happens: The role of accounts. In M. A. Rahim (Ed.), *Managing conflict: An interdisciplinary approach.* New York: Praeger.

Bies, R., Shapiro, D., & Cummings, L. (1988). Causal accounts and managing organizational conflict: Is it enough to say it's not my fault. *Communication Research, 15,* 381–399.

Biles, G.E., & Pryatel, H.A. (1978). Myths, management and women. *Personnel Journal, 57,* 572–577.

Birnbaum, J.A. (1975). Life patterns and self-esteem in gifted family-oriented and career-committed women. In M. Mednick, S. Tangri, & L. Hoffman (Eds.), *Women and achievement* (pp. 396–419). New York: Halsted.

Blake, R., & Mouton, J. (1964). *Corporate excellence through grid organization development.* Houston: Gulf Publishing Company.

Blau, F.D., & Ferber, M.A. (1985). Women in the labor market: The last twenty years. In L. Larwood, A.H. Stromberg, & B.A. Gutek (Eds.), *Women and work: An annual review* (Vol. 1, pp 19–49). Beverly Hills, CA: Sage Publications, Inc.

Bodenhausen, G.V. (1988). Stereotypic biases in social decision making and memory: Testing process models of stereotype use. *Journal of Personality and Social Psychology, 55,* 726–737.

Bodenhausen, G.V., & Lichtenstein, M. (1987). Social stereotypes and information-processing strategies: The impact of task complexity. *Journal of Personality and Social Psychology, 52,* 871–880.

Bonaguro, E.L., & Pearson, J. (1986, November). *The relationship between communicator style, argumentativeness, and gender.* Paper presented at Speech Communication Association Convention, Chicago.

Bormann, E.G., Pratt, J., & Putnam, L. (1978). Power, authority and sex: Male response to female leadership. *Communication Monographs, 45,* 119–155.

Bornstein, R.F., Leone, D.R., & Galley, D.J. (1987). The generalizability of subliminal more exposure effects: Influence of stimuli perceived without awareness on social behavior. *Journal of Personality and Social Personality, 53,* 1070–1079.

Bower, G.H. (1977). *Human memory.* New York: Academic Press, Inc.

Bowman, G., Worthy, N., & Geyser, S. (1965). Problems in review: Are women executives people? *Harvard Business Review, 43,* 14–28, 164–178.

Bradac, J.J., & Mulac, A. (1984). A molecular view of powerful and powerless speech styles: Attributional consequences of specific language features and communicator intentions. *Communication Monographs, 51,* 307–319.

Bradley, P.H. (1980). Sex, competence and opinion deviation: An expectation states approach. *Communication Monographs, 47,* 101–110.

Bradley, P.H. (1981). The folk-linguistics of women's speech: An empirical investigation. *Communication Monographs, 48,* 73–90.

Brewer, M.B. (1979). Ingroup bias in the minimal intergroup situation: A cognitive motivational analysis. *Psychological Bulletin, 86,* 307–324.

Bridges, J.S. (1988). Sex differences in occupational performance expectations. *Psychology of Women Quarterly, 12,* 75–90.

Brooks, V.R. (1982). Sex differences in student dominance behavior in female and male professors' classrooms. *Sex Roles, 8,* 683–690.

Broverman, J.K., Vogel, S.R., Broverman, D.M., Clarkson, F.E., & Rosenkrantz, P. S. (1972). Sex-role stereotypes: A current appraisal. *Journal of Social Issues, 28,* 59–78.

Brown, L.K. (1981). *The woman manager in the United States: A research analysis and bibliography.* Washington, DC: Business and Professional Women's Foundation.

Brown, V., & Geis, F.L. (1984). Turning lead into gold: Leadership by men and women and the alchemy of social consensus. *Journal of Personality and Social Psychology, 46,* 811–824.

Bruner, J.S. (1951). Personality dynamics and the process of perceiving. In R.S. Blake & C.V. Ramsey (Eds.), *Perception, an approach to personality* (pp. 121–149). New York: Ronald.

Bunker, B.B., & Bender, L.R. (1980). How women compete: A guide for managers. *Management Review, 69,* 55–62.

Bunker, B.B., & Seashore, E.W. (1975). Breaking the sex role stereotypes. *Public Management, 57,* 5–11.

Bunyi, J.M., & Andrews, P.H. (1985). Gender and leadership emergence: An experimental study. *The Southern Speech Communication Journal, 50,* 246–260.

Burgoon, J., Buller, D. & Woodall, W. (1989). *Nonverbal communication*. New York: Harper & Row.

Burke, R. (1984). Relationships in and around organizations: It's *both* who you know and what you know. *Psychological Reports, 55*, 299–307.

Burrell, N., Donohue, W., & Allen, M. (1988). Gender-based perceptual biases in mediation. *Communication Research, 15*, 447–469.

Butler, D., & Geis, F.L. (1990). Nonverbal affect responses to male and female leaders: Implications for leadership evaluation. *Journal of Personality and Social Psychology, 58*, 48–59.

Calder, B.J. (1982). An attribution theory of leadership. In B.M. Staw & G.R. Salanick (Eds.), *New directions in organizational behavior*. Malabar, FL: Robert E. Krieger Publishing Company.

Camden, C., & Witt, J. (1983). Manager communicative style and productivity: A study of male and female managers. *International Journal of Women's Studies, 6*, 258–269.

Camden, C., & Kennedy, C. (1986). Manager communicative style and nurse morale. *Human Communication Research, 12*, 551–563.

Campbell, D.T. (1967). Stereotypes and the perception of group differences. *American Psychologist, 22*, 817–829.

Campbell, J.D., & Fairey, P. (1985). Effects of self-esteem, hypothetical explanations, and verbalization of expectancies on future performance. *Journal of Personality and Social Psychology, 48*, 1097–1111.

Canary, D., Cunningham, E., & Cody, M. (1988). Goal types, gender and locus of control in managing interpersonal conflict. *Communication Research, 15*, 426–446.

Cann, A., & Siegfried Jr., W.D. (1987). Sex stereotypes and the leadership role. *Sex Roles, 17* (7/8), 401–407.

Cantor, N., & Mischel, W. (1977). Traits as prototypes: Effects on recognition memory. *Journal of Personality and Social Psychology, 35*, 38–48.

Caplow, T., & McGee, R.J. (1958). *The academic marketplace*. New York: Basic Books.

Carli, L. (1982). *Are women more social and men more task oriented? A meta-analytic review of sex differences in group interaction, reward allocation, coalition formation, and cooperation in the Prisoner's Dilemma game*. Unpublished manuscript, University of Massachusetts, Amherst.

Cash, T.F., Gillen, B., & Burns, D.S. (1977). Sexism and "beautyism" in personnel consultant decision making. *Journal of Applied Psychology, 62*, 301–310.

Chapman, J.B. (1975). Comparison of male and female leadership styles. *Academy of Management Journal, 18*, 645–650.

Chapman, J.B., & Luthans, F. (1975). The female leadership dilemma. *Public Personnel Management, 4*, 173–178.

Cheatham, H.E. (1984). Integration of women into the U. S. military. *Sex Roles, 11*, 141–153.

Chusmir, L.H. (1983). Motivation of managers: Is gender a factor? *Journal of the Psychology of Women, 10*, 153–159.

238   THE ORGANIZATIONAL WOMAN

Chusmir, L.H. (1985). Motivation of managers: Is gender a factor? *Psychology of Women Quarterly, 9*, 153–159.
Chusmir, L.H., & Koberg, C.S. (1986). Development and validation of the sex role conflict scale. *Journal of Applied Behavioral Science, 22*, 397–409.
Chusmir, L.H., & Parker, B. (1984). Dimensions of need for power: Personalized vs. socialized power in female and male managers. *Sex Roles, 11*, 759–769.
Cody, M., Canary, D., & Smith, S. (in press). Compliance-gaining goals: An inductive analysis of actors' goal types, strategies, and successes. In J. Daly & J.M. Wiemann (Eds.), *Communicating strategically: Strategies in interpersonal communication*. Hillsdale, NJ: Erlbaum.
Cohen, C.E. (1981). Person categories and social perception: Testing some boundaries of the processing effects of prior knowledge. *Journal of Experimental Social Psychology, 40*, 441–452.
Cohen, B.P., Berger, J., & Zelditch Jr., M. (1972). Status conceptions and interaction: A case study of the problem of developing cumulative knowledge. In C. McClintock (Ed.), *Experimental social psychology*. New York: Holt, Rinehart, & Winston.
Cohen, E.G., Lockheed, M.E., & Lohman, M.R. (1976). The center for interracial cooperation: A field experiment. *Sociology of Education, 49*, 47–58.
Cohen, S.I., & Bunker, K.A. (1975). Subtle effects of sex role stereotypes on recruiter hiring decisions. *Journal of Applied Psychology, 60*, 566–572.
Conrad, C. (1983). Organizational power. In L. Putnam & M. Pacanowsky (Eds.), *Communication and organizations: An interpretive approach*. Beverly Hills, CA: Sage.
Conrad, C. (1985, November). *Gender, interactional sensitivity and communication in conflict: Assumptions and interpretations*. Paper presented at the Speech Communication Association Convention, Denver, CO.
Costrich, N., Feinstein, J., Kidder, L., Maracek, J., & Pascale, L. (1975). When stereotypes hurt: Three studies of penalties for sex-role reversals. *Journal of Experimental Social Psychology, 11*, 520–530.
Crew, J.C. (1982). An assessment of needs among black business majors. *Psychology, 19*, 18–22.
Cusella, L. (1987). Feedback, motivation and performance. In F. Jablin (Ed.), *Handbook of organizational communication*. Newbury Park, CA: Sage.
Daft, R., Lengel, R., & Trevino, L. (in press). Message equivocality, media selection, and manager performance: Implications for information systems. *MIS Quarterly, 11*.
Darley, J.M., & Gross, P.H. (1983). A hypothesis-confirming bias in labeling effects. *Journal of Personality and Social Psychology, 44*, 20–33.
Day, D.R., & Stogdill, R.M. (1972). Leader behavior of male and female supervisors: A comparative study. *Personnel Psychology, 25*, 353–360.
Deal, T., & Kennedy, A. (1982). *Corporate cultures*. Reading, MA: Addison-Wesley.
Deaux, K. (1976a). *The behavior of women and men*. Belmont, CA: Brooks/Cole.
Deaux, K. (1976b). Sex: A perspective on the attribution process. In J.H.

Harvey, W.J. Ickes, & R.F. Kidd (Eds.), *New directions in attribution research* (Vol. I, pp. 335–352). Hillsdale, NJ: Erlbaum.

Deaux, K. (1979). Self-evaluations of male and female managers. *Sex Roles, 5,* 571–580.

Deaux, K. (1984). From individual differences to social categories. *American Psychologist, 39,* 105–116.

Deaux, K., & Emswiller, T. (1974). Explanations of successful performance on sex-linked tasks: What is skill for the male is luck for the female. *Journal of Personality and Social Psychology, 29,* 80–85.

Deaux, K., & Lewis, L. (1984). Structure of gender stereotypes: Interrelationships among components and gender label. *Journal of Personality and Social Psychology, 46,* 991–1004.

Deaux, K., & Major, B. (1987). Putting gender into context: An interactive model of gender-related behavior. *Psychological Review, 94,* 369–389.

Deaux, K., & Taynor, J. (1973). Evaluation of male and female ability: Bias works two ways. *Psychological Reports, 32,* 261–262.

Denenberg, V.H., Hudgens, G.A., & Zarrow, M.X. (1966). Mice reared with rats: Effects of mother on adult behavior patterns. *Psychological Reports, 18,* 451–456.

Denmark, F.L. (1977). Styles of leadership. *Psychology of Women Quarterly, 2,* 99–113.

Denmark, F.L. (1979). *The outspoken woman: Can she win?* Paper presented to the New York Academy of Sciences, New York.

DeWine, S. (1986a). Breakthrough: Making it happen with women's networks. In J. J. Pilotta (Ed.), *Women in organizations: Barriers and breakthroughs* (pp. 85–101). Beverly Hills, CA: Sage.

DeWine, S. (1986b, November). *Female leadership in male-dominated organizations.* Paper presented at Association for Communication Administrators Pre-Conference, Speech Communication Association Convention, Chicago.

DeWine, S., Alspach, S., Branch, A., Labiano, A., Liston, S., & McDaniel, N. (1982). *Women and power in the male-dominated organization: An interpretive study.* Paper presented to the Center for Continuing Studies Interdisciplinary Conference, Louisville, Kentucky.

Dickens, F., & Dickens, J. (1982). *The black manager.* New York: AMACOM.

Dion, K.L. (1985). Sex, gender, and groups: Selected issues. In V. E. O'Leary, R.K. Unger, & B.S. Wallston (Eds.), *Women, gender, and social psychology* (pp. 293–347). Hillsdale, NJ: Erlbaum.

Dipboye, R.L. (1975, May/June). Women as managers—stereotypes and realities. *Survey of Business,* pp. 22–26.

Dipboye, R.L., Arvey, R.D., & Terpstra, D.E. (1977). Sex and physical attractiveness of raters and applicants as determinants of resume evaluations. *Journal of Applied Psychology, 62,* 228–294.

Dipboye, R.L., Fromkin, H.L., & Wiback, K. (1975). Relative importance of applicant sex, attractiveness, and scholastic standing in evaluation of job applicant resumes. *Journal of Applied Psychology, 60,* 39–43.

Dobbins, G. (1985). Effects of gender on leader's responses to poor performers—

An attributional interpretation. *Journal of the Academy of Management,* *28,* 587–598.

Dobbins, G.H. (1986). Equity vs. equality. *Sex Roles, 15,* 513–523.

Dobbins, G.H., & Platz, S.J. (1986). Sex differences in leadership: How real are they? *Academy of Management Review, 11,* 118–127.

Dobbins, G., Pence, E., Orban, J., & Sgro, J. (1983). The effects of sex of leader and sex of subordinate on the use of organizational control policy. *Organizational Behavior and Human Decision-Making, 32,* 325–343.

Dobbins, G.H., Stuart, C., Pence, E.C., & Sgro, J.A. (1985). Cognitive mechanisms mediating the biasing effects of leader sex on ratings of leader behavior. *Sex Roles, 12,* 549–560.

Donnell, S., & Hall, J. (1980). Men and women as managers: A significant case of no significant difference. In J. A. Shtogred (Ed.), *Models for management: The structure of competence.* The Woodlands, TX: Teleometrics International, pp. 467–486.

Douvan, E. (1976). The role of models in women's professional development. *Psychology of Women Quarterly, 1,* 5–20.

Dovidio, J.F., & Ellyson, S.L. (1982). Decoding visual dominance: Attributions of power based on the relative percentages of looking while speaking and looking while listening. *Social Psychology Quarterly, 45,* 106–113.

Dovidio, J.F., Ellyson, S.L., Keating, C.F., Heltman, K., & Brown, C.E. (1988). The relationship of social power to visual displays of dominance between men and women. *Journal of Personality and Social Psychology, 54,* 233–242.

Dreben, E.K., Fiske, S.T., & Hastie, R. (1979). The independence of evaluative and item information: Impression and recall order effects in behavior-based impression formation. *Journal of Personality and Social Psychology, 37,* 1758–1768.

Drory, A., & Ben Porat. (1980). Leadership style and leniency bias in evaluation of employees' performance. *Psychological Reports, 46,* 735–739.

Dubnos, P. (1985). Attitudes toward women executives: A longitudinal approach. *Academy of Management Journal, 28,* 235–239.

Eagly, A.H. (1987). *Sex differences in social behavior: A social role social interpretation.* Hillsdale, NJ: Erlbaum.

Eagly, A.H., & Steffen, V.J. (1984). Gender stereotypes stem from the distribution of women and men into social roles. *Journal of Personality and Social Psychology, 46,* 735–754.

Eagly, A.H., & Wood, W. (1985). Gender and influenceability: Stereotype versus behavior. In V. O'Leary, R. Unger, & B. Wallston (Eds.), *Women, gender, and social psychology* (pp. 225–256). Hillsdale, NJ: Erlbaum.

Eakins, B., & Eakins, R. (1978). *Sex differences in human communication.* Boston, MA: Houghton, Mifflin.

Edelsky, C. (1981). Who's got the floor? *Language in Society, 10,* 383–421.

Erber, R., & Fiske, S.T. (1984). Outcome dependency and attention to inconsistent information. *Journal of Personality and Social Psychology, 47,* 709–726.

Erickson, B., Lind, E.A., Johnson, B.C., & O'Barr, W.M. (1978). Speech style and impression formation in court settings: The effects of "powerful" and "powerless" speech. *Journal of Experimental Social Psychology, 14,* 266–279.

Erkut, S. (1983). Exploring sex differences in expectancy, attribution, and academic achievement. *Sex Roles, 9,* 217–231.

Eskilson, A., & Wiley, M.G. (1976). Sex composition and leadership in small groups. *Sociometry, 39,* 183–194.

Exline, R.V., Ellyson, S.L., & Long, B. (1975). Visual behavior as an aspect of power role relationships. In P. Pliner, L. Krames, & T. Alloway (Eds.), *Nonverbal communication of aggression* (pp. 21–52). New York: Plenum.

Ezell, H.F., Odewahn, C.E., & Sherman, J.D. (1981). The effects of having been supervised by a woman on perception of female managerial competence. *Personnel Psychology, 34,* 291–299.

Fagenson, E. (1988). The power of a mentor. *Group and Organizational Studies, 13,* 182–194.

Fairhurst, G.T. (1986). Male-female communication on the job: Literature review and commentary. In M. McLaughlin (Ed.), *Communication Yearbook, 9,* 83–116.

Fairhurst, G.T., & Snavely, B.K. (1983). Majority and token minority group relationships: Power acquisition and communication. *Academy of Management Review, 8,* 292–300.

Fallon, B.J., & Hollander, E.P. (1976, September). *Sex role stereotyping in leadership: A study of undergraduate discussion groups.* Paper presented at the Annual Convention of the American Psychological Association, Washington, DC.

Fazio, R.H., Effrein, E.A., & Falender, V.J. (1981). Self perceptions following interaction. *Journal of Personality and Social Psychology, 41,* 232–242.

Feather, N.T., & Simon, J.F. (1975). Reactions to male and female success and failure in sex-linked occupations: Impression of personality, causal attributions, and perceived likelihood of different consequences. *Journal of Personality and Social Psychology, 31,* 20–31.

Feldman-Summers, S., & Kiesler, S.B. (1974). Those who are number two try harder: The effect of sex on attributions of causality. *Journal of Personality and Social Psychology, 8,* 846–855.

Ferber, M., Huber, J., & Spitze, G. (1979). Preference for men as bosses and professionals. *Social Forces, 58,* 466.

Festinger, L.A. (1954). Theory of social comparison processes. *Human Relations, 7,* 117–140.

Fidell, L.S. (1975). Empirical verification of sex discrimination in hiring practices in psychology. In R.K. Unger & F.L. Denmark (Eds.), *Women: Dependent or independent variable?* New York: Psychological Dimensions.

Fiorentine, R. (1988). Increasing similarity in the values and life plans of male and female college students? Evidence and implications. *Sex Roles, 18,* 143–158.

Fisher, B.A. (1974). *Small group decision making: Communication and the group process.* New York: McGraw-Hill.

Fishman, P.M. (1983). Interaction: The work women do. In B. Thorne, C. Kramarae, & N. Henley (Eds.), *Language, gender and society* (pp. 89–101). Rowley, MA: Newbury House.

Fiske, S.T. (1982). Schema-triggered affect: Applications to social perception. In M.S. Clark & S.T. Fiske (Eds.), *Affect and cognition: The 17th Annual Carnegie Symposium on Cognition.* Hillsdale, NJ: Erlbaum.

Fiske, S.T., Beattie, A.E., & Milberg, S.J. (1983). *A stereotype-piecemeal model of social cognition and social affect.* Unpublished manuscript, Carnegie-Mellon University, Pittsburgh.

Fiske, S.T., & Kinder, D.R. (1981). Involvement, expertise, and schema use: Evidence from political cognition. In N. Cantor & J. Kihlstrom (Eds.), *Personality, cognition, and social interaction.* Hillsdale, NJ: Erlbaum.

Fiske, S.T., & Pavelchak, M.A. (1986). Category-based versus piecemeal-based affective responses: Developments in schema-triggered affect. In R.M. Sorrentino & E.T. Higgins (Eds.), *Handbook of motivation and cognition: Foundations of social behavior* (pp. 167–203). New York: Guilford Press.

Fiske, S.T., & Taylor, S.E. (1984). *Social cognition.* Reading, MA: Addison-Wesley.

Fleishman, A., & Marwell, G. (1977). Status congruence and associativeness— Test of Galtung's theory. *Sociometry, 40,* 1–11.

Forgionne, G.A., & Nwacukwu, C.C. (1977). Acceptance of authority in female-managed organizational positions. *University of Michigan Business Review, 29,* 23–28.

Forsyth, D.R., & Forsyth, N.M. (1984, April). *Subordinates' reactions to female leaders.* Paper presented at the Eastern Psychological Association Convention, Baltimore.

Forsyth, D., Schlenker, B., Leary, M., & McCown, N. (1985). Self-presentational determinants of sex differences in leadership behavior. *Small Group Behavior, 16,* 197–210.

Frank, E.J. (1988). Business students' perceptions of women in management. *Sex Roles, 19,* 107–118.

Frank, H.H., & Katcher, A.H. (1977). The qualities of leadership: How male medical students evaluate their female peers. *Human Relations, 30,* 403–416.

Frieze, I.H., Fisher, J., Hanusa, B., McHugh, M., & Valle, V. (1978). Attributing the causes of success and failure: Internal and external barriers to achievement in women. In J. Sherman & F. Denmark (Eds.), *Psychology of women: Future directions of research.* New York: Psychological Dimensions.

Frost, P. (1987). Power, politics and influence. In F. Jablin, L. Putnam, K. Roberts & L. Porter (Eds.), *Handbook of organizational communication.* Newbury Park, CA: Sage Publications, Inc.

Fulk, J., Steinfield, C., Schmitz, J., & Power, J. (1987). A social information processing model of media use in organizations. *Communication Research, 14,* 529–552.

Futoran, G.C., & Wyer, Jr., R.J. (1986). The effects of traits and gender stereotypes on occupational suitability judgments and the recall of judgment-relevant behavior. *Journal of Experimental Social Psychology*, 22, 475–503.

Gazzaniga, M.S. (1985). *The social brain: Discovering the networks of the mind.* New York: Basic Books.

Geis, F.L., Boston, M.B., & Hoffman, N. (1985). Sex of authority role models and achievement by men and women: Leadership performance and recognition. *Journal of Personality and Social Psychology*, 49, 636–653.

Geis, F.L., Brown, V., Jennings, J.W., & Corrado-Taylor, D. (1984). Sex vs. status in sex-associated stereotypes. *Sex Roles*, 11, 771–786.

Geis, F.L., Brown, V., Jennings, J., & Porter, N. (1984). T.V. commercials as achievement scripts for women. *Sex Roles*, 10, 513–525.

Geis, F.L., Brown, V., & Wolfe, C. (1990). Legitimizing the leader: Endorsement by male versus female authority figures. *Journal of Applied Social Psychology*, 20, 943–970.

Geis, F.L., Carter, M.R., & Butler, D. (1986). *Seeing and evaluating people* (rev. ed.). Newark, DE: Office of Women's Affairs, University of Delaware.

Gersick, C. (1988). Time and transition in work teams: Toward a new model of group development. *Academy of Management Journal*, 31, 7–42.

Giacalone, R.A. (1988). The effect of administrative accounts and gender on the perception of leadership. *Group & Organization Studies*, 13, 2, 195–207.

Glick, P., Zion, C., & Nelson, C. (1988). What mediates sex discrimination in hiring decisions? *Journal of Personality and Social Psychology*, 55, 178–186.

Goktepe, J.R., & Schneier, C.E. (1988). Sex and gender effects in evaluating emergent leaders in small groups. *Sex Roles*, 19, 29–36.

Goldberg, P. (1968, April 5). Are women prejudiced against women? *Transaction*, pp. 28–30.

Goldstein, E. (1979). Effect of same-sex and cross-sex role models on the subsequent academic productivity of scholars. *American Psychologist*, 23, 407–410.

Golub, S. (1976). The effect of premenstrual anxiety and depression on cognitive function. *Journal of Personality and Social Psychology*, 34, 99–104.

Gove, W. (1972). The relationship between sex roles, mental illness and marital status. *Social Forces*, 51, 34–44.

Green, S., & Mitchell, T. (1979). Attributional process in leader-member interactions. *Organizational Behavior and Human Performance*, 23, 429–458.

Greenglass, E.R. (1985, Summer). Psychological implications of sex bias in the workplace. *Academic Psychology Bulletin*, 7, 227–240.

Gupta, N., Jenkins, Jr., G.D., & Beehr, T.A. (1983). Employee gender, gender similarity, and supervisor-subordinate cross-evaluations. *Sex Roles*, 8, 174–184.

Gutek, B.A. (1985). *Sex and the workplace: The impact of sexual behavior and harassment on women, men, and organizations.* San Francisco: Jossey-Bass.

Gutek, B.A., & Stevens, D.A. (1979). Differential responses of males and females to work situations which evoke sex role stereotypes. *Journal of Vocational Behavior, 14*, 23–32.

Haas, A. (1979). Male and female spoken language differences: Stereotypes and evidence. *Psychological Bulletin, 86* (3), 616–626.

Haccoun, D.M., Haccoun, R.R., & Sallay, G. (1978). Sex differences in the appropriateness of supervisory styles: A nonmanagement view. *Journal of Applied Psychology, 63* (1), 124–127.

Haefner, J.E. (1977). Race, age, sex, and competence as factors in employee selection of the disadvantaged. *Journal of Applied Psychology, 62*, 199–202.

Hagen, R.L., & Kahn, A. (1975). Discrimination against competent women. *Journal of Applied Social Psychology, 5*, 362–376.

Hamilton, D.L. (1979). A cognitive-attributional analysis of stereotyping. *Advances in Experimental Social Psychology, 12*, 53–84.

Hamilton, D.L., & Gifford, R.K. (1976). Illusory correlation and interpersonal perception: A cognitive basis of stereotypic judgments. *Journal of Experimental Social Psychology, 12*, 392–407.

Hansen, R.D., & O'Leary, V.E. (1983). Actresses and actors: The effects of sex on causal attribution. *Basic and Applied Social Psychology, 4*, 209–230.

Harper, N.L., & Hirokawa, R.Y. (1988, Spring). A comparison of persuasive strategies used by female and male managers I: An examination of downward influence. *Communication Quarterly, 36* (2), 157–168.

Harriman, A. (1985). *Women/men management*. New York: Praeger.

Harris, M.J., & Rosenthal, R. (1985). Mediation of interpersonal expectancy effects: 31 meta-analyses. *Psychological Bulletin, 97*, 363–386.

Haslett, B. (1987). *Communication: Strategic action in context*. Hillsdale, NJ: Erlbaum.

Haslett, B. (in press). Gender, power and communication in organizations. In B. Dervin & M. Voight (Eds.), *Progress in Communication Science (Vol. 13)*. Norwood, NJ: Ablex Publishing Corp.

Haslett, B., & Ogilvie, J. (1988). Feedback processes in task groups. In R. Cathcart & L. Samovar (Eds.), *Small group communication*. Dubuque, IA: W.C. Brown & Company.

Hastie, R. (1981). Schematic principles in human memory. In E.T. Higgins, C.P. Herman, & M.P. Zanna (Eds.), *Social cognition: The Ontario symposium (Vol. 1)*. Hillsdale, NJ: Erlbaum.

Heilman, M.E. (1983). Sex bias in work settings: The lack of fit model. In B.M. Staw & L.L. Cummings (Eds.), *Research in organizational behavior (Vol. 5)*. Greenwich, CT: JAI Press.

Hennig, M., & Jardim, A. (1977). *The managerial woman*. New York: Simon And Schuster.

Hersey, P., & Blanchard, K.H. (1969). Life cycle theory of leadership. *Training and Development Journal, 23*, 26–34.

Higgins, E.T., & King, G.A. (1981). Accessibility of social constructs: Information-processing consequences of individual and contextual variability. In N. Cantor & J.F. Kihlstrom (Eds.), *Personality, cognition, and social interaction*. Hillsdale, NJ: Erlbaum.

Hilton, J.L., & Darley, J.M. (1985). Constructing other persons: A limit on the effect. *Journal of Experimental Social Psychology, 21*, 1–18.

Hocker, J., & Wilmot, W. (1985). *Interpersonal conflict.* Dubuque, IA: W.C. Brown Co.

Hoffman, C., & Hurst, N. (1990). Gender stereotypes: Perception or rationalization? *Journal of Personality and Social Psychology, 58*, 197–208.

Hoffman, M.L. (1977). Empathy, its development and prosocial implications. *Nebraska Symposium on Motivation (Vol. 15).* Lincoln, NE: University of Nebraska Press.

Hollander, E.P. (1964). *Leaders, groups and influence.* New York: Oxford University Press.

Hollander, E.P. (1985). Leadership and power. In G. Lindzey & E. Aronson (Eds.), *Handbook of social psychology* (3rd ed., Vol. 2, pp. 485–537). New York: Random House.

Holter, H. (1971). Sex roles and social change. *Acta Sociologica, 14*, 2–12.

Horner, M.S. (1972). Toward an understanding of achievement related conflicts in women. *Journal of Social Issues, 28*, 157–175.

Huber, G., & Daft, R. (1987). The information environment in organizations. In F. Jablin, L. Putnam, K. Roberts, & L. Porter (Eds.), *Handbook of organizational communication.* Beverly Hills, CA: Sage.

Hunt, D.E. (1987). *Beginning with ourselves: In practice, theory, and human affairs.* Cambridge, MA: Brookline Books.

Hyde, J.S., & Linn, M.C. (1986). *The psychology of gender: Advances through meta-analysis.* Baltimore, MD: Johns Hopkins University Press.

Hyman, B. (1980). Responsive leadership: The women manager's asset or liability? *Supervisory Management, 25*, 40–43.

Ickes, W., & Knowles, E.S. (Eds.). (1982). *Personality roles and social behavior.* New York: Springer-Verlag.

Insko, C.A., Gilmore, R., Drenan, S., Lipsitz, A., Moehle, D., & Thibaut, J. (1983). Trade versus expropriation in open groups: A comparison of two types of social power. *Journal of Personality and Social Psychology, 44*, 977–999.

Instone, D., Major, B., & Bunker, B.B. (1983). Gender, self confidence, and social influence strategies: An organizational simulation. *Journal of Personality and Social Psychology, 44*, 322–333.

Isaacs, M.B. (1981). Sex role stereotyping and the evaluation of the performance of women: Changing trends. *Psychology of Women Quarterly, 6*, 187–195.

Jablin, F.M. (1980). Subordinate's sex and superior-subordinate status differentiation as moderators of the Pelz effect. In D. Nimmo (Ed.), *Communication yearbook 4* (pp. 349–365). Beverly Hills, CA: Sage Publications, Inc.

Jennings (Walstedt), J., Geis, F.L., & Brown, V. (1980). The influence of television commercials on women's self-confidence and independent judgment. *Journal of Personality and Social Psychology, 38*, 203–210.

Jerdee, T.H., & Rosen, B. (1976, September). *Factors in influencing the career development of women.* Paper, Annual Meeting of the American Psychological Association, Washington, DC.

Johnson, B., & O'Barr, W. (1978). Speech style and impression formation in a court setting: The effects of 'powerful' and 'powerless' speech. *Journal of Experimental Social Psychology, 14,* 266–279.

Johnson, F.L. (1983). Political and pedagogical implications of attitudes towards women's language. *Communication Quarterly, 31,* 133–138.

Johnson, P. (1976). Women and power: Toward a theory of effectiveness. *Journal of Social Issues, 32,* 99–110.

Jones, E.E., & Nisbett, R.E. (1972). The actor and the observer: Divergent perceptions of the causes of behavior. In E.E. Jones, D.E. Kanouse, H.H. Kelley, R.E. Nisbett, S. Valins, & B. Weiner (Eds.), *Attribution: Perceiving the causes of behavior.* Morristown, NJ: General Learning Press.

Jones, R.A. (1977). *Self-fulfilling prophecies: Social, psychological, and physiological effects of expectancies.* Hillsdale, NJ: Erlbaum.

Josefowitz, N. (1980). Management men and women: Closed vs. open doors. *Harvard Business Review, 58,* 57–62.

Kalin, R., & Hodgins, D.C. (1984). Sex bias in judgements of occupational suitability. *Canadian Journal of Behavioral Science, 16,* 311–325.

Kanter, R.M. (1977). *Men and women of the corporation.* New York: Basic Books.

Kanter, R.M. (1983). *The change masters.* New York: Simon & Schuster.

Kennedy, C.W., & Camden, C.T. (1981). Gender differences in interruption behavior: A dominance perspective. *International Journal of Women's Studies, 4,* 135–142.

Kimble, C.E., Yoshikawa, J.C., & Zehr, H.D. (1981). Vocal and verbal assertiveness in same-sex and mixed-sex groups. *Journal of Personality and Social Psychology, 40,* 1047–1054.

Kipnis, D., & Schmidt, S.M. (1982). *Profiles of organizational influence strategies: A diagnostic survey and profile.* (POIS). San Diego: University Associates.

Klatzky, R.L., Martin, G.L., & Kane, R.A. (1982). Influence of social-category activation on processing of visual information. *Social Cognition, 1,* 95–109.

Koberg, C.S. (1985). Sex and situational influences on the use of power: A follow-up study. *Sex Roles, 13,* 625–639.

Kohlberg, L.H. (1966). A cognitive-developmental analysis of children's sex role concepts and attitudes. In E.E. Maccoby (Ed.), *The development of sex differences.* Palo Alto, CA: Stanford University Press.

Kram, K., & Isabella, L. (1983). *Mentoring alternatives: The role of peer relationships in career development.* Paper presented to the Academy of Management Meeting, Dallas, Texas.

Kramerae, C. (1978a). Women's and men's ratings of their own and ideal speech. *Communication Quarterly, 26,* 2–11.

Kramerae, C. (1978b). Male and female perceptions of male and female speech. *Language and Speech, 20,* 151–161.

Krone, K. (1985). *Subordinate influence in organizations: The differential use of upward influence messages in decision making contexts.* Unpublished doctoral dissertation, University of Texas, Austin, TX.

Kuffler, S.W., & Nicholls, J.G. (1976). *From neuron to brain*. Sunderland, MA: Sinauer Associates.

Kuhlman, D.M., Brown, C., & Teta, P. (in press). Judgements of cooperation and defection in social dilemmas: The moderating role of judge's social orientation. In D. Messick, H. Wilke, & W. Liebrand (Eds.), *A social psychological approach to social dilemmas*. New York: Pergamon Press.

Kulik, J.A. (1983). Confirmatory attributions and the perpetuation of social beliefs. *Journal of Personality and Social Psychology, 44*, 1171–1181.

Larwood, L., & Lockhead, M. (1979). Women as managers: Toward second generation research. *Sex Roles, 5*, 659–666.

Lenney, E. (1977). Women's self-confidence in achievement settings. *Psychological Bulletin, 84*, 1–13.

Lenney, E., & Gold, J. (1982). Sex differences in self-confidence: The effects of task completion and of comparison to competent others. *Personality and Social Psychology Bulletin, 8*, 74–80.

Levine, J.M., & Murphy, G.M. (1943). The learning and forgetting of controversial material. *Journal of Abnormal and Social Psychology, 38*, 507–517.

Lewicki, P. (1985). Nonconscious biasing effects of single instances on subsequent judgments. *Journal of Personality and Social Psychology, 48*, 563–575.

Lewicki, P. (1986). *Nonconscious social information processing*. Orlando, FL: Harcourt Brace Jovanovich.

Liden, R.C. (1985). Female perceptions of female and male managerial behavior. *Sex Roles, 12*(3/4), 421–432.

Linimon, D., Barron, W., & Falbo, T. (1984). Gender differences in perceptions of leadership. *Sex Roles, 11*(11/12), 1075–1088.

Linton, R. (1966). *The study of man*. New York: Appleton-Century-Croft.

Lippa, R., & Beauvais, C. (1983). Gender jeopardy: The effects of gender, assessed femininity and masculinity and false success/failure feedback on performance in an experimental quiz game. *Journal of Personality and Social Psychology, 44*, 344–353.

Lockheed, M.E., & Hall, K.P. (1976). Conceptualizing sex as a status characteristic: Applications to leadership training strategies. *Journal of Social Issues, 32*, 3, 111–123.

Lord, C.G., Lepper, M.R., & Mackie, D.M. (1984). Attitude prototypes as determinants of attitude-behavior consistency. *Journal of Personality and Social Psychology, 46*, 1254–1266.

Lord, R.G., Binning, J.F., Rush, M.C., & Thomas, J.C. (1978). The effect of performance cues and leader behavior on questionnaire rating of leadership behavior. *Organizational Behavior and Human Performance, 21*, 27–39.

Lott, B. (1987). Sexist discrimination as distancing behavior: I. A laboratory demonstration. *Psychology of Women Quarterly, 11*, 47–58.

Lubinski, D., Tellegen, A., & Butcher, J.N. (1983). Masculinity, femininity, and androgyny viewed and assessed as distinct concepts. *Journal of Personality and Social Psychology, 44*, 428–439.

Luthans, F., Hodgetts, R., & Rosenkrantz, S. (1988). *Real managers*. Cambridge, MA: Ballinger Press.

Luthans, F., & Larsen, J.K. (1986). How managers really communicate. *Human Relations, 39*, 161–178.

Maccoby, E., & Jacklin, C.N. (1974). *The psychology of sex differences*. Palo Alto, CA: Stanford University Press.

Mainiero, L.A. (1986). Coping with powerlessness: The relationship of gender and job dependency to empowerment-strategy usage. *Administrative Science Quarterly, 31*, 633–653.

Maltz, D., & Borker, R. (1982). A cultural approach to male- female miscommunication. In J. Gumperz (Ed.), *Language and social identity*. Cambridge, UK: Cambridge University Press.

Marcel, A.J. (1982). Conscious and unconscious perception: I, Experiments on visual masking and word perception. *Cognitive Psychology, 15*, 238–300.

Markus, L. (1987). Toward a "critical mass" theory of interactive media: Universal access, interdependence and diffusion. *Communication Research, 14*, 491–511.

Massad, C.M., Hubbard, M., & Newtson, D. (1979). Selective perception of events. *Journal of Experimental Social Psychology, 15*, 513–532.

McArthur, L.Z. (1981). What grabs you? The role of attention in impression formation and causal attribution. In E.T. Higgins, C.P. Herman, & M.P. Zanna (Eds.), *Social cognition: The Ontario Symposium (Vol. 1)*. Hillsdale, NJ: Erlbaum.

McArthur, L.Z., & Baron, R. (1983). Toward an ecological theory of social perception. *Psychological Review, 90*, 215–238.

McArthur, L.Z., & Friedman, S.A. (1980). Illusory correlation in impression formation: Variations in the shared distinctiveness effect as a function of the distinctive person's age, race, and sex. *Journal of Personality and Social Psychology, 39*, 615–624.

McBroom, W.H. (1984). Changes in sex-role orientations: A five year longitudinal comparison. *Sex Roles, 11*, 583–592.

McCall Jr., M.W. (1983). What makes a top executive? *Psychology Today, 26*, 26–31.

McCallister, L., & Gaymon, D. (1989). Male and female managers in the 21st century: Will there be a difference? In C. Lont & S. Friedley (Eds.), *Beyond barriers*. Fairfax, VA: George Mason University Press.

McComas, M. (1986). Atop the *Fortune* 500: A survey of the CEO's. *Fortune, 113*(9), 26–31.

McCombs, H.G. (1989). The dynamics and impact of affirmative action processes on higher education, the curiculum, and black women. *Sex Roles, 21*, 127–144.

McMillan, J.R., Clifton, A.K., McGrath, D., & Gale, W.S. (1977). Women's language: Uncertainty or interpersonal sensitivity and emotionality? *Sex Roles, 3*, 545–560.

McPhee, R., Poole, M., & Seibold, D. (1981). The valence model unveiled: Critique and alternative formulation. In M. Burgoon (Ed.), *Communication yearbook 5* (pp. 259–278). New Brunswick, NJ: Transaction Books.

Mechanic, D. (1962). Sources of power for lower participants in complex organizations. *Administrative Science Quarterly, 7*, 349–364.

Meeker, B.F., & Weitzel-O'Neill, P.A. (1977). Sex roles and interpersonal behavior in task-oriented groups. *American Sociological Review, 42*, 91–105.

Megargee, E.E. (1969). Influence of sex roles on the manifestation of leadership. *Journal of Applied Psychology, 53*, 377–382.

Mellon, P.M., Crano, W.D., & Schmitt, N. (1982). An analysis of the role and trait components of sex-biased occupational beliefs. *Sex Roles, 8*(5), 533–541.

Merton, R.K. (1948). The self-fulfilling prophecy. *Antioch Review, 8*, 193–210.

Miller, J.G. (1984). Culture and the development of everyday social explanation. *Journal of Personality and Social Psychology, 46*, 961–978.

Mintzberg, H. (1973). *The nature of managerial work*. New York: Harper and Row.

Mischel, W. (1970). Sextyping and socialization. In P.H. Mussen (Ed.), *Carmichael's manual of child psychology* (vol. 2, 3rd ed.). New York: Wiley.

Montgomery, B., & Norton, R. (1981). Sex differences and similarities in communicator style. *Communication Monographs, 48*, 121–132.

Moore, L. (1986). *Not as far as you think*. Boston: Heath and Company.

Moore, L.M., & Rickel, A.V. (1980). Characteristics of women in traditional and nontraditional managerial roles. *Personnel Psychology, 33*, 317–333.

Morrison, A.M., White, R.P., Van Velsor, E., & The Center for Creative Leadership. (1987). *Breaking the glass ceiling: Can women reach the top of America's largest corporations?* Reading, MA: Addison-Wesley.

Moscovici, S. (1983). Social representations and social explanations: From the "naive" to the "amateur" scientist. In M. Hewstone (Ed.), *Attribution theory: Social and functional extensions*. Oxford: Blackwells.

Nadler, D. (1979). The effects of feedback on task group behavior. *Organizational Behavior and Human Performance, 23*, 309–338.

National Center for Education Statistics. (1982). Earned degrees conferred 1970-1971 and 1980-1981. *Digest of Education Statistics*.

National Research Council, Committee on the Education and Employment of Women in Science and Engineering. (1981). *Career outcomes in a matched sample of men and women Ph.D.'s: An analytical report*. Washington, DC: National Academy Press.

Nauta, W.J. (1971). The problem of the frontal lobe: A reinterpretation. *Journal of Psychiatric Research, 8*, 167–187.

Newcombe, N., & Arnkoff, D.B. (1979). Effects of speech style and sex of speaker on person perception. *Journal of Personality and Social Psychology, 37*, 1293–1303.

Nieva, V.F., & Gutek, B.A. (1980). Sex differences in evaluation. *Academy of Management Review, 5*, 267–276.

Nieva, V.F., & Gutek, B.A. (1981). *Women and work: A psychological perspective*. New York: Praeger.

Nisbett, R.E., & Bellows, N. (1977). Verbal reports about causal influences on social judgments: Private access versus public theories. *Journal of Personality and Social Psychology, 35*, 613–624.

Nisbett, R.E., & Ross, L. (1980). *Human inference: Strategies and shortcomings of social judgment.* Englewood Cliffs, NJ: Prentice-Hall.

Nisbett, R.E., & Wilson, T.D. (1977). Telling more than we can know: Verbal reports on mental processes. *Psychological Review, 84*, 231–259.

Nkomo, S.M., & Cox, T., Jr. (1989). Gender differences in the upward mobility of black managers: Double whammy or double advantage. *Sex Roles, 21*, 825–839.

Norton, R. (1983). *Communicator style.* Beverly Hills, CA: Sage.

Nyquist, L.V., & Spence, J.T. (1986). Effects of dispositional dominance and sex role expectations on leadership behaviors. *Journal of Personality and Social Psychology, 50*, 87–93.

O'Barr, W.M., & Atkins, B. (1980). 'Women's language' or 'powerless language'. In S. McConnell-Ginet, R. Borker, & N. Furman (Eds.), *Women and language in literature and society.* New York: Praeger.

O'Leary, V.E. (1974). Some attitudenal barriers to occupational aspirations in women. *Psychological Bulletin, 81*, 809–826.

Offerman, L.R. (1984). Short-term supervisory experience and LPC score: Effects of leader sex and group sex composition. *The Journal of Social Psychology, 123*, 115–121.

Offerman, L.R. (1986). Visibility and evaluation of female and male leaders. *Sex Roles, 14*, 533–543.

Olson, J.E., & Frieze, I.H. (1987). Income determinants for women in business. In A.H. Stromberg, L. Larwood, & B.A. Gutek (Eds.), *Women and work: An annual review* (Vol. 2, pp. 173–206). Newbury Park, CA: Sage.

Osborn, R.N., & Vicars, W.M. (1976). Sex stereotypes: An artifact in leader behavior and subordinate satisfaction analysis? *Academy of Management Journal, 19*, 439–449.

Pocanowsky, M., & O'Donnell-Trujillo, N. (1983). Organizational Communication as cultural performances. *Communication Monographs, 50*, 126–147.

Paludi, M.A., & Strayer, L.A. (1985). What's in an author's name? Differential evaluations of performance as a function of author's name. *Sex Roles, 12*, 353–361.

Pavitt, C., & Curtis, E. (1990). *Small group discussion: A theoretical approach.* Scottsdale, AR: Gorsuch Scarisbrick.

Pearson, J. (1985). *Gender and communication.* Dubuque, IA: W.C. Brown.

Pelz, D. (1952). Influence: A key to effective leadership in the first line supervisor. *Personnel, 29*, 209–217.

Petty, M.M., & Lee, G.K. (1975). Moderating effects of sex of supervisor and subordinate on relationships between supervisory behavior and subordinate satisfaction. *Journal of Applied Psychology, 60*, 624–628.

Petty, M.M., & Miles, R.H. (1976). Leader sex-role stereotyping in a female dominated work culture. *Personnel Psychology, 29*, 393–404.

Pfeffer, J. (1977). The ambiguity of leadership. In M.W. McCall, Jr. & M.M.

Lombardo (Eds.), *Leadership: Where else can we do?* Durham, NC: Duke University Press.

Pfeffer, J. (1981). *Power in organizations.* Marshfield, MA.: Pittman.

Pheterson, G.I., Kiesler, S.B., & Goldberg, P.A. (1971). Evaluation of the performance of women as a function of their sex, achievement and personal history. *Journal of Personality and Social Psychology, 19,* 114–118.

Piliavin, J.A., & Martin, R. (1978). The effects of sex composition of groups on style of social interaction. *Sex Roles, 4*(2), 281–296.

Poole, M. (1983). Decision development in small groups II: A multiple sequence model of group decision development. *Communication Monographs, 50,* 321–341.

Porter, N., & Geis, F.L. (1981). Women and nonverbal leadership cues: When seeing is not believing. In C. Mayo & N. Henley (Eds.), *Gender and nonverbal behavior.* New York: Springer-Verlag.

Porter, N., Geis, F.L., Cooper, E., & Newman, E. (1985). Androgyny and leadership in mixed-sex groups. *Journal of Personality and Social Psychology, 49,* 803–823.

Powell, G.N. (1987). The effects of sex and gender on recruitment. *Academy of Management Review, 12,* 731–743.

Powell, G.N. (1988). *Women and men in management.* Newbury Park, CA: Sage Publications.

Powell, G.N., & Butterfield, D.A. (1979). The good manager: Masculine or androgynous? *Academy of Management Journal, 22,* 395–403.

Powell, G.N., & Butterfield, D.A. (1986). *The good manager: Does androgyny fare better in the 1980's?* Paper presented at the annual meeting of the Academy of Management, Chicago.

Powell, G.N., & Posner, B.Z. (1983). Stereotyping by college recruiters. *Journal of College Placement, 64,* 63–65.

Powell, G.N., Posner, B.Z., & Schmidt, W.H. (1984). Sex effects in managerial value systems. *Human Relations, 37,* 909–921.

Pruitt, D.G., & Lewis, S.A. (1975). Development of integrative solutions in bilateral negotiation. *Journal of Personality and Social Psychology, 31,* 621–633.

Putnam, L. (1983). Lady you're trapped: Breaking out of conflict cycles. In J. Pilotta (Ed.), *Women in organizations: Barriers and breakthroughs* (pp. 39–54). Prospect Heights, IL: Waveland Press.

Putnam, L. (1988). Understanding the unique characteristics of groups within organizations. In R. Cathcart & L. Samovar (Eds.), *Small group communication.* Dubuque, IA: W. C. Brown.

Putnam, L., & Fairhurst, G. (1985). Women and organizational communication: Research directions and new perspective. *Women & Language, 9,* 2–6.

Putnam, L., & Jones, P. (1982). Reciprocity in negotiations: An analysis of bargaining interaction. *Communication Monographs, 49,* 171–191.

Putnam, L., & Poole, M.S. (1987). Conflict and negotiation. In F. Jablin, L.

Putnam, K. Roberts & L. Porter (Eds.), *Handbook of organizational communication*. Beverly Hills, CA: Sage.

Pyke, S.W., & Kahil, S.P. (1983). Sex differences in characteristics presumed relevant to professional productivity. *Sex Roles, 8*, 189–192.

Quattrone, G.A., & Tversky, A. (1984). Causal versus diagnostic contingencies: On self-deception and on the voter's illusion. *Journal of Personality and Social Psychology, 46*, 237–248.

Rasinsky, K.A., Crocker, J., & Hastie, R. (1985). Another look at sex stereotypes and social judgments: An analysis of the social perceive's use of subjective probabilities. *Journal of Personality and Social Psychology, 49*, 317–326.

Reardon, K. (1981). *Persuasion: Theory and context*. Beverly Hills, CA: Sage.

Reinisch, J.M., Rosenblum, L.A., & Sanders, A.S. (Eds.). (1987). *Masculinity/femininity: Basic perspectives*. New York: Oxford University Press.

Rhue, J., Lynn, S.J., & Garske, J.P. (1984). The effects of competent behavior on interpersonal attraction and task leadership. *Sex Roles, 10*, 925–939.

Rice, R.W., Instone, D., & Adams, J. (1984). Leader sex, leader success, and leadership process: Two field studies. *Journal of Applied Psychology, 69*, 12–31.

Ridgeway, C.L. (1982). Status in groups: The importance of motivation. *American Sociological Review, 47*, 76–88.

Riecken, H.W. (1958). The effect of talkativeness on ability to influence solutions of problems. *Sociometry, 21*, 309–321.

Rock, I. (1983). *The logic of perception*. Cambridge, MA: MIT Press.

Rosen, B., & Jerdee, T.H. (1973). The influence of sex-role stereotypes on evaluations of male and female supervisory behavior. *Journal of Applied Psychology, 57*, 44–48.

Rosen, B., & Jerdee, T.H. (1974). Influence of sex-role stereotypes on personnel decisions. *Journal of Applied Psychology, 59*, 9–14.

Rosen, B., & Jerdee, T.H. (1978). Perceived sex differences in managerially relevant characteristics. *Sex Roles, 4* (6), 837–843.

Rosen, B., Jerdee, T.H., & Prestwick, T. L. (1975). Dual career mutual adjustment: Potential effects of discriminatory managerial attitudes. *Journal of Marriage and the Family, 37*, 565–572.

Rosenthal, R. (1974). *On the social psychology of the self-fulfilling prophecy: Further evidence for pygmalion effects and their mediating mechanisms*. New York: MSS Modular Publications, Inc., Module 53.

Ross, L. (1977). The intuitive psychologist and his shortcomings. In L. Berkowitz (Ed.), *Advances in experimental social psychology* (Vol.10). New York: Academic Press.

Rothbart, M. (1981). Memory processes and social beliefs. In D. Hamilton (Ed.), *Cognitive processes in stereotyping and intergroup behavior*. Hillsdale, NJ: Erlbaum.

Rothbart, M., Evans, M., & Fulero, S. (1979). Recall for confirming events: Memory processes and the maintenance of social stereotypes. *Journal of Experimental Social Psychology, 15*, 343–355.

Rowe, M.P. (1977). The saturn rings phenomenon: Micro-inequities and unequal opportunity in the American economy. In P. Bourne & V. Parness (Eds.), *Proceedings of the NSF Conference on Women's Leadership and Authority.* Santa Cruz, CA: University of California Press.

Rowe, M.P. (1990). People who feel harassed need a complaint system with formal and informal options. *Negotiation Journal, 6,* 1–12.

Rowe, M.P. (in press). Options and choice for conflict resolution in the workplace. In L. Hall (Ed.), *Changing tactics.* Washington, DC: National Institute for Dispute Resolution.

Rush, M.C., Thomas, J.C., & Lord, R.R. (1977). Implicit leadership theory: A potential threat to the internal validity of leader behavior questionnaires. *Organizational Behavior and Human Performance, 20,* 93–110.

Salary Tables. (1982, February 17). *Chronicle of Higher Education.*

Sampson, E.E. (1969). Studies of status congruence. In L. Berkowitz (Ed.), *Advances in experimental social psychology,* (Vol. 4). New York: Academic Press.

Scanzoni, J. (1982). *Sexual bargaining: Power politics in the American marriage* (2nd ed.). Chicago: University of Chicago Press.

Schank, R., & Abelson, R. (1977). *Scripts, plans, goals and understanding.* Hillsdale, NJ: Erlbaum.

Scheflen, A. (1974). *How behavior means.* New York: Doubleday.

Scheidel, T., & Crowell, L. (1964). Idea development in small discussion groups. *Quarterly Journal of Speech, 50,* 140–145.

Schein, E.H. (1985). *Organizational culture and leadership.* San Francisco, CA: Jossey-Bass.

Schein, V.E. (1973). Relationship between sex role stereotypes and requisite management characteristics. *Journal of Applied Psychology, 57,* 95–100.

Schein, V.E. (1975). Relationships between sex-role stereotypes and requisite management characteristics among female managers. *Journal of Applied Psychology, 60,* 340–344.

Schein, V.E. (1978). Sex-role stereotyping, ability, and performance: Prior research and new directions. *Personnel Psychology, 31,* 259–268.

Schneier, C.E. (1978). The contingency model of leadership: An extension to emergent leadership and leader's sex. *Organizational Behavior and Human Performance, 21,* 220–239.

Schneier, C.E., & Bartol, K.M. (1980). Sex effects in emergent leadership. *Journal of Applied Psychology, 65,* 341–345.

Schriesheim, C.A., Kinicki, A.J., & Schriesheim, J.F. (1979). The effect of leniency on leader behavior descriptions. *Organizational Behavior and Human Performance, 23,* 1–29.

Schul, Y., & Burnstein, E. (1983). The informational basis of social judgments: Memory for informative and uninformative arguments. *Journal of Experimental Social Psychology, 19,* 422–433.

Seifert, C., & Miller, C.E. (1988). Subordinates' perceptions of leaders in task-performing dyads: Effects of sex of leader and subordinate, method of leader selection, and performance feedback. *Sex Roles, 19,* 13–28.

Selkow, P. (1984). Effects of maternal employment on kindergarten and first-grade children's vocational aspirations. *Sex Roles, 11,* 677–690.

Seyfried, B.A., & Hendrick, C. (1973). When do opposites attract? When they are opposite in sex and sex-role attitudes. *Journal of Personality and Social Psychology, 25,* 15–20.

Sherif, M. (1935). A study of some social factors in perception. *Archives of Psychology,* No. 187.

Shockley-Zalabak, P., Staley, C., & Morley, D. (1988). The female professional: Perceived communication proficiencies as predictors of organizational advancement. *Human Relations,* 41, 553–567.

Short, J., Williams, E., & Christie, B. (1976). *The social psychology of telecommunications.* London: John Wiley & Sons.

Sitterly, C., & Duke, C.W. (1988). *A woman's place: Management.* Englewood Cliffs, NJ: Prentice-Hall.

Skrypnek, B.J., & Snyder, M. (1982). On the self perpetuating nature of stereotypes about women and men. *Journal of Experimental Social Psychology, 18,* 277–291.

Slusher, M.P., & Anderson, C.A. (1987). When reality monitoring fails: The role of imagination in stereotype maintenance. *Journal of Personality and Social Psychology, 52,* 653–662.

Smith, E.R., & Miller, F.D. (1983). Mediation among attributional inferences and comprehension processes: Initial findings and a general method. *Journal of Personality and Social Psychology, 44,* 492–505.

Smith, H., & Grenier, M. (1982). Sources of organizational power for women: Overcoming structural obstacles. *Sex Roles, 8,* 733–746.

Snyder, M., & Cantor, N. (1980). Thinking about ourselves and others: Self-monitoring and social knowledge. *Journal of Personality and Social Psychology, 39,* 222–234.

Snyder, M., & Swann W. B., Jr. (1978). Hypothesis testing processes in social interaction. *Journal of Personality and Social Psychology, 36,* 1202–1212.

Snyder, M., Tanke, E.D., & Berscheid, E. (1977). Social perception and interpersonal behavior: On the self-fulfilling nature of social stereotypes. *Journal of Personality and Social Psychology, 35,* 656–666.

Sorentino, R.M., & Boutillier, R.G. (1975). The effect of quantity and quality of verbal interaction on ratings of leadership ability. *Journal of Experimental Social Psychology, 11,* 403–411.

Spence, J.T. (1985). Gender identity and its implications for concepts of masculinity and femininity. In T. Sondregger (Ed.), *Nebraska symposium on motivation* (pp. 59–95). Lincoln, NE : University of Nebraska Press.

Spence, J.T., & Helmreich, R.L. (1978). *Masculinity and femininity: The psychological dimensions, correlates and antecedents.* Austin, TX: University of Texas Press.

Stake, J.E. (1981). Promoting leadership behaviors in low-performance-self esteem women in task-oriented mixed-sex dyads. *Journal of Personality, 49,* 401–414.

Staley, C., & Cohen, J. (1988). Communicator style and social style: Similarities and differences between the sexes. *Communication Quarterly, 36,* 192–203.

Stangor, C. (1988). Stereotype accessibility and information processing. *Personality and Social Psychology Bulletin, 13*, 694–708.

Staw, B. (1975). Attribution of the "causes" of performance: A general alternative interpretation of cross-sectional research on organizations. *Organizational Behavior and Human Performance, 13*, 414–432.

Steinfield, C., & Fulk, J. (1986). *Task demands and managers' use of communication media: An information processing view.* Paper presented at the Meeting of the Academy of Management, Chicago, IL.

Sterling, B.S., & Owen, J.W. (1982). Perceptions of demanding versus reasoning male and female police officers. *Personality and Social Psychology Bulletin, 8*, 336–340.

Stewart, K.J., & Chester, N.L. (1982). Sex differences in human social motives: Achievement, affiliation, and power. In A.J. Stewart (Ed.), *Motivation and society* (pp. 172–218). San Francisco: Jossey-Bass.

Stewart, L.P., & Gudykunst, W.B. (1982). Differential factors influencing the hierarchical level and number of promotions of males and females within an organization. *Academy of Management Journal, 25*, 586–597.

Stewart, L.P., & Gudykunst, W.B. (1986). A field test of Festinger's substitute locomotion theory. *Central States Speech Journal, 31*, 3–7.

Stitt, C., Schmidt, S., Price, K., & Kipnis, D. (1983). Sex of leader, leader behavior, and subordinate satisfaction. *Sex Roles, 9*, 31–41.

Stogdill, R.M. (1963). *Manual for the leader behavior description questionnaire—form XII.* Columbus, OH: Bureau of Business Research, Ohio State University.

Stogdill, R.M. (1974). *Handbook of leadership.* New York: Free Press.

Stogdill, R.M. (1981). Women and leadership. In B.M. Bass (Ed.), *Stogdill's Handbook of Leadership.* New York: Wiley.

Stokes, J.P. (1983). Components of group cohesion: Intermember attraction, instrumental value, and risk taking. *Small Group Behavior, 14*, 163–173.

Strasser, G., & Titus, W. (1985). Pooling of unshared information in group decision making: Biased information sampling during discussion. *Journal of Personality and Social Psychology, 48*, 1467–1478.

Stratham, A. (1987). The gender model revisited: Differences in the management styles of men and women. *Sex roles, 16*, 409–426.

Strodtbeck, F.L., & Mann, R.D. (1956). Sex role differentiation in jury deliberations. *Sociometry, 19*, 3–11.

Suls, J.M., & Miller, R.L. (Eds.). (1977). *Social comparison processes: Theoretical and empirical perspectives.* New York: Hemisphere.

Sutton, C.D., & Moore, K. (1985). Executive women—20 years later. *Harvard Business Review, 63*, 43–66.

Swann Jr., W.B. (1984). Quest for accuracy in person perception: A matter of pragmatics. *Psychological Review, 91*, 457–477.

Swann Jr., W.B., & Ely, R.J. (1984). A battle of wills: Self-verification versus behavioral confirmation. *Journal of Personality and Social Psychology, 46*, 1287–1302.

Szilagyi, A.D. (1980). Reward behavior by male and female leaders. *Journal of Vocational Behavior, 16,* 59–72.

Tannen, D. (1987). *That's not what I meant.* New York: Ballantine Books.

Taylor, S.E., & Crocker, J. (1981). Schematic bases of social information processing. In E. T. Higgins, C. P. Herman, & M. P. Zanna (Eds.), *Social cognition: The Ontario symposium* (Vol. 1). Hillsdale, NJ: Erlbaum.

Taylor, S.E., Fiske, S.T., Etcoff, N.L., & Ruderman, A.J. (1978). Categorical and contextual bases of person memory and stereotyping. *Journal of Personality and Social Psychology, 36,* 778–793.

Taynor, J., & Deaux, K. (1975). Equity and perceived sex differences: Role behavior as defined by the task, the mode, and the actor. *Journal of Personality and Social Psychology, 32,* 381–390.

Tedeschi, J., Schlenker, B., & Bonoma, T. (1973). *Conflict, power, and games: The experimental study of interpersonal relations.* Chicago: Aldine.

Terborg, J. (1977). Women in management: A Research review. *Journal of Applied Psychology, 62*(6), 647–664.

Terborg, J.R., & Ilgen, D.R. (1975). A theoretical approach to sex discrimination in traditionally masculine occupations. *Organizational Behavior and Human Performance, 13,* 352–376.

Terhune, K. (1973). Personality in cooperation and conflict. In P. Swingle (Ed.), *The structure of conflict.* New York: Academic Press.

Thomas, K. (1976). Conflict and conflict management. In M. D. Dunnette (Ed.), *The handbook of industrial and organizational psychology* (pp. 889–935). Chicago: Rand-McNally.

Thompson, M.E. (1981). Sex differences: Differential access to power or sex-role socialization? *Sex Roles, 7*(4), 413–424.

Tidball, M.E. (1973). Perspective on academic women and affirmative action. *Educational Record, 54,* 130–135.

Trempe, J., Rigny, A., & Haccoun, R.R. (1985). Subordinate satisfaction with male and female managers: Role of perceived supervisory influence. *Journal of Applied Psychology, 70,* 44–47.

Trevino, L., Lengel, R., & Daft, R. (1987). Media symbolism, media richness, and media choice in organizations: A symbolic interactionist perspective. *Communication Research, 14,* 553–574.

Tsui, A., & Gutek, B.A. (1982, September). *A field investigation of performance between male and female managers.* Paper presented at the 90th annual convention of the American Psychological Association, Washington, DC.

Tsui, A., & Gutek, B.A. (1984). A role set analysis of gender differences in performance, affective relationships, and career success of industrial middle managers. *Academy of Management Journal, 27,* 619–635.

Tsujimoto, R.N. (1978). Memory bias toward normative and novel trait prototypes. *Journal of Personality and Social Psychology, 36,* 1391–1401.

Tuckman, B. (1965). Developmental sequence in small groups. *Psychological Bulletin, 63,* 384–399.

Tversky, A., & Kahneman, D. (1973). Availability: A heuristic for judging frequency and probability. *Cognitive Psychology, 5,* 207–232.

U.S. Bureau of Labor Statistics. (1987).

U.S. Department of Labor, Women's Bureau. (1985).

U.S. Department of Labor, Women's Bureau. (1987).

U. S. Department of Labor. (1989, August). *Handbook of labor statistics.* Washington, DC: U. S. Government Printing Office.

Vaughn, L.S., & Wittig, M.A. (1981). Women's occupations, competence, and role over-load as determinants of evaluation by others. *Journal of Applied Social Psychology, 10,* 398–415.

Vollmer, F. (1984). Sex differences in personality and expectancy. *Sex Roles, 11,* 1121–1139.

Vollmer, F. (1986). Why do men have higher expectancy than women? *Sex Roles, 14,* 351–362.

von Baeyer, P.L., Sherk, D.L., & Zanna, M.P. (1981). Impression management in the job interview: When the female applicant meets the male (chauvinist) interviewer. *Personality and Social Psychology Bulletin, 7,* 45–51.

Voudouris, N.J., Peck, C.L., & Coleman, G. (1985). Conditioned placebo responses. *Journal of Personality and Social Psychology, 48,* 47–53.

Warfel, K.A. (1984). Gender schemas and perceptions of speech style. *Communication Monographs, 51,* 253–267.

Watson, C. (1988). When a woman is the boss: Dilemmas in taking charge. *Group & Organization Studies, 13,* 163–181.

Weber, R., & Crocker, J. (1983). Cognitive processes in the revision of stereotypic beliefs. *Journal of Personality and Social Psychology, 45,* 961–977.

Weider-Hatfield, D. (n.d.). *Sex differences as a moderator in the communication–job satisfaction relationship.* Unpublished paper, University of Georgia, Athens, GA.

Wentworth, D.K., & Anderson, L.R. (1984). Emergent leadership as a function of sex and task type. *Sex Roles, 11*(5/6), 513–524.

Wexley, K.N., & Hunt, P.J. (1974). Male and female leaders: Comparison of performance and behavior patterns. *Psychological Reports, 35,* 867–872.

Wheeless, V., & Berryman-Fink, C. (1985). Perceptions of women managers and their communicator competencies. *Communication Quarterly, 33,* 137–148.

Whitely, W. (1984). An exploratory study of managers' reactions to properties of verbal communication. *Personnel Psychology,* 41–59.

Wiley, M.G., & Eskilson, A. (1982). The interaction of sex and power base of perceptions of managerial effectiveness. *Academy of Management Journal, 25,* 671–677.

Wiley, M.G., & Eskilson, A. (1988). Gender and family/career conflict: Reactions of bosses. *Sex Roles, 19,* 445–466.

Wilkie, J. (1988). Marriage, family life, and women's employment. In A. Stromberg & S. Harkness (Eds.), *Women working* (2nd ed.). Mountain View, CA: Mayfield.

Wilkins, B.M., & Andersen, P.A. (1988, February). *Managerial gender communication: A meta-analysis.* Paper presented at the Western Speech Communication Annual Convention, Spokane, WA.

Williams, J.E., & Best, D.L. (1982). *Measuring sex stereotypes: A thirty nation study.* Beverly Hills, CA: Sage Publications, Inc.

Winter, L., & Uleman, J.S. (1984). When are social judgments made? Evidence for the spontaneousness of trait inferences. *Journal of Personality and Social Psychology, 47,* 237–252.

Winter, D.A., & Green, S.B. (1987). Another look at gender-related differences in leadership behavior. *Sex Roles, 16,* 41–56.

Wood, W., Polek, D., & Aiken, C. (1985). Sex differences in group task performance. *Journal of Personality and Social Psychology, 48,* 63–71.

Wood, W., & Karten, S.J. (1986). Sex differences in interaction style as a product of perceived sex differences in competence. *Journal of Personality and Social Psychology, 50,* 341–347.

Woody, B. (1989). Black women in the emerging services economy. *Sex Roles, 21,* 45–67.

Word, C.O., Zanna, M.P., & Cooper, J. (1974). The nonverbal mediation of self-fulfilling prophecies in interracial interaction. *Journal of Experimental Social Psychology, 10,* 109–120.

Yamada, E.M., Tjosvold, D., & Draguns, J.G. (1983). Effects of sex-linked situations and sex composition on cooperation and style of interaction. *Sex Roles, 9,* 541–553.

Yerby, J. (1975). Attitude, task, and sex composition as variables affecting female leadership in small problem-solving groups. *Speech Monographs, 42,* 160–168.

Zadney, J., & Gerard, H.B. (1974). Attributed intentions and informational selectivity. *Journal of Experimental Social Psychology, 10,* 34–52.

Zajonc, R.B. (1968). Attitudinal effects of mere exposure. *Journal of Personality and Social Psychology, Monograph Supplement, 9,* 1–27.

Zanna, M.P., & Pack, S.J. (1975). On the self-fulfilling nature of apparent sex differences in behavior. *Journal of Experimental Social Psychology, 11,* 583–591.

Zimmerman, D., & West, C. (1975). Sex roles, interruptions, and silences in conversation. In B. Thorne & N. Henley (Eds.), *Language and sex: Difference and dominance.* Rowley, MA: Newbury House.

Zuckerman, M., & Evans, S. (1984). Schematic approach to the attributional processing of actions and occurrences. *Journal of Personality and Social Psychology, 47,* 469–478.

Author Index

A

Abelson, R., 60, *253*
Adams, J., 128, *252*
Adams, K., 132, *233*
Aiken, C., 109, *258*
Alexander, R.A., 135, *234*
Allen, M., 116, *237*
Allen, V.L., 69, *233*
Alperson, B.L., 41, *233*
Alspach, S., 116, *239*
Altemeyer, R.A., 39, 54, 133, *233*
Anderson, C.A., 31, *254*
Anderson, L.R., 42, 132, *257*
Anderson, P.A., 168, *257*
Andrews, P.H., 131, *236*
Argyle, M., 135, *233*
Aries, E., 107, 108, 109, 171, *233*
Arnkoff, D.B., 169, *249*
Arvey, R.D., 37, *233, 239*
Asch, S.E., 68, 70, *233*
Atkins, B., 171, *250*

B

Bacharach, P., 89, *233*
Bacharach, S., 89, 90, *233*
Baird, J.E., Jr., 106, 117, 133, 136, 163, *234*
Bales, R.F., 103, 104, 105, 106, *233*
Bandura, A., 32, *234*
Baratz, M., 89, *233*
Bargh, J.A., 28, 59, *234*
Baron, R.A., 71, 138, *234, 248*
Barron, W., 48, *247*
Bar Tal, D., 43, *234*
Bartol, K.M., 38, 42, 135, 148, 163, *234, 253*
Basow, S., 30, 33, 47, *234*
Bass, B.M., 135, *234*

Bate, B., 169, 170, *234*
Baumeister, R.F., 46, 144, *234*
Beattie, A.E., 75, *242*
Beauvais, C., 134, *247*
Beehr, T.A., 37, *243*
Bellezza, F.S., 61, 125, *234*
Bellows, N., 73, *249*
Bem, S.L., 31, 33, 46, 58, 60, *234*
Bender, L.R., 135, *236*
Bennis, W., 172, *235*
Benokraitis, N., 6, 87, *235*
Ben Porat, 74, *240*
Benson, P., *235*
Berger, J., 63, 109, 125, *235, 238*
Bernard, J., 109, 132, *235*
Berryman, C.L., 171, *235*
Berryman-Fink, C., 162, 163, *235, 257*
Berscheid, E., 65, *254*
Best, D.L., 30, *257*
Bies, R., 113, *235*
Biles, G.E., 135, 138, *235*
Binning, J.F., 126, *247*
Birnbaum, J.A., 44, *235*
Blake, R., 113, 160, *235*
Blanchard, K.H., 139, *244*
Blau, F.D., 35, 36, 37, 43, 44, 128, 131, 146, *235*
Bodenhausen, G.V., 28, 61, 62, *235*
Bonaguro, E.L., 168, *235*
Bonoma, T., 115, *256*
Bormann, E.G., 128, *236*
Bonker, R., 166, 167, *248*
Bornstein, R.F., 30, *236*
Boston, M.B., 50, 53, 129, *243*
Boutillier, R.G., 42, 124, *254*
Bower, G.H., 29, 61, 125, *234, 236*
Bowman, G., 161, *236*
Bradac, J.J., 171, *236*

Bradley, P.H., 133, 136, 139, 163, 171, 177, *234*, *236*
Branch, A., 116, *239*
Brewer, M.B., 71, *236*
Bridges, J.S., 43, *236*
Brooks, V.R., 51, *236*
Broverman, D.M., 30, *236*
Broverman, J.K., 30, *236*
Brown, C.E., 46, 113, 142, *240*, *247*
Brown, L.K., 128, *236*
Brown, V., 39, 47, 50, 51, 53, 75, 129, 139, 143, 144, *236*, *243*, *245*
Bruner, J.S., 28, *236*
Buller, D., 169, *237*
Bunker, B.B., 43, 53, 93, 134, 135, 136, 139, 141, *236*, *245*
Bunker, K.A., 37, 39, *238*
Bunyi, J.M., 131, *236*
Burgess, B., 135, *233*
Burgoon, J., 169, *237*
Burke, R., 98, 99, 100, *237*
Burns, D.S., 29, *237*
Burnstein, E., 75, *253*
Burrell, N., 116, *237*
Butcher, J.N., 41, *247*
Butler, D., 39, 41, 128, 129, 134, 216, *237*, *243*
Butterfield, D.A., 38, 125, 131, 137, 163, *234*, *251*

C
Calder, B.J., 29, 126, *237*
Camden, C., 148, 163, *237*
Campbell, D.T., 28, 46, 48, *237*
Campbell, J.D., 50, *237*
Canary, D., 113, 115, *237*, *238*
Cann, A., 130, *237*
Cantor, N., 62, 74, *237*, *254*
Caplow, T., 30, *237*
Carli, L., 108, 109, *237*
Carter, M.R., 216, *243*
Cash, T.F., 39, *237*
Chapman, J.B., 133, 136, *237*
Cheatham, H.E., 146, *237*
Chesner, S.P., 46, *234*
Chester, N.L., 135, *255*
Christie, B., 155, *254*
Chusmir, L.H., 91, 97, 139, *237*, *238*
Clarkson, F.E., 30, *236*
Clifton, A.K., 108, 134, *248*
Cody, M., 113, 115, *237*, *238*
Cohen, B.P., 125, *238*

Cohen, C.E., 62, *238*
Cohen, E.G., 50, *238*
Cohen, J., 168, *254*
Cohen, S.I., 37, *238*
Coleman, G., 51, *257*
Conrad, C., 89, 114, *238*
Cooper, E., 128, 132, *251*
Cooper, J., 65, *258*
Corrado-Taylor, D., 47, 50, 143, 144, *243*
Costrich, N., 41, *238*
Cox, T., Jr., 127, *250*
Crano, W.D., 94, *249*
Crew, J.C., 135, *238*
Crocker, J., 30, 49, 57, 58, *252*, *256*
Crowell, L., 106, *253*
Cummings, L., 113, *235*
Cunningham, E., 113, *237*
Curtis, E., 104, 107, 112, 139, *250*
Cusella, L., 119, 121, *238*

D
Daft, R., 156, *238*, *245*, *256*
Darley, J.M., 60, 66, *238*, *245*
Day, D.R., 135, *238*
Deal, T., 84, 85, 158, *238*
Deaux, K., 29, 30, 32, 34, 37, 38, 48, 94, 95, 97, 125, 126, 134, *238*, *239*, *256*
Denenberg, V.H., *239*
Denmark, F.L., 41, 135, 136, *239*
DeWine, S., 99, 116, *239*
Dickens, F., 145, *239*
Dickens, J., 145, *239*
Dion, K.L., 125, *239*
Dipboye, R.L., 35, 37, 138, *239*
Dobbins, G.H., 38, 120, 128, 135, 140, 148, *239*, *240*
Donnell, S., 139, *240*
Donohue, W., 116, *237*
Douvan, E., 50, *240*
Dovidio, J.F., 46, 141, 142, *240*
Draguns, J.G., 33, 108, 133, *258*
Dreben, E.K., 63, *240*
Drenan, S., 142, *245*
Drory, A., 74, *240*
Dubnos, P., 30, *240*
Duke, C.W., 3, *254*

E
Eagly, A.H., 6, 31, 46, 48, 72, 94, 95, 109, 110, 118, *240*
Eakins, B., 169, *240*

Eakins, R., 169, *240*
Edelsky, C., 108, *240*
Effrein, E.A., 46, *241*
Ellyson, S.L., 46, 141, 142, *240*, *241*
Ely, R.J., 66, *255*
Emswiller, T., 34, *239*
Erber, R., 28, 31, 34, *240*
Erickson, B., 170, 171, *241*
Erkut, S., 42, 43, *240*
Eskilson, A., 91, 92, 120, 131, 132, 140, *240*, *257*
Etcoff, N.L., 62, *256*
Evans, M., 60, *252*
Evans, S., *258*
Exline, R.V., 141, *241*
Ezell, H.F., 139, 143, *241*

F

Fagenson, E., 99, *241*
Fiarey, P., 50, *237*
Fairhurst, G.T., 91, 93, 114, *241*, *251*
Falbo, T., 48, *247*
Falender, V.J., 46, *241*
Fallon, B.J., 128, 131, *241*
Fazio, R.H., 46, *241*
Feagin, J., 6, 87, *235*
Feather, N.T., 41, 59, *241*
Feinstein, J., 41, *238*
Feldman-Summers, S., 30, *241*
Ferber, M.A., 35, 36, 37, 43, 44, 128, 130, 131, 146, *235*, *241*
Festinger, L.A., 67, 69, *241*
Fidell, L.S., 36, *241*
Fiorentine, R., 44, 146, *241*
Fisher, B.A., 103, 104, *242*
Fisher, J., 38, *242*
Fishman, P.M., 166, *242*
Fiske, S.T., 28, 29, 31, 34, 35, 58, 62, 63, 75, 95, *240*, *242*, *256*
Fleishman, A., 114, *242*
Forgionne, G.A., 125, *242*
Forsyth, D.R., 128, 133, *242*
Forsyth, N.M., 128, *242*
Frank, E.J., 37, 128, *242*
Frank, H.H., 144, 146, *242*
Friedman, S.A., 75, *248*
Friedman, W.J., *233*
Frieze, I.H., 35, 36, 38, 43, 128, *234*, *242*, *250*
Fromkin, H.L., 35, 37, *239*
Frost, P., 87, 89, *242*
Fulero, S., 60, *252*

Fulk, J., 156, *242*, *255*
Futoran, G.C., 32, *243*

G

Gale, W.S., 108, 134, *248*
Galley, D.J., 30, *236*
Garske, J.P., 37, *252*
Gaymon, D., 128, 146, 147, *248*
Gazzaniga, M.S., 28, 71, 74, *243*
Geis, F.L., 37, 39, 41, 47, 50, 51, 53, 75, 127, 128, 129, 132, 134, 139, 143, 144, 216, *236*, *237*, *243*, *245*, *251*
Gerard, H.B., 60, *258*
Gersick, C., 105, *243*
Geyser, S., 161, *236*
Giacalone, R.A., 165, *243*
Gifford, R.K., 75, *244*
Gillen, B., 39, *237*
Gilmore, R., 142, *245*
Glick, P., 32, *243*
Goktepe, J.R., 38, 148, *243*
Gold, J., 43, *247*
Goldberg, P.A., 34, *243*, *251*
Goldstein, E., 50, *243*
Golub, S., 128, *243*
Gove, W., 44, *243*
Green, S.B., 120, 133, *243*, *258*
Greenglass, E.R., 97, *243*
Grenier, M., 96, *254*
Gross, P.H., 60, *238*
Gudykunst, W.B., 96, 127, *255*
Gupta, N., 37, *243*
Gutek, B.A., 5, 7, 30, 37, 40, 95, 127, 143, *243*, *244*, *249*, *256*

H

Haas, A., *244*
Haccoun, D.B., 92, 161, *244*
Haccoun, R.R., 92, 161, 164, *244*, *256*
Haefner, J.E., 37, *244*
Hagen, R.L., 41, *244*
Hall, J., 139, *240*
Hall, K.P., 51, 109, *247*
Hamilton, D.l., 29, 75, *244*
Hansen, R.D., 73, *244*
Hanusa, B., 38, *242*
Harper, N.L., 165, *244*
Harriman, A., 98, 99, *244*
Harris, M.J., 66, *244*
Haslett, B., 82, 118, 119, 166, *244*
Hastie, R., 30, 62, 63, *240*, *244*, *252*

Heilman, M.E., 125, *244*
Heintz, M.A., 163, *235*
Helmreich, R.L., 70, *254*
Heltman, K., 46, 142, *240*
Hendrick, C., 41, *254*
Hennig, M., 92, 137, *244*
Hersey, P., 139, *244*
Higgins, E.T., 58, *244*
Hilton, J.L., 66, *245*
Hirokawa, R.Y., 165, *244*
Hocker, J., 112, *245*
Hodgetts, R., 153, *248*
Hodgins, D.C., 32, *246*
Hoffman, C., 47, 48, *245*
Hoffman, M.L., 117, *245*
Hoffman, N., 50, 53, 129, *243*
Hollander, E.P., 126, 128, 131, 132, 140, *241*, *245*
Holter, H., 31, *245*
Horner, M.S., 41, *245*
Hubbard, M., 28, *248*
Huber, G., 130, 156, *245*
Hudgens, G.A., 32, *239*
Hunt, D.E., 30, *245*
Hunt, P.J., 161, *257*
Hurst, N., 47, 48, *245*
Hyde, J.S., 32, *245*
Hyman, B., 133, 136, *245*

I
Ickes, W., 47, *245*
Ilgen, D.R., 163, *256*
Insko, C.A., 142, *245*
Instone, D., 43, 93, 128, 134, 136, 139, 141, *245*, *252*
Isaacs, M.B., 51, *245*
Isabella, L., *246*

J
Jablin, F.M., 165, *245*
Jacklin, C.N., 42, 46, *248*
Jardim, A., 92, 137, *244*
Jenkins, G.D., Jr., 37, *243*
Jennings, J.W., 47, 50, 53, 143, 144, *243*, *245*
Jerdee, T.H., 37, 38, 94, 97, 127, 162, *245*, *252*
Johnson, B.C., *241*, *246*
Johnson, F.L., *246*
Johnson, P., 92, 141, *246*
Jones, E.E., 72, *246*
Jones, K., 39, 54, 133, *233*

Jones, P., 116, *251*
Jones, R.A., 52, *246*
Josefowitz, N., 136, *246*

K
Kahil, S.P., 136, *252*
Kahn, A., 41, *244*
Kahneman, D., 58, *256*
Kalin, R., 32, *246*
Kane, R.A., 58, *246*
Kanter, R.M., 47, 75, 90, 96, 99, 158, *246*
Karten, S.J., 67, 163, *258*
Katcher, A.H., 144, 146, *242*
Keating, C.F., 46, 142, *240*
Kennedy, A., 84, 85, 158, *238*
Kennedy, C.W., 148, 163, *237*, *246*
Kidder, L., 41, *238*
Kiesler, S.B., 30, *241*, *251*
Kimble, C.E., 109, 132, *246*
Kinder, D.R., 35, *242*
King, G.A., 58, *244*
Kinicki, A.J., 74, *253*
Kipnis, D., 114, 136, 148, *246*, *255*
Klatzky, R.L., 58, *246*
Knowles, E.S., 47, *245*
Koberg, C.S., 97, 164, 165, *238*, *246*
Kohlberg, L.H., 32, *246*
Kram, K., *246*
Kramerae, C., 168, *246*
Krone, K., 165, *246*
Krusell, J., 135, *234*
Kuffler, S.W., 28, *247*
Kuhlman, D.M., 113, *247*
Kulik, J.A., 62, 63, *247*

L
Labiano, A., 116, *239*
Landers, A., 132, *233*
Larsen, J.K., 154, *248*
Larwood, L., 127, *247*
Lawler, E., 89, 90, *233*
Leary, M., 133, *242*
Lee, G.K., 134, *250*
Lengel, R., 156, *238*, *256*
Lenney, E., 43, *247*
Leone, D.R., 30, *236*
Lepper, M.R., 75, *247*
Levine, J.M., 61, *247*
Lewicki, P., 29, 71, *247*
Lewis, L., 32, 48, 94, *239*
Lewis, S.A., 20, *251*

Lichtenstein, M., 29, 61, *235*
Liden, R.C., 165, *247*
Lind, E.A., 170, 171, *241*
Linimon, D., 48, *247*
Linn, M.C., 32, *245*
Linton, R., 125, *247*
Lippa, R., 134, *247*
Lipsitz, A., 142, *245*
Liston, S., 116, *239*
Lockheed, M.E., 50, 51, 109, 127, *238,
    247*
Lohman, M.R., 50, *238*
Long, B., 141, *241*
Lord, C.G., 75, *247*
Lord, R.G., 126, *247*
Lord, R.R., 126, *253*
Lott, B., 39, *247*
Lowy, M.S., 163, *235*
Lubinski, D., 41, *237*
Luthans, F., 136, 153, 154, *237, 248*
Lynn. S.J., 37, *252*

M

Maccoby, E., 42, 43, 46, *248*
Mackie, D.M., 75, *247*
Mainiero, L.A., 93, 96, *248*
Major, B., 29, 43, 93, 134, 136, 139, 141,
    239, 245
Maltz, D., 166, 167, *248*
Mann, R.D., 109, 133, *255*
Maracek, J., 41, *238*
Marcel, A.J., 28, *248*
Markus, L., 156, *248*
Martin, G.L., 58, *246*
Martin, R., 106, 107, 108, 109, *251*
Marwell, G., 114, *242*
Massad, C.M., 28, *248*
McArthur, L.Z., 28, 71, 75, *248*
McBroom, W.H., 33, *248*
McCall, M.W., Jr., 140, *248*
McCallister, L., 128, 146, 147, *248*
McComas, M., 128, *248*
McCombs, H.G., 145, *248*
McCown, N., 133, *242*
McDaniel, N., 116, *239*
McGee, R.J., 30, *237*
McGrath, D., 108, 135, *248*
McHugh, M., 38, *242*
McMillan, J.R., 108, 134, *248*
McPhee, R., 118, *248*
Mechanic, D., 93, *249*
Meeker, B.F., 115, *249*

Megargee, E.E., 42, 131, *249*
Mellon, P.M., 94, *249*
Merton, R.K., 52, *249*
Milberg, S.J., 75, *242*
Miles, R.H., 163, 164, *250*
Miller, C.E., 38, 148, *253*
Miller, F.D., 58, 62, *254*
Miller, J.G., 74, *249*
Miller, R.L., 69, *255*
Mintzberg, H., 140, 151, 152, *249*
Mischel, W., 32, 62, 74, *237, 249*
Mitchell, T., 120, *243*
Moehle, D., 142, *245*
Montgomery, B., 168, *249*
Moore, K., 146, *255*
Moore, L.M., 43, 99, *249*
Morley, D., 164, *254*
Morrison, A.M., 37, 128, *249*
Moscovici, S., 62, *249*
Mouton, J., 113, 160, *235*
Mulac, A., 171, *236*
Murphy, G.M., 61, *247*

N

Nadler, D., 121, *249*
Nanus, B., 172, *235*
Nauta, W.J., 28, *249*
Nelson, C., 32, *243*
Newcombe, N., 169, *249*
Newman, E., 128, 132, *251*
Newtson, D., 28, *248*
Nicholls, J.G., 28, *247*
Nicholson, H., 135, *233*
Nieva, V.F., 5, 30, 37, 40, 127, *249*
Nisbett, R.E., 28, 72, 73, 74, *246, 249,
    250*
Nkomo, S.M., 127, *250*
Norton, R., 168, *249, 250*
Nwacukwu, C.C., 125, *242*
Nyquist, L.V., 42, 131, 132, *250*

O

O'Barr, W.M., 170, 171, *241, 246, 250*
Odewahn, C.E., 139, *241*
O'Donnell-Trujillo, N., 84, *250*
Offerman, L.R., 136, 148, *250*
Ogilvie, J., 118, 119, *244*
O'Leary, V.E., 41, 73, 130, *244, 250*
Olson, J.E., 35, 36, 128, *250*
Orban, J., 120, *240*
Osborn, R.N., 135, 136, *250*
Owen, J.W., 53, *255*

P

Pacanowsky, M., 84, *250*
Pack, S.J., 66, *258*
Paludi, M.A., 34, *250*
Parker, B., 91, *238*
Pascale, L., 41, *238*
Pavelchak, M.A., 62, 95, *242*
Pavitt, C., 104, 107, 112, 139, *250*
Pearson, J., 168, 169, *235, 250*
Peck, C.L., 51, *257*
Pelz, D., *250*
Pence, E.C., 120, 129, *240*
Petty, M.M., 134, 163, 164, *250*
Pfeffer, J., 89, 126, *250, 251*
Pheterson, G.I., 34, *251*
Piliavin, J.A., 106, 107, 108, 109, *251*
Platz, S.J., 140, 148, *240*
Polek, D., 109, *258*
Poole, M.S., 105, 112, 118, *248, 251*
Porter, N., 37, 41, 53, 127, 128, 132,
    143, *243, 251*
Posner, B.Z., 37, 127, 139, *251*
Powell, G.N., 37, 125, 127, 128, 131,
    137, 139, *251*
Power, J., 156, *242*
Pratt, J., 128, 135, *236*
Prestwick, T.L., 37, *252*
Price, K., 136, 148, *255*
Pruitt, D.G., 20, *251*
Pryatel, H.A., 135, 138, *235*
Putnam, L., 91, 103, 111, 112, 115, 116,
    128, *236, 251*
Pyke, S.W., 43, 136, *252*

Q

Quattrone, G.A., 73, *252*

R

Rasinsky, K.A., 30, *252*
Reardon, K., 165, *252*
Reinisch, J.M., 46, *252*
Rhue, J., 37, *252*
Rice, R.W., 128, *252*
Rickel, A.V., 43, *249*
Ridgeway, C.L., 130, *252*
Riecken, H.W., 132, *252*
Rigny, A., 164, *256*
Rock, I., 28, *252*
Rosen, B., 37, 38, 94, 97, 127, 162, *245,*
    252
Rosenblum, L.A., 46, *252*

Rosenkrantz, P.S., 30, 153, *236, 248*
Rosenthal, R., 64, 66, *244, 252*
Ross, L., 28, 48, 63, 72, *250, 252*
Rothbart, M., 30, 60, *252*
Rowe, M.P., 97, 201, *252, 253*
Ruderman, A.J., 62, *256*
Rush, M.C., 126, *247, 253*

S

Sallay, G., 161, *244*
Salter, V., 135, *233*
Sampson, E.E., 125, *253*
Sanders, A.S., 46, *252*
Scanzoni, J., 47, *253*
Schank, R., 60, *253*
Scheflen, A., 82, *253*
Scheidel, T., 106, *253*
Schein, E.H., 32, 86, 125, 135, 158,
    253
Schlenker, B., 115, 133, *242, 256*
Schmidt, S.M., 114, 136, 148, *246, 255*
Schmidt, W.H., 127, 139, *251*
Schmitt, N., 94, *249*
Schmitz, J., 156, *242*
Schneier, C.E., 38, 42, 133, 148, *243,*
    253
Schriesheim, C.A., 74, *253*
Schriesheim, J.F., 74, *253*
Schul, Y., 75, *253*
Seashore, E.W., 39, 53, 128, *236*
Seebohm, M.L., 163, *235*
Seibold, D., 118, *248*
Seifert, C., 38, 148, *253*
Selkow, P., 50, *253*
Senders, P.S., 46, *234*
Seyfried, B.A., 41, *254*
Sgro, J.A., 120, 129, *240*
Shapiro, D., 113, *235*
Sherif, M., 68, *254*
Sherk, D.L., 66, *257*
Sherman, J.D., 139, *241*
Shockley-Zalabak, P., 164, *254*
Short, J., 155, *254*
Siegfried, W.D., Jr., 130, *237*
Simon, J.F., 41, 59, *241*
Sitterly, C., 3, *254*
Skrypnek, B.J., 66, *254*
Slater, P.E., 133, *234*
Slusher, M.P., 31, *254*
Smith, E.R., 58, 62, *254*
Smith, H., 96, *254*

Smith, S., 115, *238*
Snavely, B.K., 93, 114, *241*
Snyder, M., 60, 65, 66, *254*
Sorentino, R.M., 42, 124, *254*
Spence, J.T., 41, 60, 70, 131, 132, *250*, *254*
Spitze, G., 130, *241*
Stake, J.E., 139, *254*
Staley, C., 164, 168, *254*
Stangor, C., 61, *255*
Staw, B., 121, *255*
Steffen, V.J., 48, *240*
Steinfield, C., 156, *242*, *255*
Sterling, C., 53, *255*
Stevens, D.A., 37, *244*
Stewart, K.J., 135, *255*
Stewart, L.P., 96, 127, *255*
Stitt, C., 136, 148, *255*
Stogdill, R.M., 135, 139, 140, *238*, *255*
Stokes, J.P., 107, *255*
Strasser, G., 29, *255*
Stratham, A., 162, *255*
Strayer, L.A., 34, *250*
Strodtbeck, F.L., 109, 133, *255*
Stuart, C., 129, *240*
Suls, J.M., 69, *255*
Sutton, C.D., 146, *255*
Swann, W.B., Jr., 65, 66, *254*, *255*
Szilagyi, A.D., 136, *256*

T

Tanke, E.D., 65, *254*
Tannen, D., 162, *256*
Taylor, S.E., 29, 37, 57, 58, 60, 62, *242*, *256*
Taynor, J., 38, *239*, *256*
Tedeschi, J., 115, *256*
Tellegen, A., 41, *247*
Terborg, J.R., 35, 97, 161, 163, 164, *256*
Terhune, K., 116, *256*
Terpstra, D.E., *239*
Teta, P., 118, *247*
Thibaut, J., 142, *245*
Thomas, J.C., 126, *247*, *253*
Thomas, K., 112, *256*
Thompson, M.E., 47, 115, *256*
Tice, D.M., 46, *234*
Tidball, M.E., 50, 143, *256*
Titus, W., 29, *255*
Tjosvold, D., 33, 108, 133, *258*
Trempe, J., 164, *256*

Trevino, L., 156, *238*, *256*
Tsui, A., 95, 127, 143, *256*
Tsujimoto, R.N., 58, *256*
Tuckman, B., 105, *256*
Tversky, A., 58, 73, *252*, *256*

U

Uleman, J.S., 47, 74, *258*

V

Valle, V., 38, *242*
Van Velsor, E., 37, 128, *249*
Vaughn, L.S., 38, *257*
Vicars, W.M., 135, *250*
Vogel, S.R., 30, *236*
Vollmer, F., 43, 134, 135, *257*
von Baeyer, P.L., 66, *257*
Voudouris, N.J., 51, *257*

W

Walters, R.H., 32, *234*
Warfel, K.A., 170, 171, *257*
Watson, C., 92, 128, 144, *257*
Weber, R., 49, *257*
Weider-Hatfield, D., 164, *258*
Weitzel-O'Neill, P.A., 115, *249*
Wentworth, D.K., 42, 132, *257*
West, C., 53, 132, 134, *258*
Wexley, K.N., 161, *257*
Wheeless, V.E., 162, 163, *235*, *257*
White, R.P., 37, 128, *249*
Whitely, W., 155, *257*
Wilback, K., 35, 37, *239*
Wilcox, J.R., 171, *235*
Wilder, D.A., 69, *233*
Wiley, M.G., 91, 92, 120, 131, 132, 140, *241*, *257*
Wilkie, J., 97, *257*
Wilkins, B.M., 168, *257*
Williams, E., 155, *254*
Williams, J.E., 30, *257*
Williams, M., 135, *233*
Wilmot, W., 112, *245*
Wilson, T.D., 73, *250*
Winter, D.A., 133, *258*
Winter, L., 47, 74, *258*
Winther, D., *235*
Witt, J., 163, *237*
Wittig, M.A., 38, *257*
Wolfe, C., 144, *243*
Wood, W., 67, 109, 163, *240*, *258*

Woodall, W., 169, *237*
Woody, B., 127, *258*
Word, C.O., 65, *258*
Worthy, N., 161, *236*
Wortman, M.S., 135, *234*
Wyer, R.J., Jr., 32, *243*

Y

Yamada, E.M., 33, 108, 133, *258*
Yerby, J., 125, *258*
Yoshikowa, J.C., 109, *246*

Z

Zadney, J., 60, *258*
Zajnoc, R.B., 51, *258*
Zanna, M.P., 65, 66, *257, 258*
Zarrow, M.X., 32, *239*
Zehr, H.D., 109, *246*
Zelditch, M., Jr., 63, 125, *235, 238*
Zimmerman, D., 53, 132, 134, *258*
Zion, C., 32, *243*
Zuckerman, M., 73, *258*

Subject Index

A

Advancement, 194–200, 208–209

Aspirations, career, *see* Stereotypes, gender, effects on women's performances; *see also* Role models, female authority, and women's careers

Authority and status assumptions, 160; *see also* Bias, perceptual, in performance, authority, and leadership

Authority role models, *see* Role models, female authority

B

Bargaining, 115–117

Bias, perceptual, 3–4, 8–21, 33–45
  changing jobs to escape, 10, 17–18
  in communication, 4
  counteracting, 212–232
  in evidence interpretation, 210
  in face-to-face interactions, 39–40
  in hiring and promotion, 36–37
  in organizations, 4–6, 177
  in opportunities, resources, and power, 38, 210–211
  in performance, authority, and leadership evaluations, 6, 17, 37–38, 211
  in product evaluations, 13, 34–35, 179
  in rules and criteria, 74
  in salaries, 1, 10, 11, 17, 20, 35–36, 209
  in strategies to overcome, 20–21, 179
  in success, failure, and ability explanations, 38–39
  in treatment and evaluation of leaders, 128–130
  as unconscious process, 71–72

Bind, double, in small groups, 110–111; *see also* Damned if she does, damned if she doesn't dilemma

C

Causes vs. reasons for decisions, 73–74

Ceiling, glass, 8–9, 15, 127–128; *see also* Bias, perceptual, in hiring and promotion

Changing jobs, 10, 17–18

Colleagues, male
  interacting with, 159–167, 180

Communication processes in organizations, 3–5, 82–103
  climate for success, 184
  formal vs. informal lines of communication, 82–83
  gender roles, social vs. professional, 8–21
  indirect messages, 8–21, 203, 209–212
  interruptions, 186, 199–200
    power of the chair, 209
    new technologies, 155–157
  nonverbal, 74–75, 141–142, 169–170
  power styles, 227–228
  presenting proposals, 183–189
  sex discrimination, 7
  small group communication, 103–122
    sex differences in, 107–111

Conflict, 111–117
  strategies in dealing with, 112–113
  sex differences in, 114–115

Consensus, social, 67–71
  defines reality, 67–68
  effects on perceptions and beliefs, 68–70
  use to break stereotypes, 70

Criticism, 187, 224–225

D

Damned if she does, damned if she
doesn't dilemma, 20, 40–41; *see
also* Bind, double
Decision making, 117–118
causes vs. reasons, 73–74
Differences, gender
absence of in leadership field studies,
135–136
in leadership, 130–137
learned vs. born, 32–33
perpetuated by status inequality,
46–49
Discrimination, *see also* Bias, perceptual
causes vs. reasons for decisions, 73–74
decreasing recently, 146–148
in leadership evaluations, 127–130
perception of rules and criteria, 74
Double bind in small groups, 117–118;
see also Bind, double

E

Empowering yourself, 212–232
Evaluation, *see also* Bias, perceptual
Exploitation, *see* Power, abuse
and exploitation
Expectation States Theory, 63
Expectations, effects on behavior, 64–67,
227–228

F

Face-to-face interactions, *see also* Bias,
perceptual, in face-to-face
interactions; Small groups
Failure, *see* Bias, perceptual, in success,
failure, and ability explanations
Family, 10–12, 18
Fundamental attribution error, 72–73

H

Harassment, sexual, 10–21, 189–191,
200–204
definition, 202, 210
options for action, 203
stopping, 201
Hiring, *see also* Bias, perceptual,
in hiring
for leadership positions, 127–128
Hostility
humor, 199
work environment, 195–200

I

Identity, social, 5
Image
credibility, establishment of, 181
professional, 180
Interview, job, 13–20

J

Job elaboration, 191–194

K

Knowledge, implicit, 28–32

L

Leadership, 123–149, *see also* Bias,
perceptual, in performance,
authority, and leadership;
Stereotypes, gender, effects
on women's performances
appointed, elected, and emergent
leaders, 124
achievement motivation, 135
definitions of, 123, 125–127
female authority role models, 143–146
gender mythology, 124–137
how female leaders are seen
and treated, 127–130
the glass ceiling, 127–128
hiring, salary, and promotion,
127–128
gender reality, 138–148
initiating structure and
consideration, 139–140
stereotypes disconfirmed, 138–139;
223–224
increasing acceptance of women,
146–148
laboratory vs. field studies, 131–137
no inherent male advantage, 131–132
participation content, task vs.
socioemotional, 133–134, 139–140
participation rates, 132–133
and power, 140–143
self-confidence, 134–135
Loopholes, mental, 71–77

M

Managers, 151–173
evaluation of, 162–164
functions of, 151–153

leadership, 157–159
new style in, 172–174
new technologies, 155–157
power of, 164–166
roles of, 151–153
sex differences in, 160–162
styles of, 159–160
tasks of, 154–155
Mentoring, 99–100
Models, role, see Role models
Motivation, achievement, 135

N

Negotiation, 188, 226–227
analysis of problem and participants,
228
recognize bottom line, 231
Networking, 98–99, 229
informal and formal, 181–182
old boy, 194, 198–199

O

Office politics, 181
Opportunities, see Bias, perceptual,
in opportunities, resources,
and power
Organizational culture, 84–87, 178
components of, 84–85
basic assumptions, 86
Organizations
changes in, 199
nature of bias, 5–6
policies
formal and informal, 182
enforcement of, 208
starting out in, 178–182
Orientation, task vs. socioemotional,
133–134, 139–140

P

Perception, 27–29
influence of gender stereotypes, 29–31,
33–41
influence of previous knowledge,
27–29
selective, 60–61
Performance, stereotype effect on
women's, 41–44; see also Bias,
perceptual, in performance,
authority and leadership

Power, see also Bias, Perceptual, in
opportunities, resources, and
power
abuse and exploitation, 142–143
and leadership, 140–143
assumption of, 228–229
barriers to, 94–98
definition of, 87–89
individual uses of, 89
need for, 91
powerlessness, 93
sex differences in, 90–93
space, 191–194
status and nonverbal communication,
141–142
strategies for, 100–101
structural barriers to, 95–98
tokens, 93
Promotion, see also Bias, perceptual,
in hiring and promotion
to leadership positions, 6–16, 127–128,
179–182, 209
perils of too rapid, 194–200
Prophecy, self-fulfilling, 45–54; see also
Expectations, effects on behavior
definition, 52
and female authority role models,
49–51, 143–146
and self-confidence, 134–135
stereotypes, sex, and social status,
45–49
stereotypes and social status structure,
52–54

R

Retaliation, 14
Risk, 197, 229–230
Role models, female authority, 49–51,
143–146
acceptance and familiarity, 51
create consensus effect, 70
and leadership, 143–146
and social support, 50–51
and women's careers, 49–50, 143–146
Rules and criteria, perception of, 74

S

Salary, see Bias, perceptual, in salary
Schema, gender, 57–63; see also
Stereotypes, gender
effects on memory, 61–63

Schema, gender *continued*
fill in gaps in evidence, 61–62
interpret evidence, 61–62
select evidence, 60–62
and stereotypes, 58–59, 207
types of schemas, 59–60
Self-confidence, 134–135, 230; *see also*
Stereotypes, gender,
effects on women's performance
increase with same sex authority role
models, 143–146
lack of caused by stereotypes, 134–135
Sex and gender differences in
managerial communication, 166–172
powerful vs. powerless speech,
170–172
small group communication, 107–111
Sexism, 205
identification of, 207–212
individual vs. organizational, 206
strategies to counteract, 212–232
process of, 213
Small groups, 103–122
characteristics of, 103–104
cohesiveness of, 107
communication in, 103–122
developmental stages in, 104–105
feedback, 118–121
mixed-sex groups, 108–109
task and socioemotional demands,
105–106
Status Characteristics Theory, 63
Status, social, 46–49, 52–54
and leadership, 130
power and nonverbal communication,
141–142
Stereotypes, gender, 29–55; *see also*
Schema, gender
in action and evaluation, 5–7, 8–21,
33–45, 225–226
and biological sex, 45–46, 223
biological sex and social status, 46–49
created by fundamental attribution
error, 72–73
disconfirmed, 138–139
effecting change, 76–77, 140, 143–146
effects on women's performance,
41–45, 208
career aspirations, 43–44
leadership, 42, 130–135
as facts, 1–6, 30

and female authority role models, 49,
214–215
as gender schema, 57–63, 207
as implicit knowledge, 29–31
influence on decisions, 73–74
influence perception of rules and
criteria, 74, 223
and leadership mythology, 124–125,
127–137
in nonverbal innuendo, 74–75
in occupational stereotypes, 31–32
perpetuated by status inequality,
46–49
select and interpret evidence, and fill
in gaps, 60–63
as social consensus, 67–71
as social expectations, 64–67
and tokenism, 75, 211
used unconsciously, 30–31
as values, 31
Strategies, 212
counteract and reduce sexism,
212–232
cope with existing sexism, 213
for career success, 213
increase number of female authority
role models, 214–215
individual action, 215
group action, 215
Structure, social, *see* Status, social
Style, managerial
power vs. personality traits, 140–143
task vs. socioemotional orientation,
133–134, 139–140
Success and Failure, *see* Bias,
perceptual, in success, failure,
and ability explanations

T
Traits, personality
"masculine" and "feminine," 29–31,
45–49
leadership traits, 139
Tokenism, 75

W
Win-win solution, 20–21, 188, 232
Workforce
discrimination statistics, 3–4
sex segregation, 4–5
return to work, 13, 19